THE ART OF CRIME

Studies in Modern Drama
Kimball King, *Series Editor*

THE ART OF CRIME

THE PLAYS AND FILMS OF HAROLD PINTER AND DAVID MAMET

Edited by
LESLIE KANE

Routledge

New York • London

Published in 2004 by
Routledge
270 Madison Ave,
New York NY 10016

Published in Great Britain by
Routledge
2 Park Square, Milton Park,
Abingdon, Oxon, OX14 4RN

Transferred to Digital Printing 2009

Library of Congress Cataloguing-in-Publication Data forthcoming.

ISBN 0-415-96830-5

Publisher's Note
The publisher has gone to great lengths to ensure the quality of this reprint
but points out that some imperfections in the original may be apparent.

For Pamela and David

Contents

Acknowledgments

I extend my appreciation to all of the contributors, a wonderful group of scholars and friends who have worked diligently with me in preparing this book. I am particularly grateful to them for their patience, their sensitive insights, and their responsiveness. I also want to express my enormous debt to Brian Hubbard, senior research librarian at Westfield State College, whose generous assistance, persistence, and professionalism I have come to rely on.

For her advice, patience, and personal commitment to this book, I want to thank my editor at Routledge, Emily Vail, in whose wise suggestions and general helpfulness I have delighted over the last several months. My thanks as well to Routledge's fine production staff for their professionalism.

As always, I am sustained by the love of my children, Pamela and David, and my husband, Stuart.

I would like to acknowledge permission to reprint from the following copyrighted material:

From *Lakeboat* by David Mamet. Copyright 1981. Used by permission of Grove/Atlantic, Inc.

From *Ashes to Ashes* by Harold Pinter. Copyright 1997. Used by permission of Grove/Atlantic, Inc. and Faber and Faber.

From *The Birthday Party* by Harold Pinter, in *Complete Works: 1*. Copyright 1976. Used by permission of Grove/Atlantic, Inc., and Faber and Faber.

From *The Caretaker* by Harold Pinter, in *Complete Works: 2*. Copyright 1977. Used by permission of Grove/Atlantic, Inc., and Faber and Faber.

From *Celebration* by Harold Pinter. Copyright 1999. By permission of Harold Pinter.

From *The Homecoming* by Harold Pinter, in *Complete Works: 3*. Copyright 1978. Used by permission of Grove/Atlantic, Inc., and Faber and Faber.

Introduction

The Art of Crime: The Plays and Films of Harold Pinter and David Mamet is the first collection of essays dedicated to a critical assessment of the centrality and pervasiveness of crime, crime stories, and criminality in the work of Harold Pinter and David Mamet, writers whose work is typically linked by their facility with language, theatricality, and distinctive idiom. Scholars and critics typically include Pinter and Mamet among the century's most influential writers, yet the aspect of criminality that is central to their work has received little critical attention. Whether contradicting or complementing one another, the international writers whose work is featured in this volume enhance this book by their expertise in the work of each—or both—writers. Collectively they initiate a compelling dialogue on criminality, con artistry, and power politics, engaging the reader in a fascinating discussion on the strategies each writer employs in order to plumb the depths of criminal behavior and intent on a personal level and in the public arena.

The Art of Crime is distinctive in its comparative approach, its thematic focus on criminality, and its inclusion of essays on works that have received little critical attention, such as Pinter's *Hothouse, Ashes to Ashes,* and *Celebration,* and Mamet's *Lakeboat, Wag the Dog*, and *The Spanish Prisoner.* The fourteen original essays that comprise this volume offer illuminating insights on how each writer conflates criminality/venality with an exploration of human motivation, personal responsibility, and moral ambiguity. Where Harold Pinter focuses upon crimes against humanity, Mamet is intrigued by the psychopathology of confidence artists. In Pinter's world the suppression of language and the loss of freedom are high crimes—criminal offenses perpetrated by individuals typically at the behest of governments. Thus his works, especially his late plays and films where violence is eroticized, dramatize gangsterism, thuggery, and a culture saturated with authoritarian implications and coercive language. For Mamet crimes typically fall under the rubric of ethical crimes or misdemeanors. The world portrayed in *House of Games*, as in most of his work, is populated by predators who succeed through personal corruption. Evincing a fascination in how artfully the con game is run, the camaraderie and betrayal of partners in crime, the con as craft, and the vulnerability (or venality) of the mark, the crimes Mamet dramatizes are typically against property (whether the stealing of jewels, money, or leads). Yet moralist David Mamet is equally inspired (and incensed) by how business corrupts individuals so that they "succeed at the cost of each other" (qtd. in Kane, *Conversation* 47). His enduring fascination with Chicago and "the gangster mythology that it spawned" (84), and the issues of corruption and corruptibility that are the subject of his work are reflected in the actions of his characters forced to defend their lives and their decisions in works as diverse as *Edmond, Homicide, The Cryptogram, Glengarry Glen Ross*, and *The Edge*.

If Pinter's work rarely strays far from the subject of crime and the criminal, from the marginalized outsider, his characters' fundamental desire for respect is aligned with justice. His work for the stage and screen raises questions about the representation of violence, repressive laws, and a culture saturated with violent imagery. Influenced by film noir and Kafka's *The Trial*, Pinter's work explores the correlation between crime and surveillance and, most recently, the erotics of torture. Yet crime, however prevalent in Pinter's work, is a slippery concept, rules being the product of power relation and negotiation. A seminal American playwright and filmmaker who is increasingly drawn to cinema as screenwriter and director, Mamet's fascination with criminality is reflected in the ways in which criminal behavior and con artistry inform his stylistic choices, structural complexity, and thematic concerns. His canon suggests that Mamet holds a more orthodox view of criminality than does Pinter as a constraint on behavior, largely because he tends to work within genres that confirm how the law operates (gangster/detective/ heist conventions).

Approaching the work of both writers from a myriad of critical/theoretical perspectives, the essays in this volume investigate the moral vision and the aesthetic sensibility evident in their work for the stage and screen, offering an unparalleled retrospective and perspective on their literary and filmic work, the cross-fertilization of film and dramatic art, and the popular arts as aesthetic endeavor. Further, these essays examine plays and filmscripts as illustrative examples of Pinter's and Mamet's fusion of thought and technique, range and complexity, and wonderfully rich ironic humor. Several essays adopt a chronological approach, seeking to place Pinter's or Mamet's screenplays within the context of his theater. Others are comparative, locating fascinating similarities and differences in the way that each writer defines and portrays criminal behavior. Most of the contributors take an in-depth approach to one or two works by a single writer, whereas others examine theatrical or filmic work spanning decades, a richly rewarding approach that yields thoughtful reflection on each writer's canon.

One of the best-known and highly respected playwrights in the English-speaking world, Harold Pinter's body of work as a playwright, screenwriter, poet, and director spans forty years. He has written twenty-nine plays, among them *The Birthday Party, The Caretaker, The Homecoming, Betrayal, Old Times,* and *Moonlight.* He has directed numerous productions of his own work, including most recently *Celebration,* James Joyce's *Exiles,* David Mamet's *Oleanna,* and seven plays by Simon Gray, and he has authored more than twenty screenplays including *The Servant, The Go-Between, The French Lieutenant's Woman, The Comfort of Strangers, The Heat of the Day,* and *The Accident.* The recipient of numerous awards, among them the South Bank Show Award for Outstanding Achievement in the Arts, the Berlin Film Festival Silver Bear, the Shakespeare Prize (Hamburg), the Pirandello Prize, the Moliere D'Honneur for lifetime achievement, Cannes Film Festival Palme D'Or, the S.T. Dupont Golden Pen Award for Distinguished Service to Literature, the David Cohen British Literature Prize, and the Commonwealth Award, Pinter's achievement has been to discover that language serves as a means of negotiation, a weapon of attack, and a source of evasion. Pinter's theatrical world is a lethal testing ground in which individuals are hunters or prey, a place characterized as much by scabrous humor as insecurity, fear, domestic battles and betrayal, and official intimidation. Patterns of dominance permeate the canon. In fact, for Pinter power/control behavior is rooted in the wish to kill one's opponent, or in the converse fear of being "killed," metaphorically annihilated. Thus for Pinter the crime enacted in plays from the first phase of his career, like *The Birthday Party,* and his most recent work, such as *One for the Road* or *Party Time,* are linked in that they depict "the destruction of an individual" (qtd. in Gussow 69). For this writer, fear and aggression are at the core of human behavior. From Pinter's perspective, violence in his work is an expression of dominance and subservience, a response to a pervasive threat. In turn that threat informs not only those who will achieve dominance but also the tools they will employ to achieve that dominance. Hence, in such works as *One for the Road* and *Mountain Language,* Pinter depicts physical and psychological torture, erotic sadism, and human rights abuses. As he told interviewer Mel Gussow, what interests him as a writer and as a citizen of the world is not the statements of contemporary politicians but "the suffering for which they [politicians] are responsible. It doesn't interest me—it horrifies me! (Pause.)" (40). In short, his plays and films are not about "ambiguities" of power or abstract crimes; they dramatize in "a series of short, sharp, brutal images" (Gussow 70) or in chillingly comic ways the abuse of power.

Pinter's vision remains the most compellingly serious of our time. Indeed, only Pinter recognizes the common cause linking criminal violence with crimes of the heart—any acts that destroy rather than promote human relationships. Hence, according to Penelope Prentice, for example, although comedy illuminates his vision to awaken consciousness, as Pinter pushes his work to frontiers of tragedy to evoke uneasy laughter, his audiences are not always sure that they have permission to laugh. In fact, Pinter's comedy magnifies the universal conflict for survival and power to illuminate how it attaches to criminal destruction. And while early works often dramatize sources of violent conflict among lower class, small time, onstage criminals, his most recent work enters the halls of power to reveal the wellspring of global violent conflict as little different from conflict at any level. Much of Pinter's earliest work dramatizes conflicts between onstage petty criminals or hoodlums who may or may not be taking orders from offstage, unseen characters engaged in malicious destruction of organized and/or political crime. Pinter's other early work and middle work, such as *The Caretaker, The Go-Between, The Homecoming,* and *Betrayal,* largely dramatize crimes of the heart. His late plays and his more recent work for stage and film, however, are distinctive in his dramatization of the sexualized, eroticized violence and the erotics of torture. *One for the Road, Mountain Language, The Handmaid's Tale, The Trial,* and *Celebration* all portray either civil, political, or war crimes or crimes of the heart, or both. Except for his torturer plays, the powerful alongside the ineffectual almost always reveal themselves as equally responsible for destruction. And while Pinter, who is a fine actor, has admitted "a yen" to play what he calls "the sinister parts" (qtd. in Gussow 23)—and he has done so brilliantly as Goldberg in *The Birthday Party,* Mick in *The Caretaker,* and the Interrogator in *One for the Road*—he is driven as a writer to focus upon the crimes perpetrated by those who "terrorize" the individual (73).

Influenced by film noir, on the one hand, and the novels of Joyce, Proust, Dostoevski, and most importantly Kafka's *The Trial,* on the other, the works of Harold Pinter are peopled with the wounded and the criminal. Pinter's education, more cinematic than theatrical, was largely influenced by British war films and the American black-and-white gangster films that he watched as a teenager, in which the thriller's "language, then, very sharp, very terse" would inform his distinctive idiom for decades (qtd. in Gussow 138). Exploring the correlation between crime and surveillance, Pinter's film adaptations, such as *The Quiller Memorandum* and *The Trial,* reveal characters who are always under suspicion and presumed guilty of having committed an offense. At first glance the hit-men and vagrants that dominate his early works behave like the Hollywood gangsters they mimic and whose influence on the young writer was profound. But as later works reveal, Pinter inverts criminal stereotypes: his thugs are not threats to, but the victims, or products, of the status quo. This is especially the case with the political criminals—the dissidents— whether in authoritarian or presumably democratic states. In fact, the "criminal" in Pinter's plays and screenplays is often the person who threatens the state. As his recent works make clear, the imprisoned are the innocent victims of oppressive governments. Police, who have populated Pinter's dramatic universe since his earliest works, make their presence known, both manifesting the power that constructs subjects through destructive force and illustrating the violence of the legal system. Pinter challenges the spectator further in films such as *The Comfort of Strangers*, in which the picture that this film presents of the victimizers is likely of central interest to most audiences, positing understanding for the victimizer. In short, the protagonist's lack of assurance about identity, masculinity, and maturity engender his cruelty and, ultimately, his criminal behavior. In fact, Pinter's fusion of restraint and violence, psychosexual aggression and interrogations, trials—both literal and metaphoric—and unverifiable stories in this film adaptation largely characterize his body of work.

Winner of three Obies, a New York Drama Critics Award, the Outer Critics Award for Distinguished Playwrighting, a Joseph Jefferson Award, the Society of West End Theatres Award, the Pulitzer Prize for *Glengarry Glen Ross*, and numerous nominations for Academy Awards for screenwriting (*The Verdict* and *Wag the Dog*), David Mamet is a seminal figure in contemporary American drama whose gift for acute social observation, depth of moral vision, and continuing productivity account for his broad critical respect. He readily credits Harold Pinter as a major influence on his early writing, and, in the years that have ensued, Pinter was influential in the National Theatre's staging of Mamet's *Glengarry Glen Ross*. He has since directed Mamet's play *Oleanna* and most recently appeared in *Catastrophe*, a Beckett one-act play in the Beckett on Film series that also starred Mamet's wife Rebecca Pidgeon and John Gielgud in his last performance.

Although the subjects and the settings of his work have clearly changed since 1975, the year in which *American Buffalo* thrust the young writer onto the national scene, the ethos that undergirds Mamet's work, the perception that ethical and legal acts are inseparable, informs his artistic creativity. From the beginning of his career, interrogatories in Mamet's plays and films have served the purpose of testing knowledge, ethics, identity, and guilt. Populated by confidence men and petty criminals, Mamet's plays and screenplays typically involve murder or burglary, and most deal with criminality that invites interpretations issuing from established genres and law that is a priori, such as the heist plot in *American Buffalo* (for which Mamet also wrote the screenplay); the whodunit in *Glengarry Glen Ross*, the Mafia in *The Untouchables, Hoffa, Things Change*, and the police procedural in *Homicide*.

Just so, the critics in this collection raise questions and invite further inquiry on Mamet's use of the con game. Moreover, they encourage further inspection of the intended misdirection of protagonist and audience in/to

Mamet's frequently enigmatic plays and screenplays. Within that context, this collection concentrates on Mamet's fascination with the con, exploring the ways in which crime, corruption (and corruptibility), confidence tricksters, and criminal behavior affect his stylistic choices, his structure, and his thematic concerns. For Mamet movies are analogous to the con game in that they have "ability to present apparently unmistakable truth . . . while hiding everything that's most essential" (Kehr 7A), an observation with broad implications for his theatrical work as well. An avid fan of movies for much of his life, Mamet wrote his first screenplay, *The Postman Always Rings Twice* in 1981, an experience he credits for influencing the structure of his Pulitzer Prize-winning play *Glengarry Glen Ross* (1982). Exploring diverse genres such as the fable, film noir, buddy films, gangster films, the detective story, drama of manners, and the romantic thriller, Mamet's plays and screenplays probe the seduction of the profit motive, the obsessive search for success, the nature of affiliation and of criminal intent. Each entails a quest—an odyssey of discovery of self and other—in which plot twists, false leads, feints, suspense, or a series of surprises—the very stuff of Mamet's con-artistry—are coupled with survival skills, high adventure, the threat of exposure or death, and con games, cabals, and codes intended to disorient characters and audience alike. A central metaphor, typically performance or gambling, shapes the action; characters are tested in a variety of ways. Usually cloaked in mystery, set in a world of crime or criminal intent, each work pairs a couple—friends, partners, or competitors—within a larger family of associates (Mafia, police department, venture capitalists). This Mamet group/family is engaged in work, play, or struggle to survive in which issues of loyalty are examined, betrayal of self or other dramatized, and ethical behavior compromised or affirmed.

Writing filmscripts and directing (*House of Games, Homicide, Things Change, Oleanna, The Spanish Prisoner, The Winslow Boy,* and *Heist*) increasingly dominate Mamet's artistic activity in this middle stage of his career. At a time when films have largely degenerated into what he terms "carnival amusement" offering thrills but no drama, Mamet views the screenplay as a "drama in schematic," one that brings individuals closer through shared experience. His filmscripts, informed by his bracingly original moral vision, strong story lines, taut dramatic structure, and criminal activity engage the audience by putting them in the position of protagonist so that, in effect, the audience and the protagonist are "in the same position . . . : led forth by events, by the inevitability of the previous actions. They don't know what they're going to do next either" (qtd. in Kane 42.) For example, like many of Mamet's works, *Glengarry Glen Ross* sparked controversy in its depiction of mendacity and moral bankruptcy in the marketplace when it premiered in the early 1980s. Mamet's sympathy for its central character, Shelly Levene, whose daughter provides ample evidence for the salesman's motivation to steal the leads from the real estate office in which he works and whose dependence infers the high price Levene will pay when he is caught, is evident. Yet, the stage play exposes the fierce competition among salesmen and their efforts to dupe unsuspecting buyers—and each other—in an effort to save their jobs. Further, in depicting the friendship between Levene and top salesman Ricky Roma, who collaborate in conning Roma's customer James Lingk, *Glengarry* conflates sharp practice with the inherent decency of hard workingmen corrupted by a system that deprives them of their ethics and soul. Similarly set in the shadowy world of crime, conspiracy and cabals, *Homicide* is a police melodrama that portrays the contentious world of ethnic hatred, cultural ignorance, and confused loyalties. Through a circuitous journey that opposes the search for a wanted criminal with the desire for home, Mamet heightens awareness of the powerful association and discourse that conjoin the figures of belonging and exile through the character of Detective Robert Gold, a highly decorated homicide investigator and hostage negotiator aptly poised between two worlds, whose efforts to be both a good cop and what he thinks is a good Jew entrap him in a tragic moral bind.

Typically Mamet uses the thriller to plumb the depths of trust and to explore the malevolent mystery of diabolical acts, of suspense and surprise, of the evil/violent side of human nature. As a writer Mamet is likely to stack the deck; his works are a marvel of deception, double-cross, and intrigue as he posits the twin poles of temptation and opportunity. As Mamet told *Playboy* interviewers, con men "are fascinating people. I've always been interested in the continuum that starts with charm and ends with psychopathology. Con artists," like the writer, "deal in human nature, and what they do is all in the realm of suggestion" (qtd. in Kane 127).

In his absorbing introduction to the topic of thuggery in Harold Pinter's works, Varun Begley contends that "proletarian assassins" and "neurotic inquisitors" encompass a spectrum of authoritarians and criminals aptly represented by the thug, "an iconic figure suggestively linking early gangsters, torturers, and fuctionaries." According to Begley, although Pinter's later plays explore a convergence of horror and civility, these plutocrats, socialites, and functionaries are affluent relations of the gangsters and sociopaths one finds in *The Birthday Party, The Dumb Waiter,* and *The Homecoming*. Examining the shift from early comic menace and erotic barbarity and enigmatic political realism in Pinter's work, Begley identifies a "pervasive overlap between early and late work." Collectively, he argues, Pinter's thugs "express and endure a violence that is both ubiquitous and invisible."

Analyzing such diverse works as *The New World Order, Party Time,* and *The Hothouse*, Marc Silverstein observes that Pinter "does not need to specify a particular criminal act" that an individual has committed. Rather, he "presents him as 'guilty' of the offense that proves most threatening to the operation of the symbolic order. . . . It is as if in such objectification of the individual and the repression of language that the Other maintains its dominance." As such the individual placed before the audience in a play like *One for the Road* is so diminished that he is "little more than a present absence." Silverstein finds that theorists such as Lacan, Derrida, Althusser, and Mac Cannell cast valuable light on the topic of subject formation, the exercise of power through violence that in Pinter's theater "never occurs without policing." Silverstein's incisive analysis further illuminates the ways in which Pinter repeatedly illustrates how those in power "keep the world clean for democracy" through "state-sanctioned criminality." Moreover, Silverstein plays particular attention to *The Hothouse*, in which the dominant ideology "takes the form of inclusion," whereby "the institution organizes itself so that its inhabitants may one day learn to recognize themselves as part of that 'humanity' in whose name they received treatment."

Steven Price's brilliant essay, "Harold Pinter Before the Law," persuasively argues that "as a political essayist Pinter oscillates between the formalist and humanist positions," but as a playwright "he dramatizes a radical-critical view of all forms of regulation, legal and otherwise." Although Pinter and his critics detect three phases/stages to his career, Price maintains that Pinter's political plays of the 1980s share with preceding *No Man's Land* and *A Kind of Alaska*, for example, "a sense of frighteningly diminishing possibilities." In the late work since *Moonlight* (1993), largely viewed by critics as a "fertile exploration of special and temporal fluidity," Price sees "unmistakable political connotations," especially in plays such as *Ashes to Ashes* that link this stage to earlier works such as *The Birthday Party*. In fact according to Price, although plays appear "less overtly political" they are "no less political"; rather, they, too, present a politicized view of the contemporary world. Opening the door to deeper exploration of this issue, Price contends that "legal, territorial, and generic boundaries" in Pinter's plays are "uncertain." Thus, although events and acts appear "criminal," the term itself constantly evolves as boundaries are "continuously renegotiated. Further, in Pinter's world, where it is more likely that a character would be accused of committing a crime, the issue itself is complicated by the uncertainty surrounding "'criminality' itself." As Price persuasively illustrates in his discussion of works as diverse as *One for the Road* and *The Caretaker*, politics and power obviously link the first and third phases of Pinter's work; the works of his middle period likewise acquire "a peculiar political resonance and rigidity."

Given the Holocaust's uniqueness as a horrific crime, Charles Grimes's essay examines the ways in Pinter's *Ashes to Ashes* "presents history allusively in the register of memory." According to Grimes, in *Ashes* Pinter addresses the temporal distance between genocide and his audience; in so doing he confronts the difficulty, if not impossibility, of bearing witness to the Holocaust. In Grimes's view, the writer presents a series of stories in this recent stage play told by the protagonist Rebecca that underscore the disjunction among history, memory, and conscience. Employing a paradigmatic technique that characterizes much of Pinter's work—the presentation of multiple versions of a story—the writer either presents and discredits or questions the credibility and validity of the narrative and narrator. Further, Grimes maintains that the act of writing the Holocaust for Pinter calls into question the "presumption of illumination," or rather, to put it differently, the expectation for increased understanding and of "truth" gleaned from writing or hearing about historical atrocities. In fact Grimes contends that Pinter's heightened sensitivity to hatred and violence, demonstrated by his outspokenness on the subject of atrocity and the abuse of power, negates the critical desire to read Rebecca's engagement with suffering in *Ashes* as triumphant or empathetic. Rather, it underscores Pinter's view that redemption is illusory.

Focusing upon two recent Pinter works for the stage, *Celebration* and *The Press Conference*, Penelope Prentice presents a compelling look at the role and place of comedy in Pinter's work. In her view Pinter "enters the halls of power to reveal the wellspring of criminal violence in global conflict as little different from the source of conflict at any level." In her unique approach to Pinter's art of crime, Prentice finds that Pinter deploys comedy as a weapon of attack against crimes of the heart, crimes against humanity, war crimes, and cowardice, the latter paradoxically functioning as a call to courage. According to Prentice, Pinter's vision is "the most compelling serious of our time." Yet, by coupling serious comedy and crime, Pinter pushes his work to the edge of horrifying tragedy. Drawing upon her vast knowledge of Pinter's work, her accessibility to Pinter's most current work, and her skill as a playwright, Prentice further argues that *Celebration*'s bawdy language "dramatizes and embraces human complexity/capacity for destruction and transformation." Thus from her perspective, comedy in Pinter's work is "an equal opportunity targeter: comedy makes terror bearable and reveals our attraction to criminal destruction for the vicarious experience that is. If in *Press Conference* education and information collapse into a single sphere, *Celebration*'s incongruity, "more deeply disturbing and more comically hilarious than any of Pinter's plays in several decades," reveals crime/power as "intimate bedfellows."

In Ann C. Hall's essay on Pinter's "longstanding fascination with Kafka's *The Trial*" and the screenplay that Pinter has written for the film, Hall astutely argues that despite Pinter's faithfulness to the original, his screenplay highlights the relationship between spectacle and crime in a way that the literary text cannot. Hall, who has previously written on the subject of spectatorship with remarkable sensitivity, recognizes that in this screenplay Pinter creates "a spectacular paranoid house of mirrors," a hierarchy of spectators and viewers in which "the chain of command" in much of the screenplay is "deliberately mystified." Examining spectatorship in Pinter's screenplay, Hall posits that by means of surveillance and sophistical observation, Josef K is "always objectified by a gaze, ours or the courts." Yet as she astutely notes, not only does "K" dwindle as a result of his "victimization/observation," but Pinter's taut screenplay also offers in her view a "hauntingly ambiguous" explanation of the parable of the doorkeeper, further confusing the diminished "K." Likewise, she contends, the final scenes offer an array of images regarding "spectacle and speculation, objectivity and subjectivity, oppression and power." Both, Hall argues, distinguish Pinter's approach to crime as portrayed in cinematic images and in the body of his work in various genres.

According to Ira Nadel, crime goes unpunished in the plays of Harold Pinter and David Mamet; only in the screenplays does punishment with cruelty become more pronounced, as illustrated by such screenplays as Pinter's *The Comfort of Strangers* or Mamet's *Hoffa*. In his incisive comparative study of the crime of lying in the work of both writers, Nadel contends that a close reading of Pinter's and Mamet's forays into the Victorian/Edwardian period in *The French Lieutenant's Woman* and *The Winslow Boy*, respectively, reveals an exception to the depiction of crime as physical violence that typically characterizes the work of these writers. In "Lie Detectors" Nadel underscores that lying as crime is not merely consistent with the motif of betrayal common to both writers, it, moreover, is typical of the historical period(s) in which both source-texts were written. Nadel's essay presents convincing commentary on the modes of adaptation employed by each screenwriter, on the visual and verbal authenticity of the screenplays, on the value placed on honesty in specific historical eras, and on the ways in which each writer rivets attention to the motifs of injustice and victimization. Whereas Pinter introduces a story within a story to bring Fowles's novel to the screen, Mamet, in Nadel's view, pares down Rattigan's play for cinematic impact in *The Winslow Boy*. And, while adaptations processes differ, their treatment of crime may in this critic's view be seen as similar in that each writer questions morality rather than violence, dishonor rather than murder.

According to Kimball King, in many, if not the majority, of Mamet's works the behavior of his protagonists may be viewed as criminal in that it is cruel or exploitative. Examining representative works—*Sexual Perversity in Chicago, The Water Engine*, and *Oleanna*—King maintains that the acts of betrayal and (ostensible) sexual harassment dramatized in these works are of questionable ethical behavior but fall short of criminal, punishable offenses. However, in plays such as *Edmond*, in which the protagonist slashes a pimp and kills a prostitute, and in *American Buffalo* and *Glengarry Glen Ross*, in which characters plan, stage, and, in the latter play, pull off a burglary, Mamet affords a vision of a "fragmented modern world" and a "rent social fabric." King contends that Mamet portrays characters who cannot construct a moral universe, a point underscored by what King terms "gradations of criminality." Further, King builds a convincing argument through myriad examples from Mamet's plays and films that in Mamet's world "actions have consequences." Yet, despite the apparent "perversion of human values" that characterize the writer's world, Mamet, in King's view, believes in the possibility of altruistic behavior, moral choice, and the values of justice, land, and community.

Taking Melville's *The Confidence Man* as a point of departure, Barry Goldensohn, Mamet's professor at Goddard College in the 1960s, considers the con game, the exchange of confidence, and the dramatic structure of the novel. In so doing he discovers striking parallels between Melville's "savage indignation at folly and duplicity, recorded through the orders and disorders of language" and central themes of truth and betrayal and "the impact of fraud and misplaced faith in American capitalist society" that one finds in Mamet works as varied as *American Buffalo, Edmond, The Cryptogram,* and *Wag the Dog.* In his perceptive reading of Mamet's work, Goldensohn amply illustrates that the language of confidence and a "satiric turn," which similarly characterizes the work of Melville and Swift, is pervasive in Mamet's canon, regardless of the genre in which he writes. Moreover, Goldensohn argues that it is not merely in the figure of the confidence man but also in the issues of betrayal, fraud, truth, and falsity that take center stage in Mamet in which we can best recognize a link to Swiftian satire and Melville's con man.

According to Anne Dean, storytelling as a means of survival is powerfully portrayed in Mamet's early stage play *Lakeboat,* which, in her view, is one of Mamet's best, largely because it is "superbly written and deftly constructed." Through an elaborate network of fantasies, notes Dean, the men who work on the lakeboat bolster their "flagging egos" and participate in a "shared moment of mutually 'lived' experience" through fictional crimes that distract the seamen and relieve them from the tedium of their daily lives. In fact, as she astutely notes, the characters themselves turn crime into art, "each of them actors in their own elaborate 'screenplay.'" However, her impressive argument gains credence when, under her careful analysis, we (re)read the play, confirming that no crime is ever committed and that the characters are "literally all talk." For Dean, these men "concoct fantasies concerning criminal activity, preferably the most violent and lurid kind," because in assuming "the macho lifestyles of their celluloid heroes"—larger in life than themselves—criminal lives need only be "tried on for size." "Theirs is a world of B-movie clichés and melodramatic twists," claims Dean, "where hard-as-nails men perform fantastic feats of strength and bravery—and always live to see another day." Her close reading of this oft-neglected Mamet stage play coupled with her thoughtful, if playful, examination of *Lakeboat*'s complexity and its pivotal relationship to Mamet's canon, opens the door to deeper exploration of the crime stories that Mamet's men in this work and in innumerable works for stage and screen fabricate and seize upon in order to fill the emptiness of their lives.

In "David Mamet's *House of Games* and the Allegory of Performance," Elizabeth Klaver, who writes frequently on semiotic systems, the convergence of artificiality and reality, and signs, finds in Mamet's first film as writer/director a world that "subverts realism." In her essay Klaver examines the functioning of "performative signs" and, specifically, how *House of Games*, using the idea of a sting operation, yields ample opportunity for "retrospective" and "reinterpretation of the 'already played.'" Of particular interest to Klaver is the unmasking of the poker game as artifice in which players trade confidences/trust "so that both the characters and viewer fall into a trusting relationship with the fictionalizer." Riveting attention to the poker game, she explores the game as Mamet plays it in the film, "the words 'house' and 'game'" functioning as "narrative generators." In fact, she contends, "it is a testament to the film's ingenuity that most viewers do not recognize the title as a 'tell' to textual forces at work and are thereby both involved in and victimized by its game-playing machinery." While Mamet's affinity for con games is touched upon by many essays in this collection, Klaver maintains that in this film the master con is "expose[d] in its ability to control and absorb meaning and intent." Her essay also offers thoughtful examinations of the role of "language as performance" in Mamet's work, notably in stage plays, such as *Speed-the-Plow* and *American Buffalo*, especially as it relates to the merging of the real with the image, theatricality with real life that Mamet masterfully captures in this film.

Thomas P. Adler uses Mamet's *Three Uses of the Knife*, three brief lectures on the nature and purpose of drama, as a springboard for his impressive essay on three Mamet works in three distinct genres. In his inspired approach to Mamet's canon, Adler's analysis illuminates diverse yet complementary works—*The Cryptogram*, *The Old Religion*, and *The Edge*—each offering a singular but related dramatic, fictional, and cinematic approach and all written within a few years of each other. Linking all three works, observes Adler, is the knife, a multifaceted sign, symbol, tool, and violent implement that figures prominently in numerous Mamet works—*Edmond*, *Prairie du Chien*, *Things Change*. In these three works in particular Adler identifies the knife as a trope signaling acts of violence, both psychological and physical. In *The Cryptogram*, for example, Adler advances the idea that the gift of a knife in exchange for a week-long assignation gains added significance as a "Combat Trophy," a sign of male friendship, a means to cut the bonds of friendship and family, a tool, "a propriation," a bribe, a totem for a boy who has lost his father. In effect, Adler reads the knife as a sign of friendship, love, loss, and betrayal. In his astute reading of the knife in *The Old Religion*, Adler takes up the subject of the "sacrificial son," alluding at once to the Old Testament and to Leo Frank's Jewishness, and he concludes that Frank's arrest is inextricably linked to the knife as a murder weapon much as Frank himself is "marked by the knife" as Other. Not only is Frank defined by the anti-Semitism that motivated his arrest, imprisonment, and lynching but also the knife becomes the instrument to cut Frank's throat and perform the act of castration that provides Mamet, in Adler's view, "two striking uses of the knife." Taking up the subject of homoerotic tension alluded to in *The Cryptogram*, Adler's essay casts light on Mamet's oft-neglected film, *The Edge*, in which a pocket knife functions as an instrument of survival, providing among its many uses a scene in which Charles Morse's newly acquired knowledge, in Adler's words, "pierces to the heart as almost nothing else in Mamet's work does."

Claire Magaha is also fascinated by *The Edge*, an immensely complex screenplay that in her view is dismissed, misread, and misjudged as a failed adventure film. According to Magaha, *The Edge* may be read as a "literal and metaphorical decent that signifies the hero's achievement of self-knowledge through enlightenment." Magaha's argument persuasively draws the reader into a rereading of the film as a dialectical engagement of man and animal-self in which Mamet constructs the protagonist's experience as an allegory. According to Magaha, through this personal rite of passage, one that is both self-destructive and self-revelatory, Mamet's film portrays the drama of the self, one in which Charles Morse's passion for the artificial and material is transformed into the spiritual. In support of her contention that Mamet's film is neither a failed nor an action film, Magaha, drawing upon Rousseau, provides ample evidence that *The Edge* is a deliberate con game, affording the opportunity for Morse and the viewer to undertake a personal journey. She contends that this journey is at first glance fearful and mysterious; however, it is dependent upon the spectator's engagement with and his or her partnership in spirituality.

Finally, in *The Spanish Prisoner*, his fifth as writer/director, I consider Mamet's serpentine screenplay that weaves a web of intrigue whereby Everyman figure, Joe Ross, a brilliant ideas man blinded by ambition and greed (which connects with our own larcenous impulses), is lured into the confidences of a mysterious stranger. A romantic, "wrong man" thriller, *Prisoner* is Mamet's most intricate and arguably his most arresting Hitchcockian fable, the perfect vehicle for the high stakes trickery played upon a credulous company man—reminiscent of his earlier *Water Engine* and *Homicide*—that invites assessment of the psychological processes and moral ambiguities inherent in Mamet's presentation of confidence games. Here game-playing as structure and element of plot is a controlling figure, much as it is in his critically acclaimed film noir, *House of Games*. Stringing us along with ruses and red herrings that repeatedly confound our expectations, the screenplay ostensibly revolves around guarded information, a theme underscored by the flirtatious secretary whose stealth and tenacity are cloaked by affability and seductiveness, further suggestive of Mamet's evocative treatment of sexuality/criminality explored in his earlier *House of Games* and stage play, *Oleanna*. Like *Prisoner*'s hero, the audience proves the perfect patsy of con artistry, learning that in Mamet's world of betrayal, deceit, and shifting loyalties the acquisition of wisdom is coequal with the acquisition of skepticism.

Pinter's and Mamet's theatrical and filmic works enjoy broad worldwide appeal, as evidenced by frequent productions and revivals of their work. *The Art of Crime* has sought to examine that appeal by its comparative approach, thematic focus on criminality, and inclusion of essays on works that have received little critical attention. In placing Pinter's and Mamet's screenplays within the context of their theater, examining both the similarities and differences in their treatment of crime and the influence that works in one medium have on the other, it seeks both to complement individual studies of Pinter's and Mamet's work and to illuminate the talent that each has for finding cinematic images for novels. Thus, it is my hope that this collection will serve as an invaluable asset for scholar and student, alike, by advancing the dialectic on the work of these writers and by expanding the level of inquiry with respect to their distinctive approaches and affinities.

Works Cited

Gussow, Mel. *Conversations with Pinter*. New York: Proscenium, 1994.

Kane, Leslie, ed. *David Mamet in Conversation*. Ann Arbor: U of Michigan P, 2001.

Kehr, Dave. "*House of Games* Stylishly Meshes Stage, Film." *Chicago Tribune,* 16 October 1987, 7.

1
A Poetics for Thugs

VARUN BEGLEY

The psychopath is not only a criminal; he is the embryonic Storm-Trooper;
he is the disinherited, betrayed antagonist whose aggressions can be
mobilized on the instant at which the properly-aimed and frustration-
evoking formula is communicated by that leader under whose tinseled
aegis license becomes law, secret and primitive desires become virtuous
ambitions readily attained, and compulsive behavior formerly deemed
punishable becomes the order of the day.
—Robert Lindner, *Rebel without a Cause*

These individuals are the most "infantile" of all: they have thoroughly
failed to "develop," have not been molded at all by civilization. . . . Here
go the hoodlums and rowdies, plug-uglies, torturers, and all those who do
the "dirty work" of a fascist movement.
—T.W. Adorno, *The Authoritarian Personality*

A brief, exemplary sequence in Alain Resnais's Holocaust documentary
Night and Fog (1955) begins with the exterior of a comfortable villa, home
to a Nazi commandant. The narrator reports that the residence was located
near one of the concentration camps. Subsequently, three snapshots depict
the wives of various commandants. One poses in the parlor, smiling, with a
group of well-dressed visitors. Another sits beside her husband, a contented
dog in her lap. The banality of these images is somehow intolerable. They
evoke real but macabre domestic dramas performed in the shadows of the
camps. Harold Pinter's later plays explore similar convergences of horror
and civility. In particular, *Party Time* (1991) enlarges the moral and political
implications of Resnais's archival photographs, dramatizing a grotesque
cocktail party for the ruling class during an evening of brutal military sup-

pression. The play's political tenor and unspecified setting are consistent with three of Pinter's other works of the period: *The New World Order* (also 1991), *One for the Road* (1984), and *Mountain Language* (1988). At the same time, however, plays like *Party Time* and *One for the Road* reveal the summit of an authoritarian class structure whose foundations date much earlier. These works extend Pinter's previous treatments of criminality, adding a new branch to an evolving genealogy of thugs. The plutocrats, socialites, and functionaries of the later plays are affluent relations of the gangsters and sociopaths in *The Birthday Party* (1958), *The Dumb Waiter* (1960), and *The Homecoming* (1965). The glib prattling of the intelligentsia echoes the enigmatic chatter of the criminals. The privileged environments of the first group complement the uncertain, alienated spaces occupied by the latter. These diverse works compose Pinter's extended meditation on the proximity of civility and barbarism. Collectively, they develop a *mise èn scene* in keeping with the villa, the dog, and the commandant.

From absurdist toughs to proletarian assassins, paranoid pimps, and neurotic inquisitors, Pinter's plays encompass a spectrum of authoritarians and criminals. These characters, I will argue, function as agents of a two-pronged critique of violence and its cultural representations. This chapter outlines the terms of this critique through the vehicle of the thug. For Pinter, the thug offers a dense, malleable cultural history, and this broad, iconic figure suggestively links the early gangsters with the torturers and functionaries of the anti-authoritarian cycle. Outwardly, however, Pinter's thugs coalesce in at least two distinct, seemingly incompatible groups. The first includes the dialogic, quasi-philosophical clowning of Gus, Ben, Goldberg, and McCann in the early plays, and the second is aligned with the monologic, eroticized self-narrations of Lenny in *The Homecoming* and Nicolas in *One for the Road*. Clearly, there is a sense of development in these characters—a shift from philosophical, comic menace to more inward, erotic modes of barbarity, from an absurd to a post-Freudian thug. Moreover, the late treatments of thuggery are distinguished by an enigmatic political realism. At the same time, however, the insidious dialogue between Des and Lionel in *The New World Order* is clearly indebted to the more comic interrogations of Goldberg and McCann in *The Birthday Party*, and in some obvious ways the political torturer Nicolas in *One for the Road* seems the offspring of Lenny, a small-time pimp in *The Homecoming*. In hindsight, Pinter has himself remarked on overlaps between the early works and subsequent political concerns. In 1988, he suggested that plays like *The Birthday Party* and *The Dumb Waiter* offer a critical look at "authoritarian postures" and "power used to undermine, if not destroy, the individual, or the questioning voice" (qtd in Page 106).

The representational genealogy of Pinter's thugs is thus enmeshed in larger questions about his politics. It is difficult to assess whether the "political" plays of the 1980s and 1990s represent a qualitative shift or an organic development. For example, despite elements of realism, the antitorture plays insist on historical indeterminacy and are less concerned with representing torture or violence than with implicating ostensibly benign linguistic, rhetorical, and social practices in murky offstage violence. The abstractness of these plays seems at odds with the notion of concrete political intervention. Jeanne Colleran argues that in *Mountain Language*, the "dramatic situation . . . is now grounded in a configuration that is at once political and ontological and which accords neither privilege" (58), yet Pinter's comment above takes a similar view of his earlier work. Indeed, in a previous interview, Pinter remarked of *The Birthday Party*: "I don't think it is all that surrealistic and curious, because this thing, of people arriving at the door, has been happening in Europe for the last twenty years. Not only the last twenty years, the last two to three hundred" (qtd. in Esslin 36).

Here Pinter echoes Robert Lindner, who suggests that the psychopath is the embryonic storm trooper. In what follows, I contend that Pinter's thugs reflect a coherent social philosophy. The later plays indicate that thuggery is political, but they retain an ontological violence derived from earlier absurdist variants. Indeed, collectively, Pinter's thugs express and endure a violence that is both ubiquitous and invisible. Assassins, gangsters, pimps, and torturers serve as equivocal links to a "real" violence, which is then deferred and mediated in the plays. In symptomatic fashion, *The Dumb Waiter* concludes with a static tableau, deferring the resolution promised by Ben's pointed gun. The tension of this unspent bullet reverberates across Pinter's dramatic universe. Physical cruelty is typically consigned to anticipation, memory, or offstage space. His work is more centrally concerned with the sublimation of urges, the sedimentation of violence in posture, gesture, and speech, and the complicity of all such symbolic displacements with unrepresented barbarities. Hence, this preoccupation has often passed under the name of menace, or, more euphemistically, "power." But apart from superficial machinations lies an inarticulate suffering that cannot, or should not, be mimetically represented. For example, when Nicolas tells Victor in *One for the Road* that his son "was a little prick" (79), the mere shift of tense signals an inexpressible ending. The guilt of a language that commands, justifies, or obscures violence extends as well to the play's trappings of civility. The imagery oscillates between etiquette and barbarism, glib urbanity and abject terror, hors d'oeuvres and the "rancid omelette," cocktails and "wet shit" (40). Even the title's inane, incongruous formality mocks the subject matter, positioning the play in a chasm between rhetoric and brutality, decomposed language and grisly reality, the visible and cruelty beyond figuring.

Of course *One for the Road* is itself a sublimation—an aesthetic, nearly abstract rendering of presumed realities, a transformed piece of dramatic speech spoken on behalf of victims. As the play demonstrates, the power to describe and narrate both masks and enables real agency ("You're a lovely woman. Well, you were" [71]). In this sense, Pinter's theatrical critique of authoritarian politics constitutes his own artistic usurpation. Clearly, Pinter's theater is alive to tensions between political and aesthetic speech, and his work resists imaginary resolutions of unresolved social contradictions, to modify a phrase from Fredric Jameson. Consider his response, in the late 1960s, to a journalist's question about politicians. "I'll tell you what I really think about politicians. The other night I watched some politicians on television talking about Vietnam. I wanted very much to burst through the screen with a flame-thrower and burn their eyes out and their balls off and then inquire how they would assess this action from a political point of view" (qtd. in States 13). In juxtaposing rhetoric and brutality, Pinter ironically undercuts his own position as commentator. His expressed opinion concerns the noxious dissembling of politicians in their representations of Vietnam. However, this intervention is accomplished through the looking glass, as it were, making the literal images of violence seem fantastic while imparting violent overtones to the rhetorical emptiness of "talking about Vietnam" or "assess(ing) this action from a political point of view." For all its nebulous influence, Vietnam itself lingers out of reach. This is not a facile resolution of the aesthetic and the political, but instead a complex rhetorical figure that Pinter offers in response to the question he chooses to answer, which is in this case less about Vietnam than about the relationship between representation and reality. His comment underlines the power of rhetoric to offer false reconciliations, for politicians *and* playwrights.

In 1953, Ionesco wondered: "But how does one manage to represent the non-representable? How do you represent the non-representational and *not* represent the representational?" (53). Pinter's plays raise similar questions about the representation of violence. His emphasis on symbolic displacement rather than visibility indicates resistance to a culture saturated with violent imagery. Yet Pinter's thugs are also political and cultural constructions assembled from available models. To dramatize thuggery is always to confront prior incarnations; Pinter's thugs comment on their predecessors, and the dramas subtly engage the conventions by which social violence is coded and represented.

But the representational history of thuggery is itself notably complex. The thug serves as a figure of collective fantasy, a symbolic negotiation of conflicting cultural attitudes toward violence, criminality, and social existence. For example, the thug's presumptive vocation is violence, yet the poignancy of thug narratives often depends on the sublimation of destructive urges. When juxtaposed with overt brutality, the hoodlum's love of his mother (*White Heat*), Beethoven (*A Clockwork Orange*), or even fresh produce (*The Godfather*) establishes contiguity between recognizable human attributes and insensible aggression. As cultural icon, the thug embodies coherent social meanings beyond opaque, pathological otherness. The disturbing quality of a film like *Henry: Portrait of a Serial Killer*—with its coldly objective, naturalistic aesthetic—rests on the absence on any figure, voice, or code to make sense of the wanton killing. More typically, however, such representations simultaneously demystify and fetishize violence by mapping its unknowability on familiar iconographies. The thug's prohibited, recalcitrant deviancy enables collective fantasies around inverse questions of authority and submission. Yet an emphasis on violent closure and narrative coherence effectively orchestrates and represses potential transgressions; most often, deviance is contained.

In the two epigraphs above, Lindner and Adorno suggest that even from the thug's point of view, violence is not a consummation but a substitution; a symbolic, compensatory release of displaced aggression. The act matters less than the symbolic work it performs in relation to trauma, maladjustment, and fantasy, triggered by actual or perceived external provocation. Pinter's thugs, by contrast, are denied vocational fulfillment. They pursue the mechanics of barbarity detached from its physical culmination. This is a dual estrangement, encompassing both characters and audience. Pinter's crime dramas withhold crime, offering the formal shell of suspense without the release of violent spectacle. What remains is a gallery of authoritarian personalities rendered without the solace of visible horror. Through the very absence of conventional gratifications, Pinter's work highlights our expectation of represented violence and our veiled authoritarian sympathies.

The social symbolism of thuggery in Pinter's work is predominantly framed by popular narratives. His thugs operate within conventions of the crime story and the dominant form of suspense. In reshaping basic patterns in the cultural aesthetics of crime, Pinter exposes the repressive ideological sublimations at work in many crime narratives that contain (and sanction) violence by making it coherent and pleasurable. Suspense usually entails the aesthetic organization of violence for purposes of pleasure, and suspense narratives typically impose strategies of closure on the more broadly social, contradictory components of the represented crimes. At the same time, suspense depends on anxiety and fear—heightened by the deferral of narrative objectives and the withholding of information—as the raw material of pleasurable resolution. Suspense narratives are dangerous because the disturbing fantasies they seek to manage are socially and psychologically hazardous if left uncontained. Pinter retools the conventions of crime narrative by exploiting this dual aspect of suspense, refiguring its ideological shape in small, perverse fragments. His plays organize responses to violence by deferring its final representation, thereby emphasizing patterns of dominance and submission in social and linguistic relationships and highlighting the psychosocial aggression that suspense both encourages and conceals.

Popular narratives form one subtext of *The Birthday Party* (1958), a play that jarringly mixes absurdist thugs with stereotypes derived from domestic drama. In this work, Pinter parodies suspense conventions through violent generic mutation, yielding a curious hybrid of music-hall comedy, absurdism, melodrama, and the crime thriller. More radically, the play injects two otherwise gratuitous interrogations, fragmented and misplaced in the domestic context. Oddly, these clichéd interrogation scenes constitute the theatrical and emotional core of the play, though their alarming incongruity resists assimilation. In seminal fashion, the interrogations inaugurate a number of characteristic tensions and displacements. Stanley, a former pianist of uncertain renown, has been living for some time in a strangely deserted seaside boarding house run by a solemn man, Petey, and his flirtatious wife, Meg, who are both in their sixties. One morning, on what may or may not be Stanley's birthday, Meg announces that two men have been inquiring about lodgings. Immediately suspicious, Stanley avoids the two men, Goldberg and McCann, when they arrive. In the evening, however, Goldberg and McCann confront Stanley, berating him with nonsensical questions, finally inducing a semi-catatonic silence. The next morning, they subject the unresponsive Stanley to a second interrogation, then abduct him, explaining to Petey: "He needs special treatment" (85).

The first interrogation begins with Goldberg and McCann forcing Stanley into a chair, asking questions like "Why did you leave the organization?" (48). The initial overtones of gangsterism and complicity are juxtaposed with Stanley's escalating confusion and the woeful insufficiency of his responses. For example, when asked to defend his choice of lodging, Stanley cryptically mentions a headache and Goldberg presses him to describe his course of headache treatment. Stanley is unable to recall the precise brand of fruit salts, nor definitively assert that he stirred them properly. "Did they fizz?" Goldberg asks portentously. "Did they fizz or didn't they fizz?" (48).

After its conventional opening, the interrogation soon withdraws from reassuring film noir or gangster clichés. Administering headache remedies acquires the force of a categorical imperative. Even in the mundane consumer space of using products and following directions the inability to stir "properly" is taken as an index of some more universal guilt. As the interrogation proceeds, the initial gangsterism takes an even more ominous shape. Goldberg and McCann inquire about the political situation in Ireland, wicket-watering on a cricket pitch in Melbourne, and "the Albigensenist heresy." They accuse Stanley of being a traitor to the cloth, of soiling the sheet of his birth (after he admits that he sleeps in the nude), before incongruously asking, "Why did the chicken cross the road?" When Stanley cannot satisfactorily respond, they demand to know "Chicken? Egg? Which came first?" that leads Stanley to an aphasic scream (51–52).

In compressed, economical fashion, the interrogation suggests a terrifying anxiety connected to even the most banal phenomena. The frame of reference oscillates between one's sleeping habits and the arcane tortures inflicted on heretics. Conventions, stereotypes, mundane references, and clichés enable a sense of familiarity, which is then subjected to the most outrageous abuses and manipulations. Certainly, there are a number of recognizable threads—religious, political, epistemological, social—sewn into Goldberg and McCann's accusations. Yet the structure of the interrogation is reminiscent of revue-sketch comedy, with its furious rhythms, incongruous responses, and conceptual free association. For example, Stanley first suffers the acute social embarrassment of not completing an ancient comic setup with a thousand possible punch lines (Why did the chicken cross the road?). Then, in a metonymic displacement via the chicken, we arrive at the clichéd recalcitrance of ontology itself (the chicken or the egg?). Thus Stanley is very nearly being "entertained" as he is humiliated, although, in the manner of Don Rickles, Goldberg and McCann ridicule him when he cannot keep pace, in what one might characterize as burlesque inquisition.

Comedy, however, does not mesh comfortably with the manifest cruelty of these exchanges. With a toehold in a realist world, the interrogations refuse the consolation of a stable frame of reference not only in relation to questions of fact but also at the level of the generic sensibility informing the audience. The second interrogation, for example, undercuts even the limited stability of the first. At the conclusion of the second interrogation, Stanley has fully regressed to a prelinguistic gurgling. Goldberg and McCann now unexpectedly employ the rhetoric of restoration and cure. They assure Stanley that he will be reorientated, rich, adjusted, a mensch, and a success. Stanley is told that he will give orders and make decisions as a magnate and statesman with yachts and animals. Here the earlier avenues of threat are unexpectedly transformed into the disembodied, sunny disposition of self-help advertising fantasy.

Taken together, the two interrogations transcode contradictory notions drawn from various social, philosophical, and commercial discourses. Goldberg and McCann represent an unnamed organization, and as Raymond Williams contends, "the fact that it is unnamed allows every effect at once: criminal, political, religious, metaphysical" (324). The broad ambiguity of menace miniaturizes suspense. Language, freed from the burdens of referential realism, is purely instrumentalized toward domination, and the deferral of physical violence effectively insinuates coercion into the naked power of speech, independent of meaning or content. This extreme, perverted form of conversation is in turn reflected on the skeletal banalities littered throughout the play, evoking what Williams terms "the dead strangeness and menace of a drifting, routine-haunted, available common life" (325).

In a purer form, Pinter's *The Dumb Waiter* (1960) presses the conventions of suspense narrative, evoking the imprint of violence on the symbolic parameters of social and cultural life. *The Dumb Waiter* clearly owes a debt to existing iconographies, engaging these traditions in complex ways. Yet the play—with its absurdist thugs, endless digressions, and final paralysis—is again concerned with symbolic crimes, with representational displacements of violence. The plot concerns a pair of ostensible assassins, Gus and Ben, who bide time in the basement of what once may have been a restaurant, waiting for instructions on their next hit. After much desultory and occasionally malevolent conversation on a variety of topics, the disused dumbwaiter in the back wall springs to life, issuing written demands for increasingly bizarre and exotic meals. Finally, Gus leaves to get a glass of water. Ben receives instructions from the heretofore silent speaking tube, indicating the target is on the way. Gus reenters, disheveled. Ben, his pistol drawn, stares at Gus in a final tableau.

The play's opening foregrounds the problem of represented cruelty and suffering. Ben disgustedly reads two newspaper stories aloud while Gus intermittently responds with astonishment: "He what?" "No?" "Go on!" "Get away." "It's unbelievable." This extended theatrical business subtly indicates the remote barbarity of an unknowable world—a gratuitous, generalized violence that permeates the apparent safety of the basement. The first newspaper story concerns an old man who unwisely tried to cross a road in a traffic jam by crawling under a stationary lorry, which then proceeded to run over him. Ben concludes that "It's enough to make you want to puke," but concedes, incredulously, that "It's down here in black and white" (86). The second, somewhat more Freudian story centers on an eight-year-old girl who allegedly killed a cat while her brother, age eleven, viewed the incident from the toolshed. Regarding this unpleasant scenario, Ben can only manage, "That's bloody ridiculous" (88).

In this first interchange, familiar expectations for suspense narrative are both established and undercut. Identification, humor, and incipient suspense are troubled by an uneasy, regressive logic behind the seemingly coherent illusion. At the level of character, one might initially detect a reassuring and comprehensible dualism, drawn from the constellation of passive/aggressive, servant/master, straight man/comedian, id/ego types. Ben, it would seem, is the more assertive and misanthropic, whereas Gus is a bit of a credulous ponce. This distinction, however, is undermined by the reciprocity of their strangeness, as though the two were halves of a singular and all-encompassing "personality," in the abstract and alienated sense of the word. Further, the manifest silliness of the news items and the snorting, exaggerated indignation of the responses are certainly funny, yet Ben's declaration "It's bloody ridiculous" is not a punch line. Instead, it betrays a symptomatic failure of the definitive insight and perspectival closure essential to ironic or sarcastic humor.

At the outset *The Dumb Waiter* presents alienated, languishing killers who read reports of violent incidents that escalate into Freudian perversity in inverse proportion to their apparent seriousness. Violence—as an index of reality beyond the play's claustrophobic codes and conventions—is available only through filters of unreliable reportage, narrative, and representation. The fulfillment of visible killing, expected ironically by both killers and audience, is immediately displaced by symbolic aggressions embedded in the newspaper. Indeed, taken together, the two newspaper items gravitate toward a gnawing unpleasantness. In regressive fashion, the cat killing suggests a more trivial yet somehow more grisly and dismal sensibility than the faux tragedy of the old man, which appears increasingly incommensurable and incongruous in light of the anecdote that succeeds it.

As the action progresses, aggression circulates around the ostensibly innocent newspaper, a mundane object that eventually divides the characters. *The Dumb Waiter* plays with the contradictory feelings aroused by newspaper reading as emblem of healthy populism and good citizenship, a triumphant ratification of the social contract, coupled with the familiar chill of seeing another person immersed in a newspaper across the now fully demarcated territories of human separation. A torso and face concealed by a newspaper engender a kind of suppressed loathing for that inviolable spectacle of self-absorption on the other side of the breakfast table or living room, eerily summed up by Gus's petulant question—"How many times have you read that paper?" (102).

The unexpected malevolence of the play's opening suggests that Pinter is less concerned with suspense as the pleasurable organization of violence than with a suspense that frustrates precisely those conventions. Aggression resides in the sphere of banal small talk and domestic objects (the newspaper, the malfunctioning toilet, the dumbwaiter itself), which now function as disturbing ideograms of a violent history. I would argue, moreover, that Pinter distills suspense to an extreme manifestation, so that it no longer constitutes a narrative category in the broad sense of plot or event but rather expresses the ill-fated microscopic impulses toward closure in the silences amid disconnected dialogue, the implied foundational uncertainty of subjects and their relationships, and the phenomenological dislocation between subject and world. These deferred, prolonged transactions and the continual move to complete them are the engine of Pinter's narrative (such as it is), at the level of the episode and the play as a whole.

As an illustration, consider the apparently semantic debate between Gus and Ben on the subject of making tea. The exchange begins with Ben directing Gus to light the kettle and Gus insisting that lighting the gas is the proper figure of speech. The argument continues to escalate, nearly precipitating a physical altercation, before Gus concludes, "I bet my mother used to say it," an assertion that Ben cryptically challenges: "Your mother? When did you last see your mother?" (97–98). The scene recapitulates the play's familiar pattern of suspenseful escalation to the brink of physical violence, simultaneously enabled and deferred by innocuous, though aggressive, linguistic gestures. The sublimating functions of language as a system for negotiating desires and resolving disputes, together with the symbolic civility of English tea, are here indicted as specious reconciliations. Further, the digressive triviality of the scene, the regressive movement from "Go and light it" to "your mother," suspends the causal strictures of narrative expectation. Like the play's final tableau, the kettle digression inhabits "dynamic" instrumentalized narrative only to boil it down to an elemental stasis. Suspense—as the expectation of resolution and as a figure of eternal waiting—is held like a gun to the audience's head.

In these early plays, Pinter's critique of suspense is expressed dialogically: through a polyphony of caricatured thugs trapped in regressive micronarratives, who can still be disavowed as types, clowns, or tokens of a larger parody. In later works, however, the thug evolves from comedic cipher to post-Freudian subject, and the problem of narrative refers not only to conventional dramatic forms but also to self-narration, to inner libidinal violence documented in self-dramatizing monologues. Nicolas, in *One for the Road*, is perhaps the central example. His two scenes with Victor are dominated by narcissistic, wheedling self-disclosures. Here, regressive gestures in dialogue are to some degree superseded by monologic digression, by the intermittent substitution of self-narration for dramatic suspense. This is a complex shift with several new points of emphasis. The appeal of represented violence partly rests on the symbolic fulfillment of prohibited aggressions and desires. For thugs, real violence likewise plays a symbolic role. In the absence of violent consummation, the thug's frustrated, digressive monologues mirror the spectator's analogous lack of fulfillment. Watching Pinter's post-Freudian thugs, the spectator's expectations are disturbingly aligned with the characters' elaborate pathologies, encouraging and highlighting unwanted identifications. The monologic mode gradually negates even the small pleasures of dialogue, plurality, and conventional suspense, and the remaining drama rests on the queasy spectacle of self-disclosure.

As we have seen, even the early works dramatize generalized aggression without visible violence, a suspension that refuses to pleasurably display its grisly referent. The new political emphasis introduces a new problem; it is difficult to represent the lived reality of political violence without perpetrating a second, artistic injustice. Pinter's late plays negotiate a line between critique and exploitation. The later work increasingly stresses psychopathic interiority and the corollary aesthetic form of monologue. This approach explores the authoritarian implications of the single, coercive voice, and the links among erotic fantasy, social ideology, and political violence. The monologic mode also interrupts the causal, interpersonal logic of popular narratives, subtly resisting the rendering of violence in conventional, entertaining forms.

Again, the thug acts as a crucial instrument of transformation. Lenny, the misanthropic racketeer of *The Homecoming* (1965), is a key transitional figure in the development of the late Pinter. His seemingly gratuitous speeches to Ruth in Act I assume importance by virtue not only of their exceptional length, strangeness, and misogyny but also by their eerie reminiscence of the cat killing recounted in *The Dumb Waiter*. We are later given to believe that Lenny is a mid-level pimp, though the final, ludicrous schemes concerning Ruth suggest a deranged, delusional underling. In any case, the erotic component of his thuggery is clear, and the confluence of frustrated sexuality, violence, and guilty confession in these two speeches underlines the complicity between pleasure and aggression in the psyche of the thug.

In contrast to earlier conventions of the soliloquy, Kristin Morrison argues: "Now the telling of a story allows characters that quintessentially 'modern,' Freudian opportunity to reveal deep and difficult thoughts and feelings while at the same time concealing them as fiction or at least distancing them as narration" (3). In Pinter, self-representations function as verbal symptoms. The thug's monologues simultaneously repress, enact, and reveal. Lenny's anecdotes compress narcissism, exhibitionism, aggression, and sexual anxiety in a single gesture. Shortly after meeting his visiting sister-in-law Ruth for the first time, Lenny's brother Teddy having gone to bed, Lenny incongruously asks if he can hold her hand. "Why?" she asks, and Lenny proceeds to tell the rambling story of a sexually aggressive, pox-ridden woman accosting him one night near the docks. Scandalized by the woman's indecent proposals, Lenny beats her and even entertains thoughts of murder, but decides against getting himself into "a state of tension," opting instead to give her "another belt in the nose and a couple of turns of the boot" (30–31).

Ruth is unimpressed by this account, and Lenny unhesitatingly launches into an even stranger anecdote, which opens on a winter morning when, feeling civic-minded, he volunteers to shovel snow in the neighborhood. He spends several enjoyable hours at this task before being rudely interrupted by an old woman during his mid-morning tea. The woman enlists Lenny's help in moving an iron mangle inconsiderately left in the wrong room by her brother-in-law. Unfortunately, Lenny can't move the mangle because "It must have weighed about half a ton." Heroically struggling with the mangle, "risking a rupture," Lenny is nonplussed by the woman's lack of assistance, precipitating the rhetorical question, "why don't you stuff this iron mangle up your arse?" Lenny is tempted to give her a "workover," but considering his good mood, he settles for "a short-arm jab to the belly" (32–33).

On the one hand, Lenny's monologues document a litany of sexual abnormalities, including fetishism, sadism, and masochistic exhibitionism. Despite desperate attempts to indicate mastery, he appears regressed, childlike, polymorphously perverse. At the same time, Lenny evinces a deep, neurotic disgust with the pox-ridden "liberties" of sexuality and a consequent inability to consummate the symbolic murder and by implication the sexual act. His anxiety when confronted with Ruth's subsequent overtures confirms the sexual panic concealed in the anecdotes. Further, his crude substitution of "clumping," "belts," and "jabs" for intercourse suggests that the deferred "murder" may stand for a terrifying, disavowed orgasm. These displacements speak to a catastrophic repression. Self-destructive sexuality is externalized through violent fantasies directed against the other.

Pinter's eroticized thug exists at the borderline of psychosis and neurosis, a space between the fantasized omnipotence described by Lindner and Adorno and the tremulous displacement of sexual and violent urges. More disturbingly, Pinter aligns the authoritarian pathology of the thug with the psychology of the spectator. He unexpectedly joins violent, sexual, and narrative desires in a single uneasy suspense. The unwanted "state of tension" that Lenny associates with murder is an apt image for the digressions, deferrals, and repressive sublimations experienced by the viewer. Fantasy images that perplex the characters become metaphors for an artistic process that implicates the audience. For example, "mangle," a noun, signifies a primitive, vaguely monstrous laundry apparatus ("they're out of date, you want to get a spin drier" [33]), while "mangle," a verb, implies mutilating disfigurement. This single image intimates archaic, repressed memories, a pronounced castration threat, and the condensed or displaced "disfigurements" necessary to symbolic representation. The mangle's resonance with Freudian dream-imagery is surely not gratuitous. Pinter's late thugs function as social and psychological surrogates, monologists of collective, authoritarian fantasy.

Pinter's expectation that we identify with post-Freudian thuggery is evident in the plays' latent psychic and social pathology. In the absence of narrative containment, closure, or violent resolution, this disturbing dynamic remains unsublimated. The question of pleasure, de-eroticized in the early suspenseful narratives, is here externalized as a polymorphous sexuality coupled with violence and aggression. This sexualized violence, incipient in *The Homecoming*, finds almost pure expression in *One for the Road* (1984), a play centered on the erotics of torture. Indeed, Lenny's descendant Nicolas, the high-ranking thug of the latter play, nakedly embodies both tendencies. *One for the Road* consists of four short scenes in which Nicolas separately interrogates a father, mother, and son. Two encounters between Nicolas and the father, Victor, open and close the play. In the first, Victor, brutalized, pleads for his own execution; in the last, prior to his release, Victor learns of the repeated rape of his wife, Gila, and the murder of his son.

One for the Road projects an alluring yet intensely problematic aura of resolution in light of Pinter's career. Its disturbing, topical subject-matter encourages the retrospective impression that the play is a kind of *Ur*-text for Pinter's thugs. It is indeed tempting to read the play as a regression from the clownish, innocent early thugs to a grim political violence at their origin. But this teleological reading is troubled by Pinter's conflicted gesture. Like other plays in the anti-authoritarian cycle, the setting of *One for the Road* is left ambiguous. Disclosure of the thug's secret, political meaning is balanced by mystification of historical context. This play about "real" torture retains a curious degree of abstraction. Moreover, *One for the Road* refrains from depicting torture and focuses instead on purposeless, digressive conversations at torture's periphery. Despite its apparent realism, the play's links to real violence remain equivocal. Again, Pinter's subject is the representation of violence; the play exposes aggressions inscribed in speech, intimations of violence deprived of spurious visible consummation.

As a verbal rather than physical torturer, Nicolas conjoins erotic and political violence in the language of fantasy. Throughout the play, his obsessive identification with father-figures is mirrored by his excoriating hatred of Gila and preoccupation with the actual and symbolic rape of the guilty maternal figure. His intermittently wheedling, seductive monologues to Victor sharply contrast the inane, dialogic interrogation of Gila, who embodies an intolerable threat that is first confronted and then disavowed. The erratic, contradictory quality of such symbolic maneuvers signals psychic instability, an impression deepened through many verbal slips. For example, an attempt at thuggish menace leads Nicolas to mention castration as an antidote to Victor's despair, but the monologic form suggests that the anxious fantasy belongs to the speaker. Similarly, Nicolas's perverse questions to Nicky about parental love echo his own half-joking maternal reference, "Do you think I'm mad? My mother did" (33). Finally, the repellent "joke" concerning Gila's sexuality is so poorly told, riddled with pauses, and punctuated by "wild" laughter that Nicolas feels compelled to explain it. Again, attempted intimidation yields to uncontained sexual anxiety, and the frantic explication reflects a desire to discipline the joke's unruliness.

More broadly, *One for the Road* centers on pathologies embedded in language. In the play's representational sphere, the civilities and sublimations of speech share reciprocal guilt with the imagined violence offstage. Nicolas's polite frankness at the outset introduces respectable discourse, and subsequent civil locutions are arrayed against the boot, castration, and "the death of others" (45) as reminders of the ineluctable suffering that rhetorical civility disguises and enables. "One has to be so scrupulous about language" (40), Nicolas remarks, and *One for the Road* blurs the boundaries between torture and the coercive power of rhetoric. For victims, speech is a luxury, and when Nicolas taunts the silent Victor with the latter's reputed fondness for "the cut and thrust of debate" (45), the context mocks the liberal ideal and the colorful image points to unsublimated realities lurking beyond the metaphor. Nor is the audience left innocent. On the one hand, the spectator is aligned with Victor, a passive, silenced victim of the narrator-as-torturer. Yet the comfort of a safe, privileged distance, the ideology of the cultural spectator, is unavailable or denied to victims, and this complicity extends to neutrally dissecting the play after the performance. To quiescently attend *One for the Road* is in some way to countenance it, and this is, I think, as Pinter intends.

Indeed, what distinguishes *One for the Road* is its perverse, insistent theatricality, an aesthetic rendering of torture that presupposes an audience. In this sense, Nicolas functions as both narrator and *metteur en scène*. His florid images, melodramatic ruminations, rhetorical posturing, psychological disclosures, and wild shifts in substance and tone, coupled with the nearly mathematical variation in monologic and dialogic modes of expression, the manipulated verbal rhythm of each distinct scene, the fully orchestrated permutations of standing and sitting figures, and the contrived erotics and politics of space—all conspire to render the interrogation as spectacle. Psychologically, Nicolas bears resemblance to psychoanalyst Christopher Bollas's description of a particular form of hysteria, namely, hysterical psychosis, which is marked by the patient's tendency to perform for the analyst, to trap the analyst in a mutually destructive dramatization of the self:

> Hysterical psychosis presents undigested images, visual scenes that defy meaning . . . Clinicians working with the psychotic actions of the hysteric do indeed find them very hard to think about, precisely because the hysteric has presented himself or herself in a grotesquely vivid manner. This is a kind of sexual psychosis, as the patient wraps these scenes in sexual lining, all too often driving the analyst into further bewilderment by an erotism gone awry. . . . For this is a psychosis that represents sexuality. Sexuality that drives the self mad. (143)

Emanating from one of the higher-ranking thugs in the Pinter canon, Nicolas's hysterical psychosis provides a psychic foundation for authoritarian violence, condensing aggression and sexuality in a single figure. At a second level, if one substitutes "author" for "hysteric" and "spectator" for "clinician," Bollas offers a fair description of Pinter's creative process. The hysterical psychotic's performances are resistant and undigested, symptomatic rather than transparent. The dramatist requires similar displacements in representing social violence, and Pinter's thugs are thus better read as symptoms than mimetic imitations. Indeed, considered realistically, Nicolas provides an easy target. Marked by his profession, visibly attached to institutional torture, the character elicits immediate and satisfying outrage. The true horror of *One for the Road* inheres less in Nicolas than in the audience's untenable relation to the spectacle. In the broad context of Pinter's work, Nicolas functions as the symptom of deeper pathologies. On the ultimate hierarchy of thugs, he ranks no higher than functionary.

In Pinter's canon the insidious thugs have purged all outward signs of thuggery and delegated the dirty work to adjutants. Insulated and invisible, the true *metteurs en scène* carouse while their militias cleanse the streets. This is the scenario of *Party Time*, the final rung on the thug's ladder. The proletarian orbit occupied by Gus, Ben, Goldberg, McCann, and Nicolas's "boys" circles an unseen center. The upper echelons of thuggery wage a campaign of symbolic terror, manipulating cultural signifiers, stigmatizing the undesirable. Cloaked in respectability, the sanitized thug enters and then propagates the cultural mainstream. In a popular culture steeped in violent imagery, violent realities are effectively displaced. The brutality of this culture lies not in what it depicts but in what it conceals.

Note: the title of this essay was suggested by the short story "A Poetics for Bullies," by Stanley Elkin.

Works Cited

Adorno, T. W., et al. *The Authoritarian Personality*. New York: Harper, 1950.

Bollas, Christopher. *Hysteria*. London and New York: Routledge, 2000.

Colleran, Jeanne. "Disjuncture as Theatrical and Postmodern Practice in Griselda Gambaro's *The Camp* and Harold Pinter's *Mountain Language*." *Pinter at Sixty*. Ed. Katherine H. Burkman and John L. Kundert-Gibbs. Bloomington: Indiana UP, 1993, 49–65.

Elkin, Stanley. "A Poetics for Bullies." *Criers & Kibitzers, Kibitzers & Criers*. New York: Thunder's Mouth Press, 1990, 197–217.

Esslin, Martin. *Pinter: A Study of His Plays*. New York: Norton, 1976.

Ionesco, Eugene. "Notes on the Theatre." *Twentieth-Century Theatre: A Sourcebook*. Ed. Richard Drain. Trans. Donald Watson. London and New York: Routledge, 1995, 53–55.

Lindner, Robert. *Rebel without a Cause*. New York: Grune and Stratton, 1944.

Morrison, Kristin. *Canters and Chronicles: The Use of Narrative in the Plays of Samuel Beckett and Harold Pinter*. Chicago: U of Chicago P, 1983.

Page, Malcolm. *File on Pinter*. London: Methuen, 1993.

Pinter, Harold. *The Birthday Party* and *The Room*. New York: Grove Press, 1968.

———. *The Caretaker* and *The Dumb Waiter*. New York: Grove Press, 1988.

———. *The Homecoming*. New York: Grove Press, 1966.

———. *One for the Road*. London: Methuen, 1986.

———. *Party Time* and *The New World Order*. New York: Grove Press, 1993.

States, Bert O. "Pinter's *Homecoming*: The Shock of Nonrecognition." *Harold Pinter*. Ed. Harold Bloom. New York: Chelsea House, 1987, 7–18.

Williams, Raymond. *Drama from Ibsen to Brecht*. New York: Oxford UP, 1969.

2

"You'll Never Be without a Police Siren": Pinter and the Subject of Law

MARC SILVERSTEIN

In Harold Pinter's *Ashes to Ashes,* Rebecca, hearing the wail of a police siren breaking the silence of a summer evening, declares that the sound leaves her "terribly upset . . . terribly insecure" (29–31). Her reaction will hardly surprise those familiar with the authoritarian police states Pinter dramatizes in the overtly political plays he has written since the mid-1980s: *One for the Road, Mountain Language, Party Time,* and *The New World Order.* In these works, such criminal acts as rape, murder, and torture are carried out by those entrusted to safeguard "law and order"; indeed, are carried out in the very name of the law. The siren provoking Rebecca's anxiety, however, does not approach her, heralding imminent arrest and the kind of horrific sexual brutality to which the police subject Gila in *One for the Road*; rather, it recedes in the distance: "It just hit me so hard. You see . . . as the siren faded away in my ears I knew it was becoming louder and louder for somebody else" (29). What makes this moment so disturbing is the palpable loss Rebecca feels, as if her subjectivity were dissolving within the siren's diminishing echo: "I hate it fading away. I hate it echoing away. I hate it leaving me. I hate losing it. I hate somebody else possessing it. I want it to be mine, all the time. It's such a beautiful sound" (31). Rebecca's (presumed) husband, Devlin, offers her the chilling consolation that "there'll always be another one. There is one on its way to you now. Believe me. You'll hear it again soon. Any minute. . . . So you can take comfort from that, at least. Can't you? You'll never be lonely again. You'll never be without a police siren" (31–33).

Not simply the siren, but the law for which it metonymically stands, functions as Rebecca's *objet petite à,* Lacan's term for the object that promises (but fails to deliver) the plenitude freeing us from lack. Since we often think of law and desire as locked in conflict, we cannot help asking how law has come to occupy the privileged position of object of desire for Rebecca, a question to which the existential pun in Devlin's response provides an answer: "You'll never *be* without a police siren." Devlin's words suggest the inextricable relation between subjectivity and the law by emphasizing that the recognition and validation of being depend upon a kind of policing; that accession to subjectivity produces our subjection to law; that we only appear as social subjects through simultaneously becoming objects of surveillance, discipline, and punishment. While the subject may elude the watchful eye of the other determined to best her in the fraught battle for power that constitutes the quintessential action of a Pinter play, she can never escape the panoptic gaze of the Other, the symbolic order both producing and produced by the dominant social/cultural/political order with which it is coextensive. As Anthony Wilden puts it, "The Other is not a person, but a principle; the locus of the 'law of desire' . . . the only place from which it is possible to say 'I am who I am'" (22). If the subject can only "be" through her recognition by the Other, that recognition demands the "gift" of the subject's desire. Not only must the subject desire in conformity with the law but she must also desire the law itself, thus ensuring the perpetuation of the symbolic order in its current form. The most important task then for those who police the symbolic order from their subject position of the Symbolic Father, as Lacan argues, "is fundamentally to unite (and not to set in opposition) a desire and the Law" (321). Only through this unity that binds subjects to the law will the symbolic order achieve the perfection of what Douglas, in *Party Time,* calls "a cast-iron peace:" "No leaks. No draughts. Cast iron. Tight as a drum. That's the kind of peace we want and that's the kind of peace we're going to get. A cast-iron peace. *He clenches his fist.* Like this" (17).

The clenched fist embodies the force of law—the force that *is* law—and tacitly acknowledges both the repressive and the ideological forms of violence exercised by the Other in its drive to "unite" desire and the law. A concrete image of this force, the fist guarantees that the subject will "freely" offer up her desire to the Other's law. If the law must resort to the fist in order to produce subjectivity as subjection, such aggression finds its justification in the subject's acquiescence to the violence directed against her. In *The New World Order,* Pinter presents us with a blindfolded man awaiting torture from Des and Lionel, who congratulate each other on their role in "keeping the world clean for democracy." Mystifying their atrocities through the language of cleansing (which, ironically, reminds us of one of the meanings of "police"—to make clean and keep in order), Des finds himself so moved by their nobility of purpose that, before commencing the man's torture, he declares to Lionel, "I'm going to shake you by the hand. . . . *He then gestures to the man in the chair with his thumb.* And so will he . . . in about thirty-five minutes" (60). For Des, torture does not so much destroy a rebellious individual as it produces a docile body who will shake Lionel's hand, an action through which the man will "freely" locate himself within the subject position the State demands he occupy.

Althusser asserts "that every 'subject' endowed with a 'consciousness' and believing in the 'ideas' that his 'consciousness' inspires in him and *freely* accepts, must '*act* according to his ideas,' must therefore inscribe his own ideas as a *free* subject in the actions of his material practice. If he does not do so, 'that is wicked'" (167–68; emphasis added). We cannot miss the irony of this passage, for it is precisely Althusser's point that nowhere does subjection to ideological interpellation, to "the indelible and constitutive mark of the Law" (211), reveal itself more clearly than in the actions through which the subject (mis)recognizes her status as a free agent. Of course, I am not suggesting we conflate subjection to ideology with subjection to torture. If the man does "inscribe his own ideas in action" by shaking Lionel's hand, he will be responding to the clenched fist rather than to internalized cultural codes. Des and Lionel will translate "the indelible mark of the Law" from metaphor into (corpo)reality as they inscribe it on the flesh of the tortured body. At the same time, however, we can read *The New World Order* as exposing the violence inherent in the process of ideological subject formation, the clenched fist forever lurking beneath the handshake sealing the "bond" between the subject and the Other.

In the Lacanian/Althusserian paradigm, accession to subjectivity fundamentally involves emerging within what Althusser calls "the order of objectifying language that will finally allow [the subject] to say: I, you, he, she or it" (210). If this language allows the subject to name herself, it simultaneously objectifies her since it is saturated with the desires, meanings, and values of the Other. Language operates as a powerful ensemble of cultural codes structuring "the determinate ideological formations in which the persons inscribed in these structures live their functions" (211). The Other will only recognize the subject *as* a subject if the latter reproduces its subjectivity as subjection through engaging in the "proper" linguistic practice learned through socialization. With this in mind, we can see why Pinter does not need to specify a particular criminal act the blindfolded man in *The New World Order* (as well as Victor and Gila in *One for the Road* and Jimmy in *Party Time*) has committed, but presents him as "guilty" of the offense that proves most threatening to the operation of the symbolic order—a transgressive appropriation of language that challenges the taxonomies through which the Other maintains its dominance. The man, Des tells us, "was a big shot, he never stopped shooting his mouth off, he never stopped questioning received ideas. Now . . . he's stopped all that, he's got nothing more to say" (58). Through questioning the status of the Other's Word as Law, rejecting the ideological codes of the authoritarian state that proclaim, as Nicolas puts it in *One for the Road,* "we are all patriots, we are as one, we all share a common heritage" (50), the man has effectively refused subjectivity. Indeed, we cannot regard the blindfolded figure before us as a subject since he lacks a name to stand as the most fundamental signifier of identity; lacks a voice to secure his place within "the order of objectifying language that will finally allow him to say: I;" lacks even the ability to hold the audience in his gaze possessed by the Protagonist, his counterpart in Samuel Beckett's *Catastrophe*. Lacking all of this, the man is little more than a present absence, a void that the state will undertake to fill so that he may recognize his "oneness" with Des and Lionel in the "democracy" they all serve, in return for which the Other will recognize him through the handshake that confirms him as a social subject.

Juliet Flower MacCannell argues that the ideological hegemony of a dominant cultural or political order demands that "the Law is 'enforced' in civil society, through its *police* . . . the policing of words (including the forms of politeness), the effort to constrain, restrain, fix meanings and men" (123). "The policing of words" Pinter dramatizes in *The New World Order* entails a physical violence that goes beyond the implicit coercion involved in the "good" subject's ideological interpellation. We can see the connections between ideological and repressive power, however, when Lionel deviates, albeit inadvertently, from state-sanctioned linguistic practice. Hurling abuse at the man as a prelude to torture, Lionel commits the "crime" of calling him first a "cunt" and then a "prick," to which Des responds in his capacity as mouthpiece for the Law: "How many times do I have to tell you? You've got to learn to define your terms and stick to them. You can't call him a cunt in one breath and a prick in the next. The terms are mutually contradictory. . . . And you know what it means to you. You know what language means to you" (57–58). Lionel's "innocent" mistake of suggesting the interchangeablity of that which must remain opposed cannot even begin to compare with the "questioning [of] received ideas" by the most feared "criminal" in such regimes—the active political dissident. As Des's response indicates, however, we can locate both Lionel and the man on a continuum of linguistic misappropriation. Lionel's momentary failure to "stick to" conventional definitions threatens to expose them *as* conventional rather than an inherent linguistic property. If, as MacCannell asserts, language functions as "the way order is *ideologized* in its everyday form" (122) by ordering, separating, and hierarchizing identity categories, then Lionel introduces a note of disorder that violates the law's demand for fixed meanings.

Since Lionel is a "good" subject, he can respond appropriately to Des's "policing of words" without the latter's resorting to the clenched fist as he must with the blindfolded man. Lionel accepts Des's correction and contemplates the violence he will enact with renewed fervor, even sobbing as he declares that he "feel[s] so pure" (60) as he "keeps the world clean for democracy." The comment about democracy reiterates the point that Pinter has made repeatedly in his speeches, interviews, and journalistic contributions of the last two decades, namely that the so-called Western democracies utilize the same methods of repression they ascribe to those criminal "rogue states" identified as the evil empire *du jour.* More subtly, however, this comment suggests that the act of torture functions ideologically for those who *perform* it. Even as they force the man's body to receive "the indelible mark of the Law," Des and Lionel re-mark themselves as subject to and subjects of that law. In "Eroding the Language of Freedom," included in his recent collection *Various Voices*, Pinter argues that "an entire range of encroachments on fundamental freedoms is taking place now in [Western democracies]. . . . I believe that the root cause of this state of affairs is that for the last forty years our thought has been trapped in hollow structures of language, a stale, dead but immensely successful rhetoric" (173). Pinter demonstrates just how successful such rhetoric can be through Des and Lionel's perceiving no contradiction between the ideals and values invoked by the codes constituting the semiotic/ideological field of democracy and the horrific violence they will inflict on the man. Indeed, the torture provides the occasion for the reinscription of their subjectivity. If the subject exhibits the success of her ideological interpellation by "inscribing her own ideas as a free subject in the actions of her material practice," the torture they perform serves as that "practice" through which they (re)produce themselves as "free subjects" and, in so doing, (re)produce the "free" and "democratic" order to which they devote themselves.

Even in as brief and relatively straightforward a work as *The New World Order* (which he calls a sketch rather than a play), Pinter offers an illuminating examination of the intersecting roles played by repressive power and ideological power in the process of subject formation. If the line demarcating these forms of power appears to collapse totally within authoritarian regimes, we can never mark the boundaries with finality in *any* process of subject formation. The "determinate ideological formations" in which we take up our subject positions—regardless of what variety of political order we inhabit—have recourse to a violence that, however latent, always presents itself as a menacing possibility. (In this connection, we need to see Lionel's linguistic lapse in relation to the blindfolded man's offense, with the implication that were he to continue to disregard fixed meanings Lionel could find himself in the same position as the man, facing a far more brutal "policing of words" than Des's mild correction.)

I

The connection I am tracing between ideology and repression suggests at least one reason why theorists like Lacan, Althusser, and MacCannell discuss subject formation in terms of metaphors of law and policing. While Althusser distinguishes between institutions that exercise power through violence (repressive state apparatuses, among which he lists the police) and those that exercise power through inserting subjects in their "proper" place within the cultural order (ideological state apparatuses), he tellingly images the act of ideological interpellation with a reference to the repressive arm of the state: "*Interpellation* or hailing . . . can be imagined along the lines of the most common everyday police . . . hailing: 'Hey, you there!' Assuming that the theoretical scene I have imagined takes place in the street, the hailed individual will turn round. By this mere one-hundred-and-eighty-degree physical conversion, he becomes a *subject*." In a footnote to this passage, Althusser adds that while hailing is a common action, it "takes a quite 'special' form in the policeman's practice of 'hailing' which concerns the hailing of 'suspects'" (174). Hailing may produce our subjectivity as subjection to the law that "fixes meanings and men," but such fixity demands the perpetual reinscription of that subjectivity. As subjects we are also "suspects," always potentially dislodging ourselves from the subject positions to which we are sentenced, always capable of placing ourselves beyond the law through an act of linguistic malfeasance that policing must punish.

Subject formation in Pinter's theater never occurs without policing. Consider, for example, the following exchange between Meg and Stanley in *The Birthday Party,* in which his simple request for a cup of tea becomes the occasion for Meg to play the role of policewoman:

> STANLEY: What About Some Tea?
> MEG: Do You Want Some Tea? (STANLEY *Reads The Paper.*) Say Please.
> STANLEY: Please.
> MEG: Say Sorry First,
> STANLEY: Sorry First.
> MEG: No. Just Sorry.
> STANLEY: Just Sorry!
> MEG: You Deserve The Strap. (27–28)

Audiences invariably laugh as Meg treats a man in his late thirties like her small child, but the comedy only underscores how the ideological terrain of the family socializes its subjects through laying down the law. Meg will only acknowledge Stanley's desire—will only acknowledge Stanley as a subject who *can* desire—once he articulates it in the proper manner (and here we should remember that MacCannell refers to imposing "the forms of politeness" as one of the most powerful examples of "the policing of words"). If this exchange parodically dramatizes the social construction of desire (and the fact that the object of desire is something as relatively insignificant as a cup of tea emphasizes the Other's totalizing drive for order), it also reminds us that the authority of the linguistic codes and forms through which we achieve intelligibility as subjects rests upon an extralinguistic violence to which the law always has recourse—the violence of the strap. Of course there is no question of Meg actually beating Stanley, but the occurrence of the threat during the language lesson, like Althusser's reference to the policeman's call as the paradigmatic example of interpellation, suggests how much ideological and repressive forms of power work in concert. The very same actions that constrain, limit, repress, and prohibit also enable and produce a "working" subject. The approved linguistic forms allow Stanley to both send and receive the messages that confirm his subjectivity, but only if he speaks with the Other's voice, thus becoming other and losing the self. Meg finally does give Stanley his tea, but altering his mode of enunciation effectively alters his desire that, in a very real sense, is not "his."

Like Lionel's slip of the tongue in *The New World Order*, Stanley's failure to adopt "the forms of politeness" hardly seems to qualify as transgressive, but just as the full significance of what Lionel says only becomes clear when considered in relation to the blindfolded man, so we must place the exchange between Meg and Stanley in relation to Goldberg and McCann, the play's chief emissaries of the Other, and their efforts to subject Stanley to the law. In the justly famous sequence in which they hurl a barrage of accusations at him, ranging from a capital offense ("Goldberg: Why did you kill your wife? . . . How did you kill her? McCann: You throttled her. Goldberg: With arsenic" (59) to the sin of gluttony ("You stuff yourself with dry toast" [61]), they act like Althusserian policemen, imposing a subjectivity on Stanley that identifies him as a suspect. Of what is Stanley under suspicion; since these charges are patently false, what crime did he commit? His refusal to say "please" and "sorry" unless compelled provides a clue—disregarding "the forms of politeness" through which subjects announce themselves as unquestioning docile bodies within the social order, Stanley attempts to evade the law. Even as he acknowledges the impossibility of locating a space that remains free from the law's demands, a space for existential self-fashioning without reference to the Other, he nevertheless insists on the need for such an utopian space:

> STANLEY (*abruptly*): How would you like to go away with me?
> LULU: Where.
> STANLEY: Nowhere. Still, we could go.
> LULU: But where could we go?
> STANLEY: Nowhere. There's nowhere to go. So we could just go. It wouldn't matter.
> LULU: We might as well stay here.
> STANLEY: No. It's no good here.
> LULU: Well, where else is there?
> STANLEY: Nowhere. (36)

Something has obviously gone drastically wrong with the process of Stanley's subject formation. As Althusser observes, "one of the effects of ideology is the practical *denegation* of the ideological character of ideology

by ideology: ideology never says, 'I am ideological'" (175). Similarly, because of this "denegation," the subject never says, "I am subjected," but, as
his exchange with Lulu demonstrates, Stanley has a sense, albeit never fully
articulated, of subjection as constitutive of the subject's experience. He
must accept that "there's nowhere to go" to extricate himself from the
Other's ideological snares, but his acknowledging this fact serves to undermine the ideological fiction of the "free subject." Such an offense cannot remain unpunished, but just as Des declares that their torture victim will shake
Lionel's hand in *The New World Order*, Goldberg and McCann present
themselves as rehabilitating Stanley, offering him a form of salvation for
which he will give thanks. While their verbal assault of often contradictory
accusations destroys the self-image to which Stanley clings, reducing him to
the silence of a "pre-subject" by depleting the linguistic resources through
which he could answer or counter their charges, their actions serve as a prelude to reinscribing Stanley's subjectivity as a model citizen: "We can save
you. . . . You'll be re-oriented. You'll be rich. You'll be adjusted. You'll be
our pride and joy. You'll be a mensch. You'll be a success. You'll be integrated" (92–94). When Goldberg and McCann exit, taking Stanley to "be re-
oriented" by the mysterious Monty—the never seen but omnipresent figure
that stands as the play's "representation" of the Other—the play completes
its dramatization of the dialectic of violent de(con)struction and constitutive
reconstruction that marks the process of subject formation. Goldberg and
McCann's promise to "watch over" (92) Stanley smacks more of the coercive regulatory gaze through which the police place suspects under surveillance than it does of nurturing protection, but without such monitoring the
subject could never secure a place within the social world. As Judith Butler
cogently phrases it, "the subjects regulated by such [ideological] structures
are, by virtue of being subjected to them, formed, defined, and reproduced
in accordance with the requirements of those structures" (2).

   The dream of a subject who always acts "in accordance with the requirements of" the Other's laws characterizes the various forms of power
Pinter's work investigates. Whether concerned with the ideological "laws"
of subject formation through which the dominant culture seeks to ensure its
perpetuation or the laws through which the authoritarian state seeks to protect itself from those who "question received ideas" while simultaneously
promoting the illusion that it operates democratically, the plays emphasize
the equivalence between the force of law and the law as force. Despite a certain dystopian element in the plays that shows the Other's ability to overcome threats to its hegemony, these threats nevertheless occur. If the law of
cultural and state power produces "good" subjects through "fixing meanings
and men"—fixing meanings in order to fix men—then it is hardly surprising
that the subjects are also suspects since meanings can never achieve the uni-
vocal, monologic finality that would place them beyond question. The only

way to ensure the fixity of linguistic forms, meanings, and practices lies in the resort to a naked show of force that belies any attempt to separate law from repression. Pinter dramatizes this kind of force in *Mountain Language,* significantly the sole example of his political plays that specifies a particular crime committed by the "enemies of the state" incarcerated in the prison that provides the play's setting. At issue here is the attempt to eradicate cultural diversity by imposing a central language ("the language of the capital") on an heterogeneous population, transforming the many into the "one" by criminalizing any recourse to a local language (the "mountain language" of the play's title) that would introduce the disruption of difference into the unanimity of the people. The Officer states the case clearly: "You are mountain people. . . . Your language is dead. It is forbidden. It is not permitted to speak your mountain language in this place. . . . You may not speak it. It is outlawed. You may only speak the language of the capital. That is the only language permitted in this place. You will be badly punished if you attempt to speak your mountain language in this place. This is a military decree. It is the law" (21).

While this law seeks to produce an ideological effect—the interpellation of subjects as the "one" who "all share a common heritage"—it does not pretend to legitimate itself in terms of ideology. Lyotard associates legitimation with "a prescriptive phrase" that "gives the *force of law* to its object . . . [and] hinges on the justice of the order given" (40, 42; emphasis added). Meg's comic threat of the strap has become deadly serious as "the order given" has entirely severed itself from even the illusory consideration of justice provided by Nicolas's humanist rhetoric of "common heritage" in *One for the Road* or Des's rhetoric of democracy in *The New World Order.* What "gives the force of law" to the prohibiting of the mountain language, is the force upon which this law rests, the force encapsulated in the phrase "military decree." Indeed, even to speak of this law as resting upon force suggests a gap between law and violence when in fact we cannot separate the status of this order as law, as a military *decree,* from the violence it can unleash as a *military* decree. This violence supplants a normative phrase as the legitimating instance of the law: "You will be badly punished if you attempt to speak your mountain language in this place." Even if this violence never rises to the level of mass extermination it effects a cultural genocide, as the Officer equates prohibiting speaking the mountain language with an act of murder: "Your language is forbidden. It is dead. No one is allowed to speak your language. Your language no longer exists" (21). If the law successfully kills the mountain language, we can only ask how long it will be before the mountain people *as* a people with their own cultural specificity "no longer exists."

Pinter has often commented on how the condition of the Kurds in Turkey, legally prohibited from speaking their language, provided the inspiration for the play. Certainly the pernicious effects of the drive for linguistic unification that Pinter dramatizes resonate with the history of fascism, imperialism, and authoritarianism, and the issues he raises speak to the role attacks on bilingual education and the question of ebonics have played in the American "culture wars" of the past two decades. Possessing a political specificity then, the play also presents in its starkest form that emphasis on the violence of the law that founds subjectivity, analysis of the "policing of words" through which regnant forms of power reproduce themselves, and exploration of how the "criminal" act of unauthorized speech threatens to deligitimate law by exposing both the ideological and repressive violence at its core, vital to Pinter's work well before his "political turn."

II

Two examples from "nonpolitical" plays illustrate the extent to which Pinter's examination of how the authoritarian state utilizes the structure of law as a weapon in his recent work grows out of his attention to the coercive nature of the demand for proper speech imposed by the dominant culture's "laws" regulating subjectivity. In *The Caretaker,* Aston's narrative of his experience in the hospital provides some of the most disturbing and powerful moments in the play. He describes his stay in what appears to be a nightmarish psychiatric ward where the chief doctor declares the necessity of "do[ing] something to your brain. He said . . . if we don't, you'll be in here for the rest of your life, but if we do, you stand a chance. You can go out, he said, and live like the others" (64). Aston's account of the medical procedure—involving being forcibly held down while gigantic pincers with wires attached to an electric machine were applied to either side of his skull—reveals the violence that the doctor's rhetoric of care mystifies, the violence through which a dominant culture attempts to ensure that each subject will "live like the others." If this hospital seems ominously like the prisons, torture chambers, and interrogation rooms of Pinter's recent plays, Aston's crime or, in keeping with the doctor's specious rhetoric, his "sickness" anticipates the blindfolded man's "questioning received ideas" in *The New World Order.* Aston experienced what the doctors insist on labeling "hallucinations" and what he calls moments of "this clear sight" (64), and he would relate the content of his vision to people in his favorite café and, perhaps more threatening to the established order, to his coworkers at the factory: "They understood what I said. I mean I used to talk to them. *I talked too much. That was my mistake.* . . . Standing there, or in the breaks, I used to . . . talk about things. And these men, they used to listen, whenever I . . . had anything to say" (63; emphasis added). Since we never know what Aston told these men, it would be too much to state unequivocally that he was some kind of agitator at the factory; nevertheless, there seems little doubt that the effect of his speech—"they understood what I said . . . they used to listen"—poses a danger that his medical treatment successfully contains. Summing up his experience in the hospital, he states, "I don't talk to people now . . . I don't talk to anyone . . . like that" (66).

In *The Homecoming,* much of the dramatic tension arises from the attempt by the male characters to compel Ruth to conform to patriarchal culture's laws regarding the gendered subject positions women may occupy. Taking Ruth's measure, Lenny uses narrative as his chosen method of intimidation, recounting his violent attack on a woman who crossed the boundaries of her proper place by "ma[king] me this certain proposal. . . . The only trouble was she was falling apart with the pox. So I turned it down. Well, this lady was very insistent and started taking liberties with me . . . which by any criterion I couldn't be expected to tolerate, the facts being what they were, so I clumped her one . . . I just gave her another belt in the nose and a couple of turns of the boot" (46–47). As often in Pinter, whether or not the narrated event really happened matters less than the effect the narrator hopes to achieve. Here, Lenny deploys narrative to silence Ruth and force her to recognize that if she attempts to "take liberties" with him—to assert a "liberty" that would threaten the play of patriarchal power relations—she will face the same violent reprisal as the woman in the story. As considerable as Lenny's narrative skills may be, however, they fall short of their mark, for Ruth challenges the legitimacy of his account: "Ruth: How did you know she was diseased? Lenny: How did I know? *Pause.* I decided she was" (47).

Lenny's response asserts a supreme power that transforms the story from a narrative about violence to a narrative that performs a kind of representational violence in the very act of its telling, not simply because it constitutes a threat to Ruth but because Lenny accesses the image-repertoire of patriarchal fantasy to produce the image of the "wicked" woman as abject, impure, disease-ridden, contaminated, and contaminating. Those empowered to police the borders of gender can "decide" upon such a representational strategy since patriarchal culture cannot countenance a woman "taking liberties" with her subject position, especially when those "liberties" take the form of impermissible speech. As Lenny observes, in a comment that defines understatement, "I tend to get desensitized, if you know what I mean, when people make unreasonable demands on me" (48). Since he claims that the woman's "pox" results from his narrative decision, the very fact that she made Lenny "a certain proposal" constitutes the "unreasonableness" of her "demand." Exercising agency through linguistic control, she violates the ideological law of patriarchy that assigns men the role of narrating subject and women the role of narrated object—a violation Lenny can control in the privileged space of narrative, even if he proves far less successful with Ruth.

As we can see, the police have populated Pinter's dramatic universe since his earliest works, for Meg, Lenny, and Aston's doctors represent the police as much as do Des, Lionel, and the Officer in *Mountain Language*. Whenever subject formation finds itself at issue, the police make their presence felt. Derrida captures the ubiquity of the police in his discussion of them as an "index of a phantom-like violence . . . the police that thus capitalize on violence aren't simply the police. They do not simply consist of policemen in uniform, occasionally helmeted, armed and organized. . . . By definition, the police are present or are represented everywhere that there is force of law. They are present, sometimes invisible but always effective" (44). They are present in Des and Lionel's profession of faith in democracy; in Nicolas's affirmation of his participation in the "one" who "all share a common heritage" (and I am thinking here of Des, Lionel, and Nicolas not *as* police, but as objects *of* policing); in the Stanley who will emerge "re-oriented, adjusted, integrated" from his stay with Monty; in Aston's ceasing to engage the world through dialogue. As an "index" of the fundamental violence inscribed at the heart of the law, the police manifest the power that constructs subjects through destructive force. The police, Derrida remarks, work "to exclude any individual violence threatening [their] order and thus to monopolize violence." The police thus exhibit "the phenomenal structure of a certain violence in the law that lays itself down, by decreeing to be violent, this time in the sense of an outlaw, anyone who does not recognize it" (33). Through the violence of the military decree, the Officer brands the mountain people as outlaws because of the "violence" they offer the state through speaking their regional language. Through the violence of representation, Lenny attempts to coerce Ruth into not overstepping the bounds of her discursive space as did the diseased outlaw of his narrative.

Pinter repeatedly illustrates how the violence of the law drapes itself in the mantle of ideology, e.g., Des and Lionel do not engage in torture, they "keep the world clean for democracy"; Nicolas does not authorize beatings and rapes, he preserves the "common heritage" that defines the national community; Aston's doctors do not destroy his "clear sight," they help him to "live like the others." For Pinter, as for Derrida, the criminal-as-outlaw demystifies this ideology. Commenting on the fascination criminals exert on people, Derrida asserts that "it is not for someone who has committed this or that crime for which one feels a secret admiration; it is someone who, in defying the law, lays bare the violence of the legal system, the juridical order itself" (33). In calling forth a show of force that exceeds the rhetoric employed to render the violence of the law invisible, the criminal threatens to undermine the strategies through which the law legitimates itself. For Pinter, this is especially the case with the political criminal—the dissident—whether in authoritarian or in presumably democratic states. In conversation with Mel Gussow, Pinter observes that in England and America, "you have the rhetoric of the free, the Christian, the democratic, but underneath the rhetoric what you have is excrement, vomit, blood, mutilation, horror" (73).

The "criminal" is often the person who threatens the state by calling this rhetoric into question, revealing it *as* rhetoric by exposing the "horror" it perpetrates in the name of "the free, the Christian, the democratic."

To say that the subject-as-criminal introduces the possibility of a legitimation crisis for the law is not to claim that the cultural, political, or ideological order supported by that law faces imminent collapse. As we have seen, the regime in *Mountain Language* eschews appeal to democracy, patriotism, or nationalism; the law of language, the law of political subject formation, must be observed because the mountain people "will be badly punished" if they fail to do so. There is certainly little suggestion in the play that the state's overt display of violence, its equation of law with force, weakens its power or threatens its chances of survival. As Pinter remarks to Gussow, however, Western democracies will go to extraordinary lengths to preserve their ideological self-image as rational bastions of law-as-justice. "What the language used by . . . the administration of this country [America], and echoed all along the line by the government of England, what the language does is debase itself. We're talking about a debased language in which the lie is simply automatic and quite persuasive and infinitely pervasive" (85) However debased, this language produces a powerful ideological effect through which "the lie" of "the free, the Christian, the democratic" has "*almost decriminalized*" (122; emphasis added) the dominant order's recourse to the very same violence that it ascribes to those it brands as outlaw.

III

Pinter provides an early examination of precisely how "debased" political language establishes a powerful ideological purchase in *The Hothouse*. While Pinter has referred (in an interview with Nicholas Hern published in the American edition of *One for the Road*) to its two predecessors *The Birthday Party* and *The Dumb Waiter* as offering a "political metaphor" (7), *The Hothouse,* set in a "rest home" run by a government ministry, is the first of his plays to be set explicitly on the terrain of the state rather than civil society. Indeed, the play ultimately questions the hard and fast distinction between the two by suggesting, in a manner similar to Althusser, that the state encompasses civil society, consolidating its political power through the construction of subjects who will recognize their place within the social totality and act on that recognition. Lush, one of the hothouse staff, explains how the institution sets about "curing" its patients: "In a rest home, you see, you do not merely rest . . . you are obliged to work and play and join in communal activity to the greatest possible extent" (27–28). Just as Althusser refers to Pascal's comment "'Kneel down, move your lips in prayer, and you will believe'" (168) to explain how the subject of ideology stands not as the point of origin but as the effect of material practices, so the overseers of the hothouse use "communal activity" to shape the subject's desire so that, upon leaving the institution, she will "freely" choose to identify herself solely in terms of "a group of people in which group common assumptions are shared and common principles observed" (35). As the site of subject formation, the hothouse promises to instill in its patients the desire for order—the Other's highest value, without which it cannot reproduce itself—while appealing to a "debased" humanist rhetoric to obscure the precise nature of how it imposes this desire. As Roote, the hothouse's director, solemnly declares, the institution's course of treatment "set[s] in motion an activity for humanity, of humanity and by humanity. And the key word [i]s order" (20).

In her discussion of the play, Rosette C. Lamont asserts that Pinter's choice of a state-run medical institution alludes to the vital role played not simply by individual doctors or the medical establishment but by a kind of medical/legal "rationality" in the Nazi form of totalitarianism. Roote's constant emphasis on the hothouse as "sanctioned by the Ministry . . . subsidized by the State" and the staff as "delegates" (20, 57) underscores both the legality of the hothouse and its function as a site for the enforcement of law. As Lamont observes, "none of [the Nazi genocide in the concentration camps] could have taken place had this program not been preceded by the legalized sterilization of 'unfit' procreators . . . [and] the mercy killing of brain damaged, deformed infants. . . . These legal murders were perpetrated in the name of 'euthanasia'" (42). Certainly, as Lamont convincingly argues, the Nazis' perpetration of the "final solution" was the specific historical event casting its shadow over the writing of *The Hothouse,* but to read the play as a meditation on Nazism runs the risk of ignoring how the play both allows us to perceive the totalitarian tendencies present even in nations constituted as democratic republics (a point to which I will return) and uses its setting to dramatize, through a kind of defamiliarization, the ideological processes of subject formation.

In terms of the latter point, I want to emphasize a fundamental difference between how the medical establishment functioned under the Nazis and the mission of the hothouse—a difference concerning the "patients" that each "treats." Nazism identifies the Aryan *Volk,* in Lyotard's words, as "a race that 'only' has to get rid of its parasites before reemerging in its primordial purity. . . . An ailing identity has to be restored to health" (68). As Lyotard perceptively suggests, the tropes through which the Nazis elaborated their racial ideology identified the "ailing identity" in need of a cure not with the actual "patients" in the hospitals and camps but with the cultural body of the Aryan people. Those upon whom Nazi doctors operated and experimented, those who fell victim to the "law of exclusion, exception, and extermination" (68), were simply "parasites"—not the diseased requiring treatment, but the disease itself requiring eradication.

In *The Hothouse,* on the other hand, the dominant ideology takes the form of a law of *inclusion;* in a rest home whose guiding principle demands "activity for humanity, of humanity and by humanity," the institution organizes itself so that its inhabitants may one day leave and recognize themselves as part of that "humanity" in whose name they received treatment. To put this another way, the hothouse undertakes the ideological project of *creating* the very "humanity" it invokes to legitimate its practices. Such a project seems far closer to republicanism or democracy than it does to Nazism, since the totality it produces encompasses everyone. There are no "parasites" infesting the social body of the play's dramatic universe, no stigmatized "others" or violent outlaws. As Roote pointedly remarks of the patients, "after all, they're not criminals. They're only people in need of help, which we try to give" (12). What kind of "help" does Roote offer? "We try to give, in one way or another, to the best of our discretion, to the best of our judgement, to help them regain their confidence, confidence in themselves, confidence in others, confidence in . . . the world. . . . One of the purposes of this establishment is to instill that confidence in each and every one of them, that confidence which will one day enable them to say 'I am . . . Gubbins,' for example" (12–13). The hothouse grants the subject the "confidence" to lay claim to her name, which means (mis)recognizing the name as a signifier of individual identity when in fact the subject is named rather than self-naming. Roote's words cast the hothouse as the site of a kinder, gentler ideological interpellation, one in which the subject enters "the order of objectifying language that will finally allow him to say: "I" not as a result of repressive policing, but through the "help" offered by the "delegates" of a compassionate state.

Much of the play's satirical humor derives from the parody of Enlightenment rationality, secular humanist universalism, and welfare state political rhetoric running through Roote's speeches. As Pinter recognizes, however, such ideologically charged language, no matter how "debased," possesses considerable power since it mystifies the coercive practices through which the patients are integrated into "humanity." Since Pinter does not include any patients among the characters, we never see precisely how the staff "help them regain their confidence," but he does take us inside number one interviewing room, a soundproof room containing a machine to which the patient is connected through electrodes and a set of earphones. When Lamb, one of the understaff, agrees "to help . . . with some little tests" (30), and allows himself to be hooked up to the machine, we see the horror underlying the humanism. Gibbs and Cutts, two members of the staff, hurl questions at Lamb with such rapidity and abrupt shifts in subject matter that he proves unable to process and respond to them. At the moments when, significantly, language fails him, when he finds himself dispossessed of his subjectivity, "*suddenly Lamb jolts rigid, his hands go to his earphones, he is propelled from the chair, falls to his knees, twisting from side to side, still clutching his earphones, emitting high-pitched cries. He suddenly stops still. . . . He looks up. He sits in the chair"* (32). This process continues until we see, in the play's concluding image, *"Lamb in chair. He sits still, staring as in a catatonic trance"* (66). Suggesting the kind of care Stanley received at Monty's, and prefiguring Aston's experience in the hospital as well as the repressive measures employed by the regimes in the recent political plays, this "treatment" reveals the violence not only obscured but also in some senses authorized by the institution's humanism. Despite Roote's rhetoric, the institution proves more than willing to resort to the kind of force exerted on Lamb in order that the patients recognize themselves as part of "humanity." Only through such force can the hothouse suture what could be a potential contradiction between the sense of individual identity that it claims to instill and the desire to submerge that identity within "a group in which common assumptions are shared and common principles observed" that it demands. Any patient emerging from number one interviewing room clearly will not "question received ideas" or raise troubling questions about the origin and legitimacy of the assumptions and principles constituting the frame of intelligibility through which we learn to recognize what counts as the "human."

The patients may not be criminals, as Roote acknowledges, but they find themselves subjected to the kind of policing that marks those branded as criminal. Ironically, when Roote does refer to criminal activity, at issue is the action of the staff and not the patients. Discovering that a female patient has given birth and that the father apparently is a member of the staff who may have raped her, Roote declares his revulsion at behavior that is "nothing short of criminal" (24). What renders the act criminal to Roote, however, is not the rape itself, but the failure to follow the "rule," the law regulating the proper conduct of rape at the hothouse: "It's in the interests of science. If a member of the staff decides that for the good of a female patient some degree of copulation is necessary then two birds are killed with one stone! . . . But we all know the rule . . . always send in a report. After all, the reactions of the patient have to be tabulated, compared with others, filed, stamped and if possible verified! It stands to reason" (21–22). Here the language of personal compassion ("for the good of the patient") and impersonal medical "reason" ("it's in the interests of science") combine not only to authorize rape but also to render it invisible *as* rape, as an offense for which the perpetrator must answer. Roote's words provide a telling example of how, as Pinter remarked to Gussow, the state has "decriminalized" its own actions through "a debased language" to such an extent that even its own "delegates" perceive no contradiction between the ideals expressed in their rhetoric and the violent brutality of their actions.

If *The Hothouse* dramatizes the criminal violence of a cultural or political order that carries out its practices in the name of "humanity," we need to ask what kind of order the play examines. Here I would agree with Lamont that we view the play as a reflection on totalitarianism, but, unlike Lamont, I want to emphasize that if we limit our sense of totalitarianism to Nazism (or even Stalinism) we run the risk of ignoring a strain of totalitarianism that exists in republics and democracies. To clarify this point, I want to extend the implications of Stephen Watt's illuminating discussion of the recent political plays in his *Postmodern/Drama*. Watt writes, "Critics of the 'political Pinter' of the 1980s and 1990s, in my view, too often ignore the fundamental differences between the regimes he represents in these plays. Not all totalitarianism states, for example . . . justify themselves in the same way . . . [totalitarianism] can be legitimated by narratives leading in totally opposite directions— one toward an origin [in terms of which Watt discusses *One for the Road*], the other toward a utopian telos of freedom and 'peace' [in terms of which he discusses *Party Time*]" (106, 109). Watt turns to Lyotard's analysis of totalitarianism's legitimating strategies in *The Postmodern Explained* for his concept of these different narrative strategies. What he doesn't say, however, is that for Lyotard these are not simply two different narrative practices, but that they legitimate two different forms of totalitarianism that, nevertheless, we cannot unequivocally oppose to each other: the despotic and the republican.

Lyotard associates legitimating narratives that point toward an origin— what he calls "mythic narration" (43)—with despotic totalitarianism, and he offers Nazism as a prime example of this form of government. "It grounded its legitimacy in . . . narratives that permitted [the German people] to identify exclusively with . . . heroes and heal the wounds inflicted by the event of defeat and crisis" (47). Faced with the "crisis" precipitated by the rapist on the staff—or, rather, by the culprit who criminally neglects to "send in a report"—as well as by the news that a patient has mysteriously died, an unnerved Roote wonders, "What's the matter with this place? Everything's clogged up, bunged up, stuffed up, buggered up. The whole thing's running down hill" (45). Roote seeks refuge from his sense of crisis in the kind of nostalgia for origins whose pernicious political effects have been amply demonstrated over the course of the twentieth century. Roote recalls a gathering he attended presided over by the hothouse's previous director: "'Order, gentlemen,' he said, 'for the love of Mike!' As one man we looked out of the window at Mike, and gazed at the statue . . . Mike! The predecessor of my predecessor, the predecessor of us all, the man who laid the foundation stone, the man who introduced the first patient, the man who . . . opened institution after institution up and down the country, rest homes, nursing homes, convalescent homes, sanatoria. He was sanctioned by the Ministry, revered by the populace, subsidized by the State" (20).

The "myth" of Mike grounds the activities of the hothouse, providing the "foundation" that legitimates and thus decriminalizes the extreme measures through which the staff restores the patients' "confidence." The peculiar power of this myth, its ability to provoke Roote's desire to return to the source—to a time before everything got "clogged up"—lies in its aesthetic representation. Indeed, Roote stands in awe less of Mike than of the statue that memorializes Mike and, through soliciting a worshipful gaze, produces the very same mass subjectivity that Roote associates with the name of "humanity:" "As *one man* we looked." Lyotard comments a propos of the place of the aesthetic in despotic totalitarianism: "The sensible representation of the people to itself encourages it to identify itself as an exceptional singularity" (53–54). Far more than a simple object, the statue embodies for Roote the validity and fundamentally ethical nature of "the aspirations of a whole community, a tradition, an ideal" (19) that he seeks to preserve—"an ideal" that he does not find incompatible with either the psychological violence of number one interviewing room or the physical violence of raping female patients (always provided the rapist files a report). Aesthetic representation of mythic figures inspires heroic acts that become the occasion for the "mythic narration" that transforms the deeds of "the predecessor" from self-contained acts into the origin of a tradition. Nothing marks the sanctification of origins more palpably than those willing to die for tradition, thus becoming part of that tradition through inspiring the kind of verbal performance Roote offers in his toast "to our glorious dead. . . . The chaps who died for us in the field of action. . . . The men who gave their lives so that we might live. Who sacrificed themselves so we might continue. Who helped keep the world clean for generations to come. The men who died in our name" (44)—the men who died, Roote might have added, "for the love of Mike." Such beautiful deaths may not bear close scrutiny, however; the one sacrifice for tradition we see in the play suggests how the invocation of tradition authorizes the kind of repressive force that would seem to have no place in "activity for humanity, of humanity and by humanity." In order to encourage Lamb to participate in the experiments with the machine in number one interviewing room, Gibbs informs him that the man whom he has replaced also used to volunteer his services for similar tests, to which Lamb enthusiastically responds that he is "glad I'm following in a tradition" (32). Pinter displays the violent results of such tradition in the play's final image of Lamb motionless, "as in a catatonic trance."

If the social formation the play dramatizes adopts despotic legitimation strategies based on origins, it also utilizes the strategies that Lyotard associates with deliberative political orders such as republicanism and democracy. The latter orders do not ground themselves through appeal to a mythic past, but through elaborating what Lyotard calls "narratives of emancipation" whose "totalizing character" proposes an answer to the question, "*what ought we to be?"* (41, 47, 49). While we can characterize despotism as archeological, deliberative sociopolitical formations are teleological, grounding their legitimacy "in a future to be brought about, that is, in an Idea to realize. This Idea . . . has legitimating value because it is universal" (50). As an institution dedicated to realizing the "Idea" of a universal "humanity," to the future-oriented project of granting the patients "that confidence which will *one day* enable them to say 'I am Gubbins'" and receive their emancipation, the hothouse seems closer to a republican than a despotic institution. Like any democratic republic whose guiding principles result from the deliberative process, the hothouse relies upon a specific system of laws to translate its goal from "Idea" to reality—laws articulated in a constitution. Even as Roote extols the lofty aim of the institution, he expresses his reservations about the law demanding that the patients must be addressed by number rather than name: "It makes it doubly difficult if they're constantly referred to as 5244, doesn't it? We lose sight of their names and they lose sight of their names. I sometimes wonder if it's the right way to go about things." Despite his doubts, Roote refuses even to consider the possibility of altering this practice, since "that was one of the rules of procedure laid down in the original constitution. The patients are to be given numbers and called by those numbers. And that's how it's got to remain" (13). Practices that might appear dehumanizing or even criminal become not only permissible but also idealized through constitutional imprimatur. Since the constitution provides for complete inclusion within the totalizing category of "humanity," it mystifies the coercive, repressive, and violent policing directed against the patients, obscuring the extent to which, as subjects of law, they are reduced to objects. The constitution may embody, as Roote puts it, the "delicately wrought concept of participation between him who is to be treated and him who is to treat" (19), but, despite its overtones of democratic equality, the language of "participation" reminds us of the "horror" perpetrated under ideological cover of the rhetoric of "the free, the Christian, the democratic."

Lyotard remarks that "in the case of totalitarianism, the opposition [of despotism] to republicanism is not absolutely distinct" (52), and the most significant political insight of *The Hothouse* consists in dramatizing the convergence between these two seemingly antithetical forms of government. As Watt convincingly argues, we can see the political plays Pinter began writing in the 1980s as individually concerned with one of these two forms, but I would suggest that no other Pinter play shows as clearly the extent to which archeological despotism and teleological republicanism or democracy can accommodate each other as does *The Hothouse*. The vehicle of this accommodation, the point of convergence between these two forms, is, perhaps unsurprisingly, the system of laws legitimating the hothouse—the constitution. While seeking to guide the hothouse's efforts to "realize" the

"Idea" of "humanity," the constitution's authority derives from the fact that, as Roote points out, it is the *"original* constitution." In other words, the answer to the future-oriented question "what ought we to be," grounds itself in the constitution's source—"the predecessor of us all, the man who laid the foundation," Mike. While despotic law criminalizes those—like the mountain people speaking their own language—who fall outside the "exceptional singularity" it attempts to preserve, and republican law operates through the language of inclusion, both forms of law essentially decriminalize the actions of the dominant political or cultural order by granting them legal sanction, no matter how violent or repressive the act.

That despotism should have recourse to violence comes as little surprise; that republicanism should resort to violence in the attempt to realize its "Idea" may perhaps strike us as counterintuitive. It is precisely in such violence, however, that Lyotard locates the totalitarian tendency within republicanism. While republicanism speaks the idealistic language of constitutions, rights, justice, law as enabling and generative rather than as prohibitive and repressive, it must turn to the "phantom-like violence" of those who police subjectivity (and what is the hothouse if not ultimately a kind of police station?) because of a gap insinuating itself between the "Idea" and any reality offering itself as the embodiment of that "Idea." This violence, Lyotard writes, raises itself to the level of terror: "For the ideal of absolute freedom, which is empty, any given reality must be suspected of being an obstacle to freedom. . . . Terror acts on the suspicion that nothing is emancipated enough. Every particular reality is a plot against the [Idea]" (54). This passage can aid us in understanding why Pinter, throughout his works, links the ideological processes of subject formation to violence, why he locates violence at the very heart of the law of the subject. Lyotard's words remind us that even as Roote extols the "delicately wrought concept" to which the hothouse dedicates itself, he never mentions whether or not the institution has met with success. Indeed, we never hear of any patient ever leaving the hothouse except, in the case of 6457, through a death so mysterious that we are left to wonder if perhaps his treatment went too far, if the devices in number one interviewing room were applied too zealously. We have no evidence from the text that any patient has ever reached the stage of being "emancipated enough" to count as a full-fledged member of "humanity," a term that, despite the privilege granted it within the hothouse's ideology, is left curiously undefined and empty, suggesting it remains in excess of any subject offered as its embodiment.

The violence directed against the patients, like much of the violence in Pinter's works, may be prescribed by the ideological law determining appropriate subjectivity, but it also signals the deep suspicion that the "law" can never with any certainty produce the subjects it needs. After all, if Stanley, Aston, the patients in the hothouse, the mountain people, and Des and

Lionel's prisoner must be "reoriented," then, obviously, their initial interpellation must have failed. What guarantee exists then that this time the
subject will play the role assigned her in the ideological drama the Other
demands she enact? As Lyotard's discussion of terror suggests, no such
guarantee exists—the "free" assembly of individual subjects around the
"Idea" made flesh never occurs; the patients will never be, *can* never be,
"human" enough. When the interrogator Nicolas proclaims to the dissident
Victor in *One for the Road,* "I have never been more moved, in the whole of
my life, as when . . . the man who runs this country announced to the country: We are all patriots, we are as one, we all share a common heritage. Except you, apparently" (50), Pinter takes us to the very heart of terroristic
violence. While overtly Nicolas chastises his prisoner for refusing to acknowledge his place within the "one," his words also suggest that the material reality of the nation fails to match up to the ideal of the Nation; that
Victor exposes the fact that the nation is not and ultimately never can be "as
one." The violence the state inflicts upon Victor and his family—his torture, Gila's repeated rapes, and the murder of Nicky, their son—seeks to effect what Lyotard calls "the suppression of reality" (55); the suppression,
that is, of the knowledge of the unbridgeable chasm between "Idea" and reality. We can, I think, see more clearly now why both Althusser (with his
comparison of ideological interpellation to the policeman's hailing) and
Pinter see the subjects emerging from interpellation as "suspects," as always already guilty of the crime of exposing the lack within the cultural/so-
cial/political real.

In the interview with Nicholas Hern printed in the American edition of
One for the Road, Pinter responds to drama critic Michael Billington's ob-
jection that the play never lets the audience know of what specific offense
Victor and Gila stand accused: "Well, I must say that I think that's bloody ridiculous, because these people, generally speaking . . . ninety per cent of
them have committed no offence. There's no such thing as an offence, apart
from the fact that *everything* is" (15–16). While Pinter refers here to political dissidents, his comments encapsulate the precarious nature of subjectivity itself dramatized in his works, always under suspicion by the very police
who enforce the law of subject formation. Nor does such suspicion limit itself to those whom the Other seeks to "integrate" within its cultural field;
even those who exercise power in the Other's name are, as Lyotard reminds
us, "contingent in the light of th[e] ideal, and therefore suspect" (55). Pinter
alerts us to this contingency in those moments of a kind of doubling when
the line between the police and the suspect dissolves. In *One for the Road,*
the following exchange occurs when Nicolas begins questioning Nicky, Victor and Gila's seven-year-old son: "Nicolas: What's your name? Nicky:
Nicky. Nicola: Really? How odd. *Pause*" (55). In *Mountain Language,* the
Prisoner tries to make the Guard see that they share a common humanity:

GUARD: I'll tell you another thing. I've got a wife and three kids. And you're all a piece of shit. *Silence.*
PRISONER: I've got a wife and three kids.
GUARD: You've what? *Silence.* You've got what? *Silence.* What did you say to me? You've got what? *Silence.* You've got *what? He picks up the telephone and dials one digit.* Sergeant? I'm in the Blue Room . . . yes . . . I thought I should report, Sergeant . . . I think I've got a joker in here . . . *The* SERGEANT *comes in.*
SERGEANT: What joker? *Blackout.* (31–35)

When the lights come up on this scene again, the Sergeant has left the stage, but we have no need to ask what occurred during the blackout since "*the* PRISONER *has blood on his face* [*and h*]*e sits trembling*" (43). In both examples, the "odd" doubling suggests that Nicolas and the Guard could very easily find themselves in the position of their prisoners; that their role as the Other's "delegates" does not exempt them from suspicion. No matter how devotedly they serve their regimes, even they, simply by their existence, may prove traitors to the "ideal" of the "one," "common heritage" and "humanity" by revealing the extent to which that "ideal" has failed to materialize. The violence with which they respond to the sudden sense of their own contingency—Nicky's murder and the Prisoner's beating—certainly exhibits the repressive power of the law, but it cannot guarantee the security of their position, nor, more importantly, can it guarantee that absolute coincidence between "Idea" and reality the law seeks to enforce. This lack of coincidence does not signal the imminent collapse of the institutions of social and political power in Pinter's plays. On the contrary, Pinter's vision remains largely dystopian as he unearths the totalitarian tendencies present just below the surface of our society. Such tendencies ensure that the subject of law will always remain a suspect; always vulnerable to the various kinds of violence that accompany ideological interpellation; always susceptible to the multiple forms of policing that mark the subject's subjection. In the world with which Pinter confronts his audience it is the subject's fate, as Devlin puts it, to "never be without a police siren."

Works Cited

Althusser, Louis. *Lenin and Philosophy.* Trans. Ben Brewster. New York: Monthly Review Press, 1971.

Butler, Judith. *Gender Trouble: Feminism and the Subversion of Identity.* New York: Routledge, 1990.

Derrida, Jacques. "Force of Law: The 'Mystical Foundation of Authority.'"*Deconstruction and the Possibility of Justice.* Ed. Drucilla Cornell, Michel Rosenfeld, and David Gray Carlson. New York: Routledge, 1992.

Gussow, Mel. *Conversations with Pinter.* New York: Grove Press, 1996.

Lacan, Jacques. *Ecrits.* Trans. Alan Sheridan. New York: W. W. Norton, 1977.

Lamont, Rosette C. "Harold Pinter's *The Hothouse:* A Parable of the Holocaust." *Pinter at Sixty.* Ed. Katherine H. Burkman and John L. Kundert-Gibbs. Bloomington: Indiana UP, 1993.

Lyotard, Jean-Francois. *The Postmodern Explained: Correspondence, 1982–1985.* Trans. Don Barry. Minneapolis: U of Minnesota P, 1993.

MacCannell, Juliet Flower. *Figuring Lacan.* Lincoln: U of Nebraska P, 1986.

Pinter, Harold. *Ashes to Ashes.* New York: Grove Press, 1997.

———. *The Birthday Party. Complete Works: 1.* New York: Grove Press, 1976.

———. *The Caretaker. Complete Works: 2.* New York: Grove Press, 1977.

———. *The Homecoming. Complete Works: 3.* New York: Grove Press, 1978.

———. *The Hothouse.* New York: Dramatists Play Service, 1980.

———. *Mountain Language.* London: Grove Press, 1988.

———. *One for the Road.* New York: Grove Weidenfeld, 1986.

———. *Party Time; and, The New World Order: Two Plays.* New York: Grove Press, 1993.

———. *Various Voices: Prose, Poetry, Politics, 1948–1998.* New York: Grove Press, 1998.

Watt, Stephen. *Postmodern/Drama: Reading the Contemporary Stage.* Ann Arbor: U of Michigan P, 1998.

Wilden, Anthony. *System and Structure: Essays in Communication and Exchange.* London: Tavistock, 1972.

3

Harold Pinter's "Before the Law"

STEVEN PRICE

In Kafka's parable a man from the country arrives at the doorway to the Law, to which he seeks admission. His path is barred by a doorkeeper, who tells him that, although it is possible he will be allowed in later, he cannot enter now. Nor should he try: all the hallways are guarded, each by a doorkeeper more terrible than the last. The man from the country resolves to wait. Year after year he waits until, with death approaching, he thinks of a question he has never asked before. Why, he asks, since everyone seeks admission to the Law, has no one but he ever come to the door? "No one else could ever be admitted here," replies the doorkeeper, "since this gate was made only for you. I am now going to shut it" (3–4).

The words strike with the finality of a death sentence and with the force of revelation; yet their meaning is elusive, demanding exegesis even within *The Trial* itself, the novel into which "Before the Law" was incorporated and which was a formative influence on Harold Pinter (Billington 15). Among its implications might be the following:

> the Law may not exist, and yet is omnipotent;
> the Law is a place, and yet is inaccessible;
> the Law will punish unto death those who come in search of it.

All of these possibilities will seep into the fabric of Pinter's plays, as will another that would barely need stating were it not that Pinter's ongoing critique of American foreign policy is couched in explicitly legal terms:

> the Law provides no certainty of justice.

The dire warning of "Before the Law"—that power is inaccessible and mysterious, capricious in its abuse of helpless individuals, and lacks both moral authority and the need for self-justification—is felt throughout the first of what Pinter discerns as three phases in his own writing:

> I think in the early days, which was 30 years ago in fact, I was a political playwright of a kind. But I then took a break from being so for about 17 years. I wrote a lot of plays between 1970 and 1985 which can't be said to be political plays—things like *Old Times* and *Betrayal* and *Landscape* and *Silence*, which were concerned with memory and youth and loss and certain other things. They didn't concern themselves with social and political structures whereas the earlier plays did. (Gussow 82)

In that "break" the dynamics of the earlier work give way to explorations of stasis in place and in time. In *Landscape* and *Silence* (1969) the characters remain, Beckett-like, in their own areas of the stage; *No Man's Land* (1975) is an expansive meditation on old age and impotence, and the culmination of this process is *A Kind of Alaska* (1982), in which Deborah awakes from a "sleeping" sickness that has lasted for twenty-eight years. Most would agree with Pinter that a decisive change then occurs with *Precisely* (1983), *One for the Road* (1984) and *Mountain Language* (1988), which introduce overtly the political ideas he had begun to address in essays, letters, and interviews and continues to advance today. These ideas, Pinter suggests, are implicit in the plays of the first period.

An example is Petey's plea to Stanley in *The Birthday Party*: "Stan, don't ever let them tell you what to do" (96). In 1988 Pinter told Mel Gussow that "I've lived that line all my damn life. Never more than now" (71), and he responded to Gussow's suggestion that the play "has the same story as *One for the Road*" by commenting: "It's the destruction of an individual, the independent voice of an individual. I believe that is precisely what the United States is doing to Nicaragua" (69). In the same interview he also refers to *The Dumb Waiter* and *The Homecoming* in these contexts, and clearly the incarceration of dissenters in *The Hothouse* and Aston's electric shock treatment in *The Caretaker* take on a starker meaning in the light of Pinter's political essays. Austin E. Quigley, too, has recently cited Petey's remark in an essay that argues for a consistent political position in Pinter's thought. Quigley's earlier identification in *The Pinter Problem* (1975) of the "interrelational function" and speech-act dynamics, rather than referential exposition, as the means by which meaning is produced on Pinter's stage is recalled in the terms in which he now discusses Pinter's politics:

> In a world of local and contingent social contracts persisting negotiation takes precedence over presumed authority, every contract that emerges from social interaction involves rights as well as responsibilities that may or may not hold for the duration of the contract and even those not directly involved in the negotiation have a stake, as Petey does, in the principles and procedures that emerge in the process. (16)

Contracts, rights, authority, negotiations: a legal discourse underlies both the early plays and the later essays.

On the other hand, Pinter reminds Gussow in Lawrentian vein that the author is not "making a speech" but "writing a play. . . . Something is being said, but the playwright isn't necessarily saying it," and he draws a distinction between the playwright and the citizen (70–71). Clearly it would be a partial and reductive reading that argued for continuities in the career without drawing attention to the differences between the plays, or between drama and political debate. There being analogies but no simple equation between the earlier plays and the later politics, it is at least as productive to read the politics dramatically as it is to read the plays politically; and for the purposes of this essay it will be crucial to distinguish various ways in which one might conceive of the law as either an a priori set of codes and statutes, or an evolving dramatic situation subject to interpretation, moral pressure, and authoritarian power.

Stanley Fish, for example, draws a threefold distinction between "formalistic," "humanistic," and "radical" or "critical" conceptions of law. The formalist position he finds exemplified in a quotation from Hans Kelsen's *The Pure Theory of Law*, according to which "legal theory becomes an exact structural analysis of positive law, free of all ethical-political value judgments." The "humanistic" response to this would object to the severance of law from value, whereas Fish's "radical" or "critical" response "would simply declare that a purely formal position is not a possibility" because "any specification of what the law is will already be infected by interpretation and will therefore be challengeable" (143–44).

One can see fluctuations between all three of these positions in Pinter's work. To overgeneralize: as a political essayist Pinter oscillates between the formalist and the humanist positions; as a playwright, as Quigley's analyses suggest, he dramatizes a radical-critical view of all forms of regulation, legal and otherwise. One must qualify this, however, by recalling the peculiar three-stage development Pinter detects in his dramatic career. He regards the middle period as a "break" from politics, and therefore elides it in tracing connections between the first and third phases. Seen differently, however, the political plays of the 1980s share with the preceding *No Man's Land* and *A Kind of Alaska* a sense of frighteningly diminishing possibilities. In place of the ambiguities and uncertainties of the first phase is an anxiety, as the second period draws to an end, that the mind will become, almost literally, frozen; and this anxiety persists, as the third period gets underway, in the political conviction that there is a single, empirical reality that language must either acknowledge or evade. As a citizen Pinter still adheres to this view; as a playwright, since *Moonlight* (1993) he has returned to what most would see as the more fertile exploration of spatial and temporal fluidity, though there remain unmistakable political connotations in the images of the Nazi period that haunt *Ashes to Ashes* (1996). In what follows I shall argue that the politics of Pinter the citizen and Pinter the playwright, which coincided for a relatively brief period between 1983's *Precisely* and 1991's *Party Time*, are otherwise divergent, and that the less overtly political plays in fact offer a different but no less political view of the contemporary world situation.

From the start of his public entry into political debate in the early 1980s Pinter was concerned to remove the cloak of legitimacy from acts he regarded as basically criminal. As the Reagan-Thatcher axis was emerging he was preoccupied, though by no means exclusively, with violations of human rights by the military dictatorships of Turkey and Latin America, whose abuses were made possible by the support of the United States. In the 1990s, as Yugoslavia disintegrated in a series of civil wars, his focus remained on the United States and therefore—worryingly, for both his critics and many of his supporters—his attention shifted away from internal repression and toward the actions of NATO that culminated in the bombing of Serbia in 1999. Pinter again saw this as "essentially a criminal act, showing total contempt for the United Nations and international law" (quoted in Gillan). Fiachra Gibbons reported in the *Guardian* of 26 July 2001 that, to widespread dismay, Pinter had joined the International Committee to Defend Slobodan Milošević, a man he had previously characterised as "undoubtedly ruthless and savage" (*Guardian* 8 April 1999). Pinter explained his reasons in a detailed interview with Matthew Tempest. Although "an international criminal court is really very much to be desired," the court as constituted is "illegitimate and, in fact, with no proper international substance" because it is "American-inspired . . . a really partial court." Moreover, Milošević "was more or less abducted and taken to the Hague" in return for a bribe of $1.3 billion, and Clinton and Blair were "criminals" whose governments were "acting like thugs." On the other hand, although "I am absolutely not saying that Milošević might not be responsible for all sorts of atrocities," in his case Pinter perceived mitigating circumstances: "there is an enormous amount of propaganda about Milošević," "there was a civil war going on there," and the Kosovo Liberation Army "was actually also responsible, and still is, now even more so, for this ethnic cleansing which has been going on in Kosovo for the last nine months" (Tempest 2001).

While there is evidence to support each of these statements, taken in the round their tendency is clear: Milošević has a defense but Clinton and Blair do not; in his "Degree Speech to the University of Florence" on 10 September 2001, Pinter ridiculed the idea that the bombing was a "humanitarian intervention" as a kind of Orwellian euphemism, like "collateral damage." It is an argument capable of gross misrepresentation—Pinter has never said that Milošević is innocent, for example—but many who are broadly sympathetic to Pinter's view of the United States have been troubled by his tone and bewildered by the apparent tendency to apply double standards, objections that in Britain led to him being placed, by John Sweeney and Henry Porter, in a gang of three alongside two other respected writers of the radical left, John Pilger and Tariq Ali. One of the most convincing critiques of Pinter's current position, however, is to be found not in the comments of his detractors but in his own plays, in particular, in their suspicion of definitive statements of law, in their dramatization of the interrelationship of law and power, and in their explorations of the anxieties informing the construction of territorial boundaries and the figure of the outsider.

A contrast may be drawn here between Pinter's work and that of the other subject of this book, David Mamet. Although the American's stage is populated by confidence men, petty criminals, and rule-benders generally, these figures can be identified as such because they are subject to an established national, criminal law that is a priori and known to all. For example, in *American Buffalo* Teach and Don, planning the robbery of a coin collection, are constantly on the lookout for the police whose cars drive past Don's resale shop with disturbing frequency. Therefore, although in what he says Teach constantly blurs the boundaries between criminal aggression and lawful self-protection, and regards burglary as "tak[ing] what's ours" (77), in fact he knows that laws exist and that he is planning to break them. In *Glengarry Glen Ross* the real estate salesmen may be committing fraud on a grand scale by presenting worthless tracts of land as valuable investments, but they, like the wife of their proposed victim Lingk, are fully aware of the regulation of the industry by outside bodies that Lingk confusedly remembers as the Attorney General or the "Consumer office" (49). The exception that proves the rule occurs in the play's second scene, in which Aaronow is surprised to discover himself branded a criminal by Moss just because he has listened to Moss proposing a break-in. If Moss is right, this is indeed what David Worster describes as a "speech-act play" in which rules do not refer to an existing state of affairs but are constantly brought into being and renegotiated through dialogue. In fact, however, the play refutes Moss's argument: Levene commits a robbery along the lines Moss has proposed, in the second act the police inspector, Baylen, investigates it, and by the end of the play Levene's guilt has been established. The plots of almost all of Mamet's screenplays involve murder or revolve around burglary and robbery, concepts that only make sense in a world in which territory and private property are clearly marked, whereas the occasional references to crossing the state line draw attention to a long history of American tales in which the fugitive from justice knows his rights under federal and state laws. Audiences, too, know where the line is because most of the plays and films that deal with criminality invite interpretations that observe the conventions of established genres, including the heist plot (*American Buffalo, Heist*), the whodunit (*Glengarry Glen Ross*), the Mafia film (*The Untouchables, Hoffa, Things Change*) and the police procedural (*Homicide*), all of which draw on socially sanctioned legal codes to establish a world in which the law is known and the distinction between the agent and the transgressor of the law is clear, if routinely contravened.

The situation is quite different in Pinter's plays, in which legal, territorial, and generic boundaries are all uncertain. The dictionary appearance of the word "Pinteresque" establishes the irreducibility of these plays to generic conventions, in whose absence the world appears to be operating without any criteria by which the behavior of its characters may be assessed. In a situation like this the law is not going to help. The concluding action of *The Room* is shocking, but it is doubtful that Bert's assault on Riley should be referred to the police; few have attempted to determine the legal ramifications of Ruth's "contract" in *The Homecoming*, and no impoverished ambulance chaser has yet come forward to suggest that Spooner might have a case of false imprisonment in *No Man's Land*. Such events may look criminal, but to think of the law at moments like these would be to play the wrong language game: Questions of legality or illegality do not arise because these are plays in which rules and contracts simply do not preexist, and instead lines are continuously renegotiated according to developments in the dramatic situation.

Far from exploiting the dramatic potential of the criminal along the lines of some of Mamet's characters (the eponymous hero of *Edmond* is another stark example), the protagonist of a Pinter play is frequently someone who, like Josef K., finds himself accused of something unknown: Stanley in *The Birthday Party*, the inmates of *The Hothouse*, Victor in *One for the Road*. The reason for such plays' pervasive feelings of anxiety and guilt is not that the characters have committed any crime, but that "criminality" itself is uncertain: There is no legal framework by which their guilt or innocence may be assessed. The fear is not simply that the innocent may be accused, but that the accused have no access to justice in a state in which, as Pinter told Nicholas Hern, "[t]here's no such thing as an offence, apart from the fact that *everything* is—their very life is an offence, as far as the authorities go. Their very existence is an offence, since that existence in some way or another poses critical questions or is understood to do so" (15–16).

If this is so, then neither is there a reliable standard according to which the accusers and abusers of such characters can simply be dismissed as criminals themselves. The mysterious organizations that employ Goldberg and McCann in *The Birthday Party* and Ben and Gus in *The Dumb Waiter*, like the multifarious scams pursued by Max and family in *The Homecoming*, may imply the conflation of business and crime that Mamet would later make explicit in *American Buffalo*; but in the absence of any reference to the legal agents and mechanisms that would enforce such an identification the audience's attention is directed to less realistic possibilities in interpreting the action. In the more overtly political *One for the Road*, Nicolas is unambiguously a torturer and killer but crucially, as Pinter has pointed out, not necessarily a criminal:

> he believes that it is right, for him, to possess this power, because, as far as he's concerned, he's acting for his country legitimately and properly. When he refers to the country's values, those are his values. And because of those values, he will kill, allow rape, everything he can think of. And torture. In order to protect the realm, anything is justified. (Hern 16–17)

Moreover, in 1985 state sovereignty would almost certainly protect Nicolas from any legal retribution, although more recent developments such as the creation of the International Criminal Tribunals for Rwanda (ICTR) and Yugoslavia (ICTY) and the establishment of the International Criminal Court (ICC) could now bring him the sleepless nights that may possibly have troubled General Pinochet. International criminal law, as the authors of a recent textbook on the subject have remarked, is "metamorphosing before our eyes" (Ratner and Abrams xlii).

As we shall see, the law became effective in these areas only when it was prepared to rethink the boundaries between the sovereign state and the will of international communities and to subject established legal principles to radical, even questionable, reinterpretation. In other words, the law is changing under a radical-critical analysis of itself. Pinter, meanwhile, has moved in quite the opposite direction. In 1962, in a speech published as "Writing for the Theatre," he famously suggested that "there can be no hard distinctions between what is real and what is unreal, nor between what is true and what is false," and he described reality as a "quicksand" (11–12). By 1985, however, his view had changed, or at least the emphasis had changed toward asserting a reality that is both knowable and independent of discourse:

> There's only one reality, you know. You can interpret reality in various ways. But there's only one. And if that reality is thousands of people being tortured to death at this very moment and hundreds of thousands of megatons of nuclear bombs standing there waiting to go off at this very moment, then that's it and that's that. (Hern 21)

Few would seriously dispute that these are facts, but one might still ask similar questions to those one might ask of any character in a Pinter play: What legitimizes these facts? What is their citation designed to bring about? In what ways are these facts in competition with others, and why should they be given priority among the myriad other facts daily competing for attention?

These are akin to the questions that J. L. Austin posed in speech-act theory when, in *How to Do Things with Words*, he rejected the notion of "constative" (value-free, proposition-bearing) facts and instead emphasized the invariably "performative" function of their citation. The citation of facts is, of course, essential in constructing any case against an alleged criminal, not least in recent examples such as those of Pinochet, Miloševic, or Christopher Hitchens's regrettably hypothetical *The Trial of Henry Kissinger*, in which the defendant has used a political mask to evade responsibility under the law. Pinter's political writing belongs in this context. But however deep one's despair at New Labor's role in delivering the British electorate to the multinationals, a legal methodology that establishes Tony Blair as a war criminal while campaigning for the freedom of Slobodan Miloševic at the very least invites the citation of other, competing facts that would arrive at the reverse conclusion.

It is in this sense that the separation of facts from interpretation that Pinter made in 1985 is open to question. Mireia Aragay notes that in the representative sample of political essays from the 1980s and 1990s collected in *Various Voices*, Pinter "draw[s] a line between discourse and reality. Not surprisingly, terms such as 'reality,' 'facts' or 'truth' and their distortion in language are recurrent motifs" (252). To these one must add "law," and especially "international law," a phrase that occurs in the second sentence of the section and is used in that section a further eight times, in each case with reference to the alleged crimes of the United States. Pinter's conviction of the persuasive power of facts is inextricable from an apparently "formalistic" conception of law (it exists, and under it the facts establish the guilt of the United States), which is in fact, like any view of law, deeply implicated in moral judgments. This is to contest neither the existence of facts nor a morality that judges U.S. foreign policy to be criminal, but merely to insist that facts are always cited in some discourse or other that can never be entirely value free. The difference is between the playwright's acute suspicion of definitive statements and the citizen's faith in the persuasive value of facts and law.

Pinter's assertion of a single reality, then, is underpinned by a confidence in the citation of existing law to establish a case against the accused. Without this confidence, indeed, the law would not exist, the "principle of legality" stating, as a matter of both logic and procedure, that without law there is no crime:

A fundamental precept of international criminal law is the prohibition in international and domestic law on assigning guilt for acts not considered as crimes when committed. The maxim *nullum crimen sine lege, nulla poena sine lege*, or "no crime without law, no punishment without law," captures this notion, which finds different forms in various legal contexts. (Ratner and Abrams 21)

While this principle provides some protection against the capricious abuse of state power, in international law it encounters serious problems. An act may be criminal in one territory but not in another; moreover, international communities have not always been willing to accept the principles of *nullum crimen sine lege, nulla poena sine lege*, which can conflict with ideas of "humanistic" and natural law.

The hardest case concerns the postwar trials of Nazi leaders at Nuremberg, trials recalled in Pinter's *Ashes to Ashes* via Gitta Sereny's study of *Albert Speer: His Battle with Truth* (1995). Troublingly, the Nuremberg Tribunal, while exacting retribution for monstrous acts that for the first time were labelled "crimes against humanity," did not itself strictly adhere to the principle of legality in arriving at its judgments:

> the defendants asserted that the charges against them—in particular that of waging a war of aggression—were not crimes as of 1939. The International Military Tribunal took an extremely loose and controversial view of *nullum crimen* in 1946 with regard to the criminality of aggressive war. The court saw it as a "principle of justice" and merely stated that it would be unjust to let those who violate treaties go unpunished since "the attacker must know that he is doing wrong." (Ratner and Abrams 22)

The Nuremberg Tribunal violated the principle of legality for the first time, leading to complaints of illegitimacy and "victor's justice" that are recalled in Pinter's objections to the trial of Miloševic. Yet in so doing it satisfied the demands of natural law, recognized that international law "evolves like the Common Law of the Anglo-American tradition to reflect the moral judgments of the community of nations" (Kittichaisaree 20), and established precedents by which future war crimes might be redressed.

Such arguments, of course, do not contradict the view that law is dictated by the victorious and powerful. The U.S. government's current refusal to have its citizens subject to the ICC is an obvious example, symptomatic of the current behavior of what Pinter in his "Degree Speech" calls "the most dangerous power the world has ever known," "[a]rrogant, indifferent, contemptuous of International Law, both dismissive and manipulative of the United Nations." With George W. Bush in the White House, few on the left would disagree; but Pinter here reveals a problem in appealing to external arbiters. Geoffrey Robertson, a barrister with impeccable credentials as a defender of human rights, argues that both international law and the United Nations are in many respects the causes, not the cure, of crimes against humanity: the former is "that most airyfairy of disciplines, at worst a mirage and at best a hostage to international politics" (xx), while "human rights might have a healthier future if it parted company with the United Nations, if that body were replaced or marginalized by a democratic 'coalition of the willing'" (447).

For Robertson, the "systemic defect" of the UN is its "[o]beisance to member state sovereignty" (xix), which is the major obstacle to the formulation and exercise of international law. The increasingly critical international stance against the former near-immunity granted by state sovereignty is illustrated in Robertson's lengthy and detailed analysis of the NATO bombing of Serbia. For Pinter and others, NATO's actions are not only murderously criminal but violate this key principle; yet, after considering all of the specific charges against NATO and the United States, Robertson, who is no admirer of the US record on human rights, concludes that NATO demonstrated an "unprecedented attention to obeying the laws of war" (416) and that "[o]n balance . . . Kosovo was a just and lawful war" (423). Pinter's vehement opposition, albeit on legal as well as moral grounds, lends weight to the suggestion that his political views are animated by an entrenched anti-Americanism, characterized by his wife Antonia Fraser as a hatred of "injustice or unfairness" (Billington 288), that predetermines the position he will take whenever there is a conflict between the often contradictory legal principles that bedevil international law.

Here again, a study of the plays produces different readings of the tension between state and international powers from those in Pinter's political analysis, not least because Pinter himself tends always to read such situations in terms of American power, whereas the plays unfold either in an unspecified place and time or in a location (such as North London) infrequently associated with state terror and repression. Characters fight for possession of the onstage space while offstage is an area of unspecified threat from which undesirable intruders may invade. The pertinence of this to what Pinter sees as American attempts to erode the territorial integrity of sovereign nations, and to what others would regard as humanitarian interventions in genocidal internal conflicts, is clear. At the most prosaic level, the characters' struggle for territorial possession involves questions of legal ownership that, extended, hint at the control of states and their citizens by the economically and politically powerful. In *The Room* it is not altogether clear that Mr. Kidd is the landlord, or that the Hudds have the right to remain in the room; in *The Dumb Waiter* Gus wonders whether "Wilson" owns the properties in which the killings take place, and why no neighbors ever complain about the noise. In *The Caretaker* Mick, speaking of Aston, tells Davies:

> I could tell him to go. I mean, I'm the landlord. On the other hand, he's the sitting tenant. Giving him notice, you see, what it is, it's a technical matter, that's what it is. It depends how you regard this room. I mean it depends whether you regard this room as furnished or unfurnished. [. . .] All this furniture, you see, in here, it's all his, except the beds, of course. So what it is, it's a fine legal point, that's what it is. (80)

Such local, comic "fine legal points" rapidly take on a wider significance. In *The Room*, the invisible figure Mr. and Mrs. Sands encounter in the basement may be Riley, the enigmatic black man beaten up by Bert at the end of the play. While Riley is clearly not a realistic figure, his status both as intruder and possibly as landlord hints at the racist, often economically based bigotry experienced by immigrants that Pinter had experienced firsthand as a Jew growing up in the East End. Racial tensions increased in the 1950s with the large-scale immigration from the colonies alluded to in *The Caretaker* in the underclass, homeless character Davies's xenophobic mistrust of "blacks" and Indians. Such anxieties would later be exploited in Enoch Powell's infamous "rivers of blood" speech in 1968, and it requires no great imaginative leap to see connections to the ethnic massacres of the twentieth century. Economic pressures are also evident in *The Homecoming*, in which the question of legal ownership is explicitly extended from property to human beings: Ruth resists the roles of wife and (problematically) prostitute, and instead negotiates a "contract" with the aim of establishing herself not as a sexual worker for the family but as a relatively independent businesswoman using the men as a kind of merchant bank.

If these internal struggles may recall political struggles for territory, status, and citizenship within sovereign states, it has distressed many that having objected to American interference in the internal affairs of numerous Latin American states, in the former Yugoslavia Pinter appears disproportionately more concerned about the external threat posed by the United States than the internal threat posed by dictators, death squads, and the secret police. The external threat, of course, should not be minimized: Pinter observed that one of the seeds of *The Birthday Party* was the fear of the Gestapo knocking on the door (Gussow 71); the plays' dramatization of anxieties about the threat from the outside world may owe something to the experience of wartime bombing raids on London or, today, from the threat of destruction from invisible weapons fired from other continents while the fear of unseen assailants has clear implications in the light of the ongoing "war against terrorism." Yet whatever lurks beyond the stage in Pinter's plays is often a good deal less threatening than what is already on it: the assaults on defenseless characters in *The Room* and *The Caretaker*, Ben and Gus's preparations for murder in *The Dumb Waiter*.

What is offstage is murky and unquantifiable, the boundaries between it and the onstage space fluid and uncertain, marked often by the closed blinds and curtains that flimsily seek to keep the outside world at bay. In *The Room* Mr. Kidd is unable to state how many floors there are in the building; in *The Dumb Waiter* it is unclear from where the eponymous contraption with its gnomic instructions arrives, while at the end of the same play Gus exits left yet seconds later inexplicably enters right, suddenly a shattered man; in *Old Times* Anna enters the present-day world of Deeley and Kate not through the door but as if summoned by memories; in *No Man's Land* Briggs tells the story of Bolsover Street, difficult to find and impossible to leave.

If this murkiness makes the offstage space mysterious and threatening, equally it can mask an astonishing ineffectuality. When the feared character finally arrives it could be Goldberg or McCann, but equally it could be the seemingly benign Riley in *The Room*, who in asking "Sal" to "come home" speaks to Rose as if he were a friendly relative seeking to save her from an abusive husband, and gets beaten up for his pains (124); the just departed and comparatively innocent *raisonneur* Gus, in *The Dumb Waiter*; or even the comically mute and possibly nonexistent Matchseller in *A Slight Ache*. Extending the ambivalent representation of onstage and offstage forces in Pinter's plays once more into the geopolitical realm, one may note the near-total powerlessness of international bodies to end the massacres in Rwanda or, prior to the NATO bombing, in the former Yugoslavia; the continuing tensions between principles of sovereignty and international law; the United Nations as alternately instrument of and obstacle to humanitarian intervention; and the fluidity of international partnerships themselves, with some voices in the United States challenging the idea of fixed coalitions such as NATO and advocating the creation of impermanent, ad hoc alliances to combat individual local challenges. Many of these developments lend weight to Pinter's anxieties about the growing power of the United States—the impotence or strength of international bodies tends to be proportionate to the degree of interest America shows in them—but there are at least grounds for optimism in the establishment of the ICTR, the ICTY, and the ICC, and in the worldwide condemnation of America's unilateral abrogation of international agreements on matters from global warming to arms control.

If the political issues of power and territory most obviously connect the first and third phases of Pinter's writing, the plays written in the seventeen-year "break" are hardly irrelevant to the contemporary nightmare of "ethnic cleansing" and the attempt to erase layers of the territorial palimpsest by turning back the clock, freezing time at whatever historical moment the killers elect as the golden age, expelling whichever population is identified as the invader, and redrawing the lines on the map in accordance with a predetermined idea of what should constitute the rigid and immutable boundaries of the sovereign state. It is in this sense that the explorations of stasis in the plays of the middle period acquire a peculiar political resonance, in particular the illuminatingly entitled *No Man's Land*, that condition of old age and impotence that, as Spooner says, "never moves, which never changes, which never grows older, but which remains forever, icy and silent" (157). This, the penultimate speech of the play, comes shortly after Hirst has made the fateful decision to "change the subject. *Pause.* For the last time" (153). The play's terrifying vision of psychic paralysis is made concrete in *A Kind of Alaska*, in which Deborah awakes after twenty-eight years from a condition that her doctor Hornby can only hope was "not entirely static, was it? You ventured into quite remote . . . utterly foreign . . . territories" (337). The disabling rigidity of the mental states explored in these plays is described in geographical metaphors that in retrospect seem prescient both of the demands for secure territorial borders and of the destabilization and redrawing of borders in conflicts such as those in the former Yugoslavia and in Israel-Palestine.

But the "no man's land" of Hirst and Spooner also recalls Kafka's man from the country, who spends a lifetime paralyzed before the doorway to the Law before asking his final, fateful question. The parable stands as an image of the political world Pinter came to inhabit in the 1980s, as he asked what was to be done in the face of a heedless and inaccessible, near-totalitarian, power. Many explanations have been advanced for Pinter's political radicalization: his marriage to Antonia Fraser; the death of his close friend, the Marxist playwright David Mercer; a delayed artistic response to current events, particularly the Pinochet coup in Chile in 1973 (Billington 287). Another possibility is that the form Pinter's political thinking took on in the 1980s is an extension of the form his plays took on in the 1970s. In 1993 he remarked of the plays from *One for the Road* through *Party Time*:

> These plays, all of them, are to do not with ambiguities of power, but actual power. Now maybe this is not as appealing to some people as ambiguities of power, or shifting power, or how actual power is susceptible to all sorts of influences, psychological changes. But if I chose to write plays like *Mountain Language*, where you have the army and you have the victims, there's no ambiguity there. It is crude; that's the whole point. (Gussow 152)

And yet Pinter himself may read actual brutality differently depending on the context. He has stated in *Various Voices* that "I don't believe in the relativity of human rights" (226), but some allowances, it seems, may be made for the actions of the Serbian death squads, because Miloševic was engaged in a civil war, whereas no such allowances may be made on the NATO side. Pinter's unambiguous comments on "actual power" are accompanied by an unambiguous interpretation of the nature of and responsibility for war crimes, even though quite different legal and moral interpretations may be put on those events even by those who are generally sympathetic to Pinter's position. It is as if, in the early 1980s, Pinter as a political citizen finally changed the subject—for the last time. And yet as a playwright, despite the diminished quantity of new plays, he remains wonderfully creative and versatile, producing in *Ashes to Ashes* and *Celebration* plays that show the dramatist continuing to avoid stasis, turning away from a doorway that, to his detractors, is all too easily caricatured as having been made only for him.

Works Cited

Anon. "Artists against the War." *Guardian* (London), 8 Apr. 1999.

Aragay, Mireia. "Pinter, Politics and Postmodernism (2)." *Cambridge Companion to Harold Pinter*. Ed. Peter Raby. Cambridge: Cambridge UP, 2000, 246–59.

Austin, J.L. *How to Do Things with Words*. Oxford: Oxford UP, 1962.

Billington, Michael. *The Life and Work of Harold Pinter*. London: Faber, 1996.

Fish, Stanley. *There's No Such Thing as Free Speech: And It's a Good Thing Too*. Oxford: Oxford UP, 1994.

Gibbons, Fiachra. "Free Milošević, Says Pinter." *Guardian* (London), 26 July 2001.

Gillan, Audrey. "Bombing Shames Britain, Pinter Tells Protesters." *Guardian* (London) 7 June 1999.

Gussow, Mel. *Conversations with Harold Pinter*. London: Nick Hern, 1994, 7–23.

Hern, Nicholas. "A Play and Its Politics: A Conversation between Harold Pinter and Nicholas Hern." *One for the Road*. London: Methuen, 1985.

Kafka, Franz. "Before the Law." Trans. Willa and Edwin Muir. *The Penguin Complete Stories of Franz Kafka*. Ed. Nahum N. Glatzer. Harmondsworth: Penguin, 1983, 3–4.

Kittichaisaree, Kriangsak. *International Criminal Law*. Oxford: Oxford UP, 2001.

Mamet, David. *American Buffalo*. London: Methuen, 1984.

———. *Glengarry Glen Ross*. London: Methuen, 1984.

Pinter, Harold. "Degree Speech to the University of Florence 10th Sep. 2001." http://www.haroldpinter.org/home/florence.html. 10 Sep. 2001.

———. *The Caretaker. Plays: One*. London: Methuen, 1976.

———. *A Kind of Alaska. Plays: Four*. London: Faber, 1993.

———. *No Man's Land. Plays: Four*. London: Faber, 1993.

———. *The Room. Plays: One*. London: Methuen, 1976.

———. *Various Voices: Prose, Poetry, Politics 1948–1998*. London: Faber, 1998.

————. "Writing for the Theatre." *Plays: One*. London: Methuen, 1976.

Porter, Henry. "Radical Mistakes." *Guardian* (London), 9 June 1999.

Quigley, Austin E. "Pinter, Politics and Postmodernism (1)." *Cambridge Companion to Harold Pinter*. Ed. Peter Raby. Cambridge: Cambridge UP, 2000, 7–27.

Ratner, Steven R., and Jason S. Abrams. *Accountability for Human Rights Atrocities in International Law: Beyond the Nuremberg Legacy*. 2nd ed. Oxford: Oxford UP, 2001.

Robertson, Geoffrey. *Crimes against Humanity: The Struggle for Global Justice*. Harmondsworth: Penguin, 2000.

Sweeney, John. "Why Can't They See?" *Guardian* (London), 30 May 1999.

Tempest, Matthew. "Pinter: I Won't Be Silenced." *Guardian* Unlimited. www.guardian.co.uk/Archive/Article/0,4273,4233451,00.html). 3 Aug. 2001.

Worster, David. "How to Do Things with Salesmen: David Mamet's Speech Act Play." *Glengarry Glen Ross: Text and Performance*. Ed. Leslie Kane. New York: Garland, 1996, 63–79.

4

Harold Pinter's *Ashes to Ashes*: The Criminality of Indifference and the Failure of Empathy

CHARLES GRIMES

Ever since Theodor Adorno's famous, though often misunderstood, injunction against writing poetry after Auschwitz, the propriety of using art to depict the Holocaust has been fiercely debated.[1] It has often been argued that any writing about the Holocaust, either as history or art, results in falsification. As Emily Miller Budick puts it, "To survivors and nonsurvivors alike, the Holocaust has always seemed to be beyond our ability to know it and therefore to represent it. Writing about the Holocaust . . . has seemed . . . not simply to miss it but to violate it: to distort or trivialize or even to deny it" (329–30). Efraim Sicher notes that current Holocaust remembrance "once more stir[s] up the questions Theodor Adorno and Elie Wiesel raised about legitimacy and authenticity" ("Introduction" 7).

The so-called historical uniqueness of the Holocaust, often adduced as a cause of its inability to be interpreted or represented, may not stand up to historical scrutiny, given the genocidal impulses of the twentieth century. Yet, there lingers a sense of the Holocaust's uniqueness as an horrific crime against human morality and dignity. The sheer scale of the Nazis' crimes, their deliberate nature, and the unprecedented means of genocidal murder they invented render Holocaust "intransigent" to "puny human interpretation" (Clendinnen 18). What happens, then, when artists try to imagine and to represent horrors and crimes that have been forcefully termed unimaginable, inexpressible, and unrepresentable?

The idea that the Holocaust should not be the subject of art has hardly prevented writers and artists from attempting to represent it. In recent years, critics of Holocaust literature have described several qualities that art, and other forms of discourse, should display in order to avoid the dangers of illegitimacy and inauthenticity first described by Adorno. One such criterion is a kind of indirection that frequently takes the form of allusiveness. As Inga Clendinnen aptly observes, "The most effective imagined evocations of the

Holocaust seem to proceed either by invocation . . . or by indirection" (165).
Another element in "successful" Holocaust writing is a meta-discourse that
declares and confronts its inherent paradoxes and difficulties. Sicher believes that authentic Holocaust literature "succeeds in showing the impossibility of [its] representation. . . . [N]o account claiming to have found words
to express the truth can be genuine" ("The Holocaust" 321). And, Berel
Lang in *Act and Idea in the Nazi Genocide* claims that any writing of the
Holocaust must question our "presumption of illumination" (145), that is,
our desire for increased knowledge or comprehension. Equally important to
nonreductive, serious Holocaust art is an ability to contemplate atrocity
without allowing oneself to escape such bleakness by constructing positive
or redemptive meanings that lead away from genocide's deep depravity and
evil. Lawrence Langer is a persuasive advocate of this idea, arguing in
Holocaust Testimonies and subsequent books that the deepest, most authentic engagement with the Holocaust is also the most dangerous, the most psychologically self-wounding.

In *Ashes to Ashes*, Harold Pinter presents history allusively in the register of memory. Highlighting the impossibility of verifying what may or may
not be historically accurate, he employs a style of indirection, referring, for
example, to specifics of the career of the war criminal Albert Speer, Hitler's
architect and arms minister, without detailing names, places, or dates. *Ashes
to Ashes* invokes Holocaust history but never shows Nazi criminal behavior
nor uses the words Nazi or Jew. Pinter investigates his own artistic medium
through and in this play, showing how sustained empathy with the legacy of
atrocity is made problematic by the circumstances of bourgeois comfort and
by the social and temporal distances between the events of the genocide and
his audience. Budick claims that "increasing temporal distance has made
speaking about the Holocaust that much more precarious and forgetting it
all that much easier" (330). My intent here is to show how Pinter has dramatized this precariousness, the uncertain place authentic commemoration of
the past is granted in contemporary society.

Ashes to Ashes dramatizes the difficulty of bearing witness to the Holocaust, suggesting that a self-conscious witness, aware of his or her own distance from the Holocaust, is the only kind now possible. Pinter emphasizes
the forces (internal and external, psychological and social) that seek to silence this witness. As Pinter's play underlines the challenge of moral engagement, it urges us to transvalue our perceptions of what is real and unreal
in our daily lives and in the constitution of our moral selves. For Rebecca,
the embattled protagonist of *Ashes to Ashes*, life's most familiar moments—
going to the movies, a marital spat, children growing up—seem foreign,
even alienating, whereas at the same time they appear trivial and clichéd.
Pinter wants us to see the events of Rebecca's life as she does—tiredly familiar and horribly alien. Thus, he depicts her attempts to confront the Holo-

caust as far more profound than anything associated with her domestic roles. Haunting the play is the premise that normal life is drained of moral substance while conversely it seems as if compassionate contemplation of the Holocaust makes it too profound, too big, for our everyday lives. This moral paradox, which amounts to the impossibility of "thinking" the Holocaust, is the dilemma with which the play confronts us.

In her narrative, Rebecca recounts a sexual affair with a man who took part in an "atrocity" reminiscent of the Nazi genocide. Her description of ritualized abuse at the hands of this "lover" suggest perhaps she was raped (13). The enormity of these events is dressed in everyday terms, however, as she quite factually describes her lover as a "courier" for a travel agency and then as a "guide" (19, 21). In her second story, the man takes her to a factory where the workers show him elaborate deference, "doff[ing] their caps" (23). Rebecca next tells a story, apparently from a different time, when she witnessed a mass suicide as guides led fur-coated refugees into the waters off Dorset. Later, she recounts what seem like normal events: a movie matinee, a visit to her sister. Devlin, both jealous and concerned, seeks to clarify these references to a man in his wife's past and attempts through a combination of flattery, reassurance, and anger to talk Rebecca back into the everyday life from which she is so radically alienated. However, near the end of the play, Devlin attempts briefly to emulate the violence Rebecca accepted from her lover. In her final story, which takes place on a train platform, Rebecca tries to rescue a baby by disguising it as a bundle but gives the baby up to her lover, now a guard. She then denies she has abandoned the baby. An echo repeats her phrases. Once she reaches the point in her narrative in which she once again has failed to have impact, she steps out of the story, repeating its final line: "I don't know of any baby." Pinter uses this moment to emphasize the disjunction of history, memory and conscience, and after a "Long silence," the play ends (85).

Ashes to Ashes, like *Old Times*, is a play "about" an unhappy marriage but also, perhaps more importantly, it enacts a debate about historical knowledge. As the play ends, we are confronted with questions. In regard to Rebecca's historical allusions, we might wonder what parts of her stories could truly have happened to her or to others whom she may or may not have known. What is the meaning of these stories if they are not grounded in (her) experience? Asserting the interpersonal meaning human experience should provide, Arthur Miller described his play *All My Sons* as an assault upon "the fortress of unrelatedness," the idea that our lives have no necessary connection one to another, that we have no responsibility for each other (131). Rebecca's fabric of being is a battle against this prevailing unrelatedness. In analogous fashion to Miller, Pinter's *Ashes to Ashes* raises what might be termed "pastlessness," the idea that the past has nothing to do with the present. Through Rebecca's stories, Pinter critiques our definition of knowledge and questions our opportunities for confronting, or evading, history. In a discussion of the play after a 1996 New York reading (21 October, 92nd Street Y), Pinter commented that intellectual understanding exists alongside emotive or intuitive knowledge. Rebecca assumes that human knowing can neither be solely rational nor be properly ahistorical. Jumping the gap between reflection and immediate experience, she seeks to relieve "cognitive unknowing," caused by distance in time from the events themselves, with a kind of "emotional knowing" (Horowitz 290) prompted by the fact that as the Holocaust recedes into the past, into "history," those who would reflect upon it must do so indirectly as members of generations after the events. Rebecca tells her stories as a way to test her own moral-imaginative capacity to apprehend history in the present. "Nothing has ever happened to me" (41), she admits under Devlin's interrogation of her conduct; thus, narrative becomes her only entry into the past and imagination her only route to moral engagement.

By linking historical truth with inventive and emotive memory, Pinter undermines conventional distinctions between history as factual record and history in more subjective, allegedly less "verifiable," forms. From the viewpoint of Holocaust historians, identification with the subjects of history is not a guarantee of knowledge. Eva Hoffman points to the importance of the separation between an event and its historical perception: "[T]he distance between ourselves and that event needs to be taken account of in the ways we remember it. The gulf cannot be closed by insistence on 'identification'" (22). Even sympathetic people may be "unable to identify intellectually or to experience vicariously the feelings, thoughts, and attitudes of the victims," not to mention those of the perpetrators of genocide or of their passive or approving bystanders (Magurshak 424). The inherent difficulty of Rebecca's attempts at empathy is made clearer by these cautionary statements. Finally, Rebecca's difficulties in communication lead to problematic relationships with her husband in the play and (according to some reviewers) with the audience watching it. Through these difficulties and through her final isolated silence, Pinter raises the possibility that imaginative, emotive knowledge of history may be so personally consuming as to end in stalemate and futility, a state very few of us would be able to sustain.

Pinter uses the character of Devlin, who is apparently a scholar or professor, to introduce one perspective on the theme of knowledge:

> You understand why I'm asking you these questions. Don't you? Put yourself in my place. I'm compelled to ask you questions. There are so many things I don't know. I know nothing . . . about any of this. Nothing. I'm in the dark. I need light. Or do you think my questions are illegitimate? (11)

Here the clear knowledge Devlin hopes for, enlightenment in the traditional sense, equates to light and ignorance to darkness. In voicing rational curiosity about Rebecca's stories, Devlin is a proxy for the audience, who also desire to assess her truthfulness. Her refusal to enter the discussion on Devlin's terms—"What questions?" she asks—threatens to leave us in the dark. Pinter specifies the stage lighting to supplement the play's concern with defining knowledge. He writes: *"The room darkens during the course of the play. The lamplight intensifies."* Pinter insists on this contradiction: *"By the end of the play. . . . The lamplight has become very bright but does not illumine the room"* (1). The ability of darkness to overcome light suggests that darkness is not just an absence of light but an encroaching, positive force in itself, phenomenologically prior to light. The lasting power of darkness echoes Berel Lang's phrase that any act of writing the Holocaust must call into question the "presumption of illumination" (145), that is, the expectation for increased understanding of "the truth," that we bring to any representation of history. (The symbolism of light and darkness in moral terms also is relevant here: how Pinter lights his play seems a metaphorical illustration of the triumph of evil [darkness] over goodness [light], a triumph suggesting that ideals of morality may never overcome evil.)

According to Michael Billington's authorized biography of Pinter, the playwright began writing *Ashes to Ashes* after reading Gitta Sereny's *Albert Speer: His Battle with Truth* (1995), which recounts an affair Speer had with a young German woman in his last years.[2] Speer's liaison suggested to Pinter Rebecca's connection with an older man who may be a war criminal (Billington 373) Additionally, Pinter, who often traces his impulse to write his plays to a particular visual image, was inspired to write *Ashes to Ashes* by a specific moment in Sereny's book. Rebecca's story about a visit to her lover's factory is born out of Speer's 1943 visit to a secret work camp called Dora—a successor facility to Peenemunde established to build V-2 rockets and supplied with slave labor from the Buchenwald concentration camp and European deportees. Thus Pinter's play dramatizes an historical reference, although the language of the play avoids such traditionally "historical" details as to date, place, or other localizing context. Rebecca relates, with delicate vagueness, her unsettling visit to this factory which "wasn't the usual kind of factory" (23). Rows of workers in caps removed their caps in apparent deference to their commander, Rebecca's lover. She notes the factory was cold and "exceedingly damp" but had no toilets: "I wanted to go to the bathroom. But I simply couldn't find it" (27).

Rebecca's somewhat anodyne language conflicts with an eyewitness view of conditions at Dora. According to Jean Michel, a French slave laborer, the Nazis provided "No heat, no ventilation, not the smallest pail to wash in. . . . the latrines . . . were barrels cut in half with planks laid across" (*Dora* 62–63). In *Albert Speer*, Sereny allows Speer to give his version, querying him in 1978 about the 1943 visit to Dora. She describes his powerful shame on the subject: "immediately and impossible to fake, his face went pale; again he covered his eyes for a moment with his hand" (404).

Speer told her that at the time, "I was outraged. I demanded to see the sanitary provisions." He ordered that rations be increased, facilities built, and workers not be threatened with execution as a motivating tool. In his memoirs *Inside the Third Reich*, Speer portrays himself as the recipient of such a salute as Rebecca describes: "Expressionlessly, they [the prisoners] looked right through me, mechanically removing their prisoners' caps of blue twill until our group had passed them" (370). Not even Speer himself describes this moment in the terms of respect and warmth evoked by the image of these prisoners "doffing" their caps to him. The slave-laborers' actions conflict in tone with Rebecca's account, providing an ironic contrast between differently narrated versions of the same event, and illustrating that Rebecca herself adopts Speer's ability to construct history in a way that is partial and self-absolving.

Although there are so many facts—so many truths—available in the historical record of the Holocaust, paradoxically, there is no one truth that is generally agreed upon—if indeed the "truth" concerning anything about the Holocaust can be understood by those who did not live through it. In *Ashes to Ashes*, Pinter dramatizes a fact of Holocaust history as if it were one person's bizarre, vague, unverifiable story. How one views the facts of the genocide is a problem of perspective, which Pinter confronts directly. If Pinter aims to draw our attention to genocidal crimes, his audience, with its post-Holocaust political perspective, might object that such nightmares have nothing to do with us—we aren't slave drivers like Speer; we are not war criminals, we don't even know anyone who is. Through Devlin's attack on Rebecca's lack of authority to refer to the Holocaust, Pinter voices a likely response by an audience asked to ponder material that would assault its moral complacency. Thus Pinter incorporates an attitude of resistance to the material the play explores, rendering problematic the process of opening oneself to knowledge of historical oppression. Specifically, Devlin believes Rebecca unreliable in how she uses language to formulate experience:

> DEVLIN: Now let me ask you this. What authority do you yourself possess which would give you the right to discuss such an atrocity?
> REBECCA: I have no such authority. Nothing has ever happened to me. Nothing has ever happened to any of my friends. I have never suffered. Nor have my friends.
> DEVLIN: Good. (41)

Rebecca's remarks here reflect society's (or human beings') efforts to deny historical atrocities, even in the case of individuals who do try to "admit" them into consciousness. Lawrence Langer argues that human memory almost inevitably rejects extreme victimization. "[H]umiliated memory," he writes in *Holocaust Testimonies*, "negates the impulse to historical inquiry. Posterity not only can do without it; it prefers to ignore it" (79). Given how frequently the Holocaust has been documented and memorialized in recent years (through movies, television, museums, history books), however, everyone has access to images of the genocide; the issue is how deeply or seriously we permit them to inhabit our psyches, our moral imaginations.[3] Langer writes that the concern must be with how much we allow ourselves to "admit" these images and their resonances. Devlin personifies a willed ignorance (a paradox, admittedly, but one Devlin is committed to). His behavior reveals the collusion between an autonomous, bourgeois self, and a cultural preference for denying history. (Pinter himself experienced this kind of denial in the audiences at his political plays. According to the playwright, these audiences pretended they already knew and "did not need to be told" about the facts he was dramatizing [Hern 18].) We flatter and lie to ourselves, Pinter suggests, if we believe our consciences extend further than does Devlin's. Through him, Pinter illustrates how the atomized, insulated selves we seek out of self-protection or social conformity bar engagement with the depths of history. A society that values the truth and privacy of personal experience will only with difficulty be able to learn from the past.[4]

Contrary to Devlin's manner of rejecting experience he defines as outside his personal sphere of knowledge, Rebecca embraces a kind of historical determinism in which everyone's life is connected with everyone else's. She tries to will historical fate into her personal life, attempting to know the past through emotion, imagination, memory. Yet, though Rebecca wishes to connect with history, and specifically with the Holocaust, the play shows how this attempt is fraught with difficulty. In his 1996 discussion of the play, Pinter asserted the moral heroism of Rebecca's actions, but in a way that nearly characterizes her as obsessed. "We dare not think about these things," he said in reference to historical crimes, "but Rebecca can't *not* think about them." Pinter seems to suggest that personally to acknowledge such guilt as manifested in the Holocaust is to risk being overwhelmed. Such an attempt threatens our very selves, leading to an emotional state that Clendinnen identifies as "the Gorgon effect," a paralysis caused by Holocaust contemplation (18). Rebecca provides such an image of paralysis when describing a fellow cinemagoer:

> But there was a man sitting in front of me, to my right. He was absolutely still throughout the whole film. He never moved, he was rigid, like a body with rigor mortis, he never laughed once, he just sat like a corpse. I . . . moved as far away from him as I possibly could. (65)

Though Rebecca apparently distances herself from this ostracized "corpse," it may, nevertheless, double for Rebecca herself, who also denies a capacity for humor and who is generally immobile and self-isolating.[5] We may conclude that she represents an impossible sort of freedom that requires remaining apart. Rebecca's sense of obligation to others coincides with her estrangement from them; hence, it cannot be acted on and is difficult to emulate. Pinter attempts to estrange us from Rebecca's historical sympathy by associating it here with death and, in the passage on "mental elephantiasis," (51) with a disabling awareness of guilt. To have guilt, or to experience responsibility for another, comes to connote paralysis and self-death. Pinter also qualifies Rebecca's "compassion" for others by placing this word in the context of the subjugation she imagines as part of her relationship with her "lover." "No, no, he felt compassion for me," she says of her lover-oppressor, denying that the violence perpetrated against her can be seen as criminal aggression. This heterodox portrait of compassion is not Pinter creating a morally masochistic character, but rather a means of investigating skeptically the efficacy of empathy in life and art. Pinter does not allow his audience to take consolation from a triumph of empathetic responsibility. He suggests that in a post-Holocaust world, redemption is illusory.

In previous criticism of *Ashes to Ashes*, empathy has been privileged as an effective route from suffering toward transcendence. Katherine H. Burkman, in her essay "Harold Pinter's *Ashes to Ashes*: Rebecca and Devlin as Albert Speer" (*Pinter Review* 1997/1998), argues that Rebecca's storytelling may lead to an existentially fuller life, perhaps to the ownership of suffering and to healing, loving capabilities. Burkman parallels the play to Gitta Sereny's biography; in so doing, she equates Speer's ability to love late in his life with Rebecca's growth at the end of the play: "Perhaps, like Speer, she will now be able to love" (94). Just as Speer is able to overcome the emotional paralysis that blinded him to his odious actions for the Third Reich, Rebecca makes a similar rediscovery of feeling and personal growth leading to her expressions of empathy for the victims of history.[6]

The impulse to see empathy as a transcendent, positive process parallels deep assumptions about the moral efficacy of art. Theater especially is thought to offer moral benefits based upon its ability to bridge the gap between the experiences of differing selves. Additionally, when dealing with material as dark and depressing as the Holocaust, one experiences an impulse to escape from such darkness to a more hopeful, positive endpoint (thus leading Langer to prefer an artistic "discourse of ruin" to one of "consolation" fostering only our self-protection [*Admitting the Holocaust* 6].) Francis Gillen, for example, like Burkman, seems driven to a more positive reading than the play warrants, claiming Rebecca strengthens herself (and us as viewers too) through identification and empathy. By means of empathy, he writes, she "discovers her own power . . . to reshape herself as non-victim" (91). Both Gillen and Burkman note that Pinter provides Rebecca with one important triumph: She declines to kiss Devlin's fist when he emulates this tactic of her "lover." However, this moment of resistance to Devlin's potential violence need not be privileged as the definitive moment of his and Rebecca's relationship, nor should its meaning be overrated. Rather, it should be set against two other events: how Devlin denies Rebecca a psychologically secure space in which she can utter her words of witness, and (as I shall examine later in this essay) how Rebecca embraces silence and withdrawal at the end of the play.

If critics of *Ashes to Ashes* valorize empathy and its empowering effects, the very possibility of real empathy has been questioned in important ways. Elaine Scarry argues throughout *The Body in Pain* that accounts of suffering always provoke doubt in their hearers: attending to reports of how others suffer is nearly impossible. The Holocaust's extreme subjugation brings the problem of identification with suffering to its highest pitch. Its victims were utterly stripped of will and were threatened that their narrations would never be believed. The Holocaust's extremity as a vast criminal enterprise, arising not from the margins of society but from the heart of a supposedly civilized country, also uniquely endangers our view of ourselves as moral individuals whose use of words like "compassion" and "empathy" has been irrevocably altered by the fact of genocide.

Surely it is a mark of Rebecca's success in imagining the Holocaust if she can see herself as a victim, albeit a disabling "success." In considering the question of what Rebecca ultimately becomes, I believe it is necessary to note two things about her stories. First, they end in a way that impresses on us the fact and finality of that ending; second, they narrate the abdication or "denial" of moral responsibility. When Devlin confronts Rebecca about her lack of "authority," she seems to renounce her own project of sympathetic historical knowledge. Possibly her overall aim in the play is to complete this renunciation: She speaks in order to be able to not speak. Although the final moments of the play, with Rebecca's narrative of abandoning her baby and her denial that she has done so, may in Burkman's view only "seem negative," it is instead a negativity that is both lasting and pervasive, engulfing any "possibility of redemption" (94). Such redemption might represent the kind of inappropriate, yet understandable, consolation that Adorno, Langer, and Cynthia Ozick have warned us against: "We want to escape from the idea of having to quit in the bottomless muck of annihilation, with nothing else on the horizon" (Ozick 278). But the nature of the Holocaust makes such escape false, wishful. Pinter's consciousness of hate and violence—both its intensity and persistence—means to disallow such escape. Moreover, the critical desire to read Rebecca's engagement with suffering as triumphant misrepresents the burden of that suffering as a convenient stepping stone to spiritual growth.

Pinter underlines Rebecca's closure and isolation through her status as passive spectator in the stories she tells. From her window, Rebecca watches refugees being led into the sea. Likewise, she hands over her baby without protest. Her final renunciation of responsibility for the "baby" parallels her earlier retreat under Devlin's attack. Rebecca's action of abandoning her own storytelling mirrors the abandonment she narrates. Even in her imagination, she cannot picture herself as morally effective. Her inward turn, finally, comes up empty. Both the plot of her narration and her abandonment of her story illustrate how Rebecca doubly internalizes the failure of moral outreach, the indifference that many historians have located at the heart of the genocide. The role she constructs is the mythically innocent, fatally ineffective bystander. Rebecca's final story inverts the narrative of rescue now so familiar to us from movies such as *Schindler's List* and *Life is Beautiful*. Rainer C. Baum, who argues that the moral indifference that permitted the Final Solution is rooted in social circumstances both deeply ordinary and absolutely contemporary, writes that "modern life simply generates no demand for conscience" (82, 56). "[L]et us use memory," he posits, "to realize just how deeply we have woven the opportunities for amoral conduct into the social fabric of modern life, how easy we have made it for ourselves to adopt the role of passive bystander" (84). Our role as spectators to the play may even, in allusive fashion, parallel this role of passive onlooker.

Rebecca's experience in the play confirms the notion of Zygmunt Bauman in *Modernity and the Holocaust* that the practice of morality is socially and temporally circumscribed: "Morality tends to stay at home and in the present" (200). Bauman argues that key aspects of social modernity represent a necessary condition of the Holocaust, maintaining that genocide could have occurred in any bureaucratically advanced Western nation. Bauman defines three methods by which society manages and restricts morality:

> social production of distance, which either annuls or weakens the pressure of moral responsibility; substitution of technical for moral responsibility, which effectively conceals the moral significance of the action; and the technology of segregation and separation, which promotes indifference to the plight of the Other. (199)

These aspects of social practice are visible in *Ashes to Ashes* and in other Pinter plays. *Ashes* dramatizes the social distance and separation between "home" and "world," between oneself and others, a separation internalized by Rebecca whose position in her stories is distanced and spectatorial. The "technology of segregation and separation" defines the settings of *Mountain Language* and *Party Time*—settings hidden from public view, serving in the first case as prison for the out-group and in the second as fortress for the in-group. Also, Albert Speer exemplifies what Bauman calls "the substitution of technical for moral responsibility." In Speer's words: "[T]he habit of thinking within the limits of my own field provided me, both as architect and as Armaments Minister, with many opportunities for evasion" (*Inside the Third Reich* 113). Devlin, too, substitutes duty for conscience and thereby defends both indifference and aggression to others: "Fuck the best man, that's always been my motto. It's the man who ducks

his head and moves on through no matter what . . . who gets there in the
end. . . . A man who doesn't give a shit. A man with a rigid sense of duty"
(47). Devlin embodies mental habits that culminate in a "plausible deniabil-
ity" of moral responsibility to others.

Bauman ties the Holocaust to the present day in ways that strengthen
the link to prominent Pinter themes. In the present,

> the ancient Sophoclean conflict between moral law and the law of society
> shows no sign of abating. If anything . . . odds are shifted in favour of the
> morality-suppressing societal pressures. . . . [M]oral behavior . . . means
> resistance to societal authority. (199)

His notions of morality and power describe Pinter's overall political stance
that values outsiders against a morally deadening society forcing all to conform. An irony arises: antisocial behavior is moral, whereas actions conjoined by society may be immoral. Pinter expressed the necessity of such
defiance, famously and economically, in Petey's plea to the defeated Stanley
at the end of *The Birthday Party*: "Stan, don't let them tell you what to do"
(86). This definition of morality as defiance roots Pinter's overall politics in
his conception of the Holocaust.

Ashes to Ashes illustrates the link between genocide and life in the
now—a connection that is, paradoxically, both inescapable and tenuous.
The fact of genocide has a lingering yet uncertain presence in contemporary
consciousness. Late in the play, Devlin (like Deeley in *Old Times*) joins his
mate in singing a romantic tune:

> REBECCA: (*singing softly*) 'Ashes to ashes'—
> DEVLIN: 'And dust to dust'—
> REBECCA: 'If the women don't get you'—
> DEVLIN: 'The liquor must.' *Pause.* I always knew you loved me.
> REBECCA: Why?
> DEVLIN: Because we like the same tunes. (69)

Despite Devlin's assertion of community, this moment illustrates fracture
and misunderstanding. While Rebecca does not correct Devlin's musical
memory, as she did earlier in the play (17), we still see that Rebecca's understanding of "ashes to ashes" has nothing to do with Devlin's. To Rebecca, obsessed by genocidal imagery, these ashes are the ashes of Jews (or
Bosnians or Hutus or Kurds). To Devlin they are simply the cue for a popular (also misogynist) song, worthy of no more thought than one gives to any
cliché.

The words that title Pinter's play evoke the Holocaust for Rebecca,
measuring her psychological and epistemological distance from Devlin to
whom they evoke simply a sentimental song or a wistful allusion to love.

Words that many of us think of as unexceptional are granted powerful meaning by Rebecca because these words are somehow, at least potentially, connected to the Holocaust. In the same vein, Norma Rosen writes in "The Second Life of Holocaust Imagery" that particular words—"trains," "camps," and so forth—whenever they are uttered, in whatever context, may evoke memory of the Holocaust. "For a mind engraved with the Holocaust, gas is always that gas. Shower means their shower. Ovens are those ovens" (58). Possibly such references, including that to the song lyric "ashes to ashes," if woven into the texture of daily life by those who never stop contemplating the Holocaust, can be slight but effective memorials to its victims. Rosen's conception that everyday life affords opportunities for moral contemplation of the Holocaust enlarges the ways in which postgenocide generations may confront its legacy.

Pinter himself uses the crimes of the genocide as the basis for his moral denunciation of contemporary Western governments. In an interview with Mireia Aragay, he correlates Nazi oppression with the death-dealing actions of present nations: "It's not simply the Nazis that I'm talking about in *Ashes to Ashes* . . . it's also that what we call our democracies have subscribed to . . . repressive, cynical and indifferent acts of murder" (11). Pinter's eagerness to move from the Nazi genocide to contemporary political crimes suggests a move to find certitude and to embrace a particular abstract conclusion as the end result of Holocaust contemplation. This conclusion is at some temporal-historical distance from specifically Nazi crimes, crimes that in Pinter's interpretation here figure as analogues to other acts of oppressive power.[7] In contrast to Pinter's public pronouncements on current geopolitics, the play itself resists such interpretive certainty. Rather, it opens a space in which the Holocaust must, impossibly, be "thought" as an event that challenges and denies the assumptions that we can comprehend and interpret experience through language or in any other way.

This empty space is privileged in our experience of the play by its status as conclusion. Rebecca's attempts to merge history with self end with a final silence memorably dramatized by Pinter. Rebecca's final moment of renunciation lasts through the "Long silence" specified in the penultimate stage direction (85). Rebecca has previously reminded us that an ending can be not a point in time but a lasting process (67). Her final silence, in similar fashion, ends at great length, as the echo we have come to expect fails to arrive. The pause between her two denials, "I don't know of any baby," marks one utterance as being inside her story and the other outside it, that is, from Rebecca as "herself." Silence is the ground from which language may or may not emerge; in Rebecca's final silence (mirroring the play's opening) Pinter makes us attend to the absence, the disappearance, of language. This empty space, characterized as void of language, is a site in which genocide is conceived as challenge to meaning and articulation.

Holocaust literature, writes Lang, is "always to be judged as having displaced the value of silence" (161). However, perhaps anything other than silence, any discourse at all, may have only negative value in this context; to return to Langer's terms, there may be no such thing as a "discourse" of ruin, in that any use of language implies reconstruction and consolation. Language always fails to communicate the truth of traumatic events. The untranslatability of trauma into words derives from the essence of trauma, the nature of which is that it cannot be articulated: Contemplation of extreme suffering escapes both recollection and words, leading perhaps to extreme psychological numbness. That Pinter's Holocaust play ends in pronounced silence is aesthetically and morally appropriate as an index of a catastrophe about which one of its victims predicted, "The truth was always more atrocious, more tragic than what will be said about it" (qtd. in Blanchot 83).

Rebecca's final state can be conceived as a silence that is externally imposed upon as well as internally sought by her. Maurice Blanchot in *The Writing of the Disaster* argues that a unique type of silence is the condition of contemplating our survival after the Holocaust, a condition in which we cannot be ourselves. "The thought of the disaster," Blanchot writes, removes us from conventional life; "it replaces ordinary silence—where speech lacks—with a separate silence, set apart, where . . . the other, keeping still, announces himself" (12). In describing the moral pressure Rebecca puts on herself in his 1996 public discussion, Pinter noted that she strips herself naked, echoing the idea that Rebecca's project is about divesting herself of herself. "Passivity . . . is being worn down past the nub" (17), a state composed of "anonymity, loss of self, loss of sovereignty but also of all subordination; utter uprootedness; exile" (17–18). Rebecca carries this exile within her. She intensifies this condition for herself, even mourning over a police siren that moves away from her toward others, leaving her bereft, lonely, and as she puts it, "insecure" (31). According to Blanchot, extreme suffering owns the individual who attempts to own it. Such is the end, the limit, and also the personal cost of empathizing with victims of the Holocaust. Acknowledging responsibility "interrupt[s] our speech, our reason, [and] our experience" (18). The impossibility of contemplating the Holocaust is that it separates us from our selves.

The theme of Pinter's political plays in the 1980s and early 1990s is the suppression of dissident voices by overwhelming structures of established power. Rebecca's can be seen as such a dissident voice, also ultimately stilled. As her attempts at imaginative empathy conclude, we witness what could be termed the end of witness as we enter a frozen world with little or no room for remembering atrocity. Contrary to earlier plays such as *Old Times* and *No Man's Land*, Pinter is no longer dramatizing the persistence of the past in the present; memory now can no longer sustain the presence, the presentness, of the past.[8] "Never forget," is one famous purported lesson of the Holocaust. Pinter's play is a testament to the impossibility as well as the necessity of commemorating the dead. Rebecca's isolation indexes profound loss and gestures to the irremediable absence that both provokes and concludes engagement with atrocity's legacy. Faulkner wrote, "The past is never dead. It's not even past," yet *Ashes to Ashes* refutes Faulkner's view. *Ashes to Ashes* summons us to make the past meaningful in our present, as it simultaneously demonstrates how attempting to obey such a calling has complex, threatening, and self-destructive consequences.

Notes

1. Adorno also writes in "Commitment": "the abundance of real suffering tolerates no forgetting. . . . It is now virtually in art alone that suffering can still find its own voice, consolation, without immediately being betrayed by it" (188).
2. Laudatory reviews include those by Dennis L. Noble (*Library Journal*, 15 Oct. 1995, 74) and Boyd Tonkin (*New Statesman and Society*, 8 Dec., 1995, 32).
3. Geoffrey Wheatcroft writes in the *Times Literary Supplement*, 9 June 2000: "It seems that the further the event recedes in time, the larger it grows in our consciousness. 'The Holocaust' is everywhere, impossible to ignore in the newspapers or bookshops, on radio and television" (9).
4. There is, as other critics have noted, an irony here: Even as Devlin privileges "privacy," he nevertheless pursues verification of Rebecca's stories as if they had meaning. See Marc Silverstein's "'Talking about Some Kind of Atrocity'": *Ashes to Ashes* in Barcelona" (*Pinter Review* 1997/98, 74–85) for an astute analysis of this aspect of Devlin and of other issues in the play.
5. This impression was reinforced for me by this moment as performed by Anastasia Hill in the production of the play at Lincoln Center's 2001 Pinter Festival (directed by Katie Mitchell). Hill gave a short, cautious smile here, as if Rebecca found a subtle humor in the implied relationship between herself and the moviegoer. In the final moments of the play, also, Hill's physical pose evoked paralysis and rigidity. Her version of Rebecca was always quiet, never overtly dramatic, and yet extremely intense. The voice of the echo was a sly, quiet whisper—a taunting call to conscience Rebecca clearly experienced as painful.
6. If Burkman reads Sereny partially and overoptimistically, it may also be that Sereny herself tells the story of Speer too reassuringly. Ian Buruma (*New Republic*, 13 Nov. 1995, 33–38) and Richard J. Evans (*Times Literary Supplement*, 29 Sept. 1995, 4–7) argue against Sereny's view of Speer's moral progress, which, to them, distorts the evidence. Buruma argues that, seeking a positive conclusion to her involvement with Speer, Sereny falsely convinced herself that she caused cathartic self-awareness in him. Evans concludes similarly, "Despite Gitta Sereny's attempt to prove otherwise, Albert Speer lived his lie to the last" (6).
7. Pinter's comments in this interview on what he views as the colonialist tactics of Israel, England's treatment of unwed mothers, the U.S. death penalty. The Holocaust per se drops as a topic in the latter part of the interview. In a letter to The

New York Review of Books (9 June 1994), Pinter similarly springboards from Nazism to what he terms the illegalities of American foreign policy. Pinter's rhetoric here is part of a current trend in contemporary usage, in which the Holocaust becomes precedent or analogy for subsequent experiences. Pinter's play, as I have outlined here, nevertheless arises from and contains (albeit allusively) historiographical representation of the Holocaust.
8. My thanks to Stanton B. Garner, Jr., for the phrasing of this insight.

Works Cited

Adorno, Theodor. "Commitment." Trans. Frances McDonagh. *Aesthetics and Politics*. Ernst Bloch, et al. London: NLB, 1977, 177–95.

Baum, Rainer C. "Holocaust: Moral Indifference as *the* Form of Modern Evil." *Echoes of the Holocaust: Philosophical Reflections on a Dark Time*. Ed. Alan Rosenberg and Gerald E. Myers. Philadelphia: Temple UP, 1988, 53–90.

Bauman, Zygmunt. *Modernity and the Holocaust*. Ithaca NY: Cornell UP, 1989.

Blanchot, Maurice. *The Writing of the Disaster*. Trans. Ann Smock. Lincoln: U of Nebraska P, 1986.

Budick, Emily Miller. "Acknowledging the Holocaust in Contemporary American Criticism." *Breaking Crystal: Writing and Memory After Auschwitz*. Ed. Efraim Sicher. Urbana: U of Illinois P, 1998, 329–43.

Burkman, Katherine H. "Harold Pinter's *Ashes to Ashes*: Rebecca and Devlin as Albert Speer." *The Pinter Review* (1997/1998): 86–96.

Clendinnen, Inga. *Reading the Holocaust*. Cambridge: Cambridge UP, 1998.

Faulkner, William. *Requiem for a Nun*. New York: Random House, 1966.

Gillen, Francis. "History as a Single Act: Pinter's *Ashes to Ashes*." *Cycnos* 14 (1997): 91–97.

Hern, Nicholas. "A Play and Its Politics: A Conversation between Harold Pinter and Nicholas Hern." *One for the Road*. Harold Pinter. New York: Grove Press, 1986, 7–23.

Hoffman, Eva. "The Uses of Hell." *New York Review of Books*, 9 Mar. 2000, 19–23.

Horowitz, Sara R. "Auto/Biography and Fiction after Auschwitz: Probing the Boundaries of Second-Generation Aesthetics." *Breaking Crystal: Writing and Memory After Auschwitz*. Ed. Efraim Sicher. Urbana: U of Illinois P, 1998, 276–94.

Lang, Berel. *Act and Idea in the Nazi Genocide*. Chicago: U of Chicago P, 1990.

Langer, Lawrence L. *Holocaust Testimonies: The Ruins of Memory*. New Haven: Yale UP, 1991.

———. *Admitting the Holocaust: Collected Essays*. New York and Oxford: Oxford UP, 1995.

———. *Preempting the Holocaust*. New Haven: Yale UP, 2000.

Magurshak, Dan. "The 'Incomprehensibility' of the Holocaust: Tightening Up Some Loose Usage." *Echoes of the Holocaust: Philosophical Reflections on a Dark Time*. Ed. Alan Rosenberg and Gerald E. Myers. Philadelphia: Temple UP, 1988, 421–31.

Michel, Jean. *Dora*. Written in association with Louis Nucera. Trans. Jennifer Kidd. New York: Holt, Rinehart, and Winston, 1980.

Miller, Arthur. *The Theater Essays of Arthur Miller*. New York: Viking, 1978.

Ozick, Cynthia. "Roundtable Discussion." *Writing and the Holocaust*. Ed. Berel Lang. New York: Holmes and Meier, 1988, 277–84.

Pinter, Harold. "The Art of Drama" (Remarks in conversation with Austin Quigley). 92nd Street Y, New York. 21 Oct. 1996.

———. *Ashes to Ashes*. London: Faber, 1996. New York: Grove Press, 1997.

———. *The Birthday Party* and *The Room*. New York: Grove Press, 1968.

———. *Mountain Language*. New York: Grove Press, 1988.

———. *Party Time* and *The New World Order*. New York: Grove Press, 1993.

Rosen, Norma. "The Second Life of Holocaust Imagery." *Midstream* 33.4 (1987): 56–59.

Rosenfeld, Alvin H. *A Double Dying: Reflections on Holocaust Literature*. Bloomington: Indiana UP, 1980.

Scarry. Elaine. *The Body in Pain: The Making and Unmaking of the World*. New York: Oxford UP, 1985.

Sereny, Gitta. *Albert Speer: His Battle with Truth*. New York: Knopf, 1995.

Sicher, Efraim, ed. "The Holocaust in the Postmodernist Era." *Breaking Crystal: Writing and Memory After Auschwitz*. Urbana: U of Illinois P, 1998, 297–328.

————. Introduction. *Breaking Crystal: Writing and Memory After Auschwitz.* Urbana: U of Illinois P, 1998, 1–16.

Speer, Albert. *Inside the Third Reich.* New York: Bonanza, 1982.

van der Vat, Dan. *The Good Nazi: The Life and Lies of Albert Speer.* Boston: Houghton Mifflin, 1997.

5
Comedy and Crime: Pinter's Primal Power

PENELOPE PRENTICE

They turned out to be a bunch of criminals like everyone else.
—HAROLD PINTER, *The Homecoming*

Playwrights love to watch audiences die laughing. Harold Pinter's comedy, especially his recent *Celebration* (1999), kills us with laughter. We laugh helplessly at his darkly delightful *Celebration,* at painful truths beneath the crude remarks of loveless men who traffic in crime—the guns, money, and drugs that run the world. He wages comedy against crimes of the heart, crimes against humanity, war crimes, and, culminating, in *Press Conference* (2002), perhaps our worst crime born of unconfronted fear: cowardice. Yet paradoxically, his comedy does so as a call to courage, to equitable justice. Pinter deploys comedy as an attack weapon aimed at the destructive portions of the heroic vision we live by, which drives the conflict for survival and power in every beat and scene of his plays.[1] His core conflict driven by that heroic vision perpetuates often deadly hierarchical conflict.

The art of comedy is the art of incongruity, and crime is the ultimate incongruity.[2] Comedy conspires incongruously with crime in Pinter's signature conflict to allow us to embrace seeming contradictions—fear and desire, laughter and terror. Pinter's comedy attacks crimes that originate in destructive portions of our vision with laughter that requires us to act with courage. Where heroic vision looks to one leader to cleanse a particular society, rewarding him or her with personal glory, Pinter shows how that vision disenfranchises and devalues human beings, endorsing individual human powerlessness and engenders pervasive insecurity and fear at the same time it promotes power struggles. At the core, *both* Pinter's powerful and submissive characters reveal how human beings are diminished or destroyed by engaging in win/lose, zero-sum conflicts.[3] Pinter's comedy illuminates our vision, and excises its destructiveness. Where Freud and Jung observed how playfulness can bring into consciousness the most disturbing, yet elusive psychic content (Helitzer 22), Pinter's comedy performs that very act, one source of his primal power. Evoking the heightened, contradictory, yet essential human emotions—terror and joy—that drive almost all human thought and action,[4] Pinter's vision remains the most compellingly serious of our time. By coupling serious comedy with crime, Pinter pushes his work to the edge of horrifying tragedy to evoke uneasy laughter so that audiences are not always sure they have permission to laugh as his characters access our own darkest depths. Except in his torture plays, the savagely powerful *alongside* the ineffectual almost always reveal themselves as equally responsible for destruction to bring down what is productive, what is best in civilization.

That apparent incongruity, the awful paradox central to Pinter's work, reveals how our very survival strength, when driven by a desire for power over another, destroys precisely what it seeks to preserve: life.[5] Paradox is, however, seeming contradiction, and Pinter's comedy wedded to his life-and-death conflict, rather than endorsing powerlessness that threatens survival, conveys choice where we may see none in order to ask: How do we best live? Pinter's primal power originates at the interface of comedy and tragedy played out along the immense continuum of that primal conflict for survival. That desire for love, including the erotic, that drives all action in his work explicitly links with justice, or more correctly, the lack of love links to injustice. The conflict for love and respect that plays out along a continuum linked to justice, where love, even the erotic, explicitly connects to justice (or more correctly in Pinter's work the lack of love links to injustice) informs his vision. In his torture plays *Mountain Language* and *One for the Road*, both the language of love and acts of love are subverted to brutal destruction, torture, rape, and killing so addictive to the torturer. Nicholas proclaims, "I love death. . . . Sexual intercourse is nothing compared to it" (11). In *Party Time* the least just characters proclaim their "justice" and superior "morality" as they all slaughter any who oppose their views. Yet at the core, *both* Pinter's dominant and subservient characters reveal how humans are diminished or destroyed by engaging in win/lose, zero-sum conflicts.

Comedy, delivered through Pinter's terrifying yet delightful primal conflict for survival, gives his tragic conflict its breadth, yielding not a comic-tragic bastardization but a strengthening of both comedy and tragedy,[6] Pinter's comic wit, which commends to our affection those we might otherwise condemn—Lambert in *Celebration* no less than Max in *The Homecoming*—immediately endears his characters to his audiences. The primal power in Pinter's work originates at the interface of comedy and the tragic conflict, his terrifying, yet often wittily delightful, life-and-death signature conflict that delivers both hope and despair. These polar opposites create the breadth and depth in Pinter's work underscoring the contradictory, yet essential human emotions—terror and joy—that drive almost all human thought and action. Laughter evoked by Pinter's work illuminates both the moment and the vision we live by.[7] That laughter connects the audience to the work and it turns the audience into a community. The laser of comic laughter throws light on Pinter's dark vision and brings into our consciousness unconscious destructiveness, making the terror bearable. Comic laughter that tempers high seriousness and horror of his tragic vision conveys a tone (defined as the author's attitude to life) of optimism: hope necessary to inspire courage, which is nicely defined by philosopher Jan Narveson as brave action in service of what is good (71).

I

Even after Pinter was galvanized by America's role in Chile under Allende and fully awakened to the horror of torture in Turkey,[8] he also expressed the reverse side of revulsion: the attractions of criminal destruction. Consider the torture-master Nicholas in *One for the Road*, Pinter says; imagine having all that power. His comedy and crime dramatize the necessity of acknowledging both in the self as necessary for truth and transformation.

Pinter's comedy defines itself in the best sense, as Chekhov does, as dramatizing those who overcome weaknesses. But because Pinter's characters, like those of Chekhov, seldom do, his comedy does not impose itself as a comic vision. Rather, Pinter's comic wit collaborates with crime to promote change less in his characters than in us; seeing why his characters fail throws that task to the audience. Wit, the highest form of comedy, combines the intellect with emotion. Pinter's comic wit, a prime source of his primal power, shifts us intellectually and emotionally because his comedy, which locates fear as the prime cause of destruction, does not excuse harm or approve crime.

The earliest OED entry for *cryme,* derived from the Latin *crimen* meaning judgment or accusation, defines crime in terms of law and injury rather than ethics or morality: "An act punishable by law, as being forbidden by statute or injurious to the public welfare," and cites *to cryme,* as a verb from at least 1670 through a 1957 entry: "He'd crime a man as soon as look at him." Pinter's characters dramatize crime as the harm they do that springs from the desire to maintain power over another. Unconscious of the insecurity and fear propelling the conflict, or of the resulting destructiveness, the characters' power plays cause suffering and destruction by casting human relationships as adversarial. Crime is generally defined as requiring *mens rea*, deliberate intention. Pinter's characters, though less deliberately malicious (evil) than unconsciously destructive, are caught in a struggle for preservation of the self. Pinter's onstage criminal (as opposed to offstage boss or leader) does not deliberately set out to destroy until threatened, often unaware of the triggering threat; however, when threatened the criminal views destruction as defensive, even heroic, cleansing for the good of the individual and/or society. Even his torturers destroy in the name of good or God. But all engage in a desperate struggle for power to maintain status and to survive, fighting viciously to maintain what they have rather than to gain what they do not. Because they harm in ignorance, they seem to know not what they do.

Pinter's consistent portrayal of that unconscious, often comic, ignorance asks not for forgiveness but demands productive action. His comedy targets crimes less against laws of man than against humanity—against love and justice essential to and for the preservation of the self and society—and includes characters as, for example, Emily in *The Dreaming Child,* who refuses her lover only to imagine after his death increasingly passionate lovemaking while her real-life lovelessness destroys her marriage and kills her adopted child. Likewise, the loveless unconsciously destroy in others the love they lack to preserve what position or power they have: from Burt in *The Room*, the torturer in *One for the Road*, the dying Andy in *Moonlight*, Lambert in *Celebration* (however wistfully he recalls having loved and been in love),[9] through the Minister in *Press Conference*. But the critical moments of choice are often comic.

Pinter is not the first to link crime with love, both comically and quite seriously, to dramatize responsibility that may go against received mores. The comedy that lets us laugh at Lambert's lusty destruction of his wife in *Celebration,* in his loveless yet lustful marriage, also poignantly touches us with Lambert's real pain even as we also laugh at his lost loves. In *Betrayal* we still sympathize with Robert's pain as he lashes out in Venice, "I've always liked Jerry. To be honest, I've always liked him rather more than I've liked you" (87), a sadly comic triple entendre intended to cut her, to cover his pain, and to conceal his double loss of friend and wife. But it is also funny, and through his pain, Robert may mean just the opposite, as do the lovers when they later part. Pinter's comedy reveals how crimes of the heart can kill the human spirit no less than crimes against humanity can kill the body, and that comedy discovers the failure to love at the root of both.

Pinter's work has grown to extend beyond private rooms into the public world.[10] Much of his earliest work dramatizes conflicts between onstage petty criminals or hoodlums who may or may not be taking orders from offstage, unseen characters engaged in deliberately malicious destruction sometimes suggestive of organized and/or political crime. Attempting to maintain position and to survive, these dominant characters oppose more subservient characters we may sympathize with, who, equally struggling to survive, oppose and therefore threaten them in return only to escalate the conflict. Consider Rose's husband's employer in *The Room*, possibly Solto in *Night School,* Ben in *The Dumb Waiter,* Goldberg and McCann in *The Birthday Party.* Unlike the interrogators in *Quiller Memorandum* who deliberately torture to discover secrets and truths that threaten them, Ben and Burt, like Goldberg and McCann, do not attack until provoked, their authority threatened with disrespect. Pinter's other early and middle works dramatize crimes of the heart in which conflict is provoked by a character's inability to respect or love: Edward in *A Slight Ache,* Davies in *The Caretaker,* Richard in *The Lover,* the husband in *The Pumpkin Eater,* Teddy in *The Homecoming.* Other works reflecting this paradigm are *À la Research du Temps Perdu: The Proust Screenplay, The French Lieutenant's Woman, The Last Tycoon,* and *Betrayal.* Pinter's more recent work ascends (he might say, descends) into the halls of power to reveal crimes that link love and justice. How the loveless destruct is portrayed in terrifying, sometimes comic scenarios in which the complexities of crime, even the worst human malice—torture—is dramatized. Works such as *Precisely, One for the Road, Mountain Language, Victory, The Handmaid's Tale, Reunion, The Heat of the Day, The Trial, The Remains of the Day, The Comfort of Strangers, Party Time, The New World Order, Moonlight, Ashes to Ashes, The Dreaming Child,* and *Celebration* dramatize civil, political, or war crimes or crimes of the heart, or both.

As Pinter's focus has turned to violent crimes against humanity conducted in the name of justice, the comedy has almost disappeared, but the wit never vanishes. Where Pinter's earliest work often locates sources of violent conflict among lower class, small-time, on stage criminals working for offstage syndicate bosses, and his middle work deals in middle-class crimes of the heart, his most recent work enters the halls of power to reveal the wellspring of criminal violence in global conflict as little different from the source of conflict at any level.

II

Laughter in Pinter's work, like the Zen slap of enlightenment that produces change and transformation, has roots in the birth of Western drama. Comic laughter in Pinter's conflict culminates in a felt/thought that opens fresh perspectives. It offers/forces us to confront unbidden truths, which can lead to a fresh vision that moves action. His quest for truth, one that leaves no illusions intact, further reveals that without freedom there is no comic laughter and, thus, no transformation.

Pinter's recent three-page *Press Conference* horrifyingly dramatizes how, as our separate spheres of education, information, and entertainment collapse into a single sphere, entertainment climbs in bed with naked aggression in the name of Free Trade economics to suppress freedom. The

Press Conference interview with the Minister of Culture turned head of the Secret Police who sees no "contradiction between those two roles" (1), depicts through The Press, as a collective voice, how easily fear is evoked and unconfronted becomes instantly contagious, pervasive, paralyzing. As the play unmasks repressive brutality, itself sprung from fear and cowardice in the guise of Free Press, we appreciate the extraordinary personal and collective courage necessary to preserve freedom. The Minister "defending ourselves against the worm" to "protect and to safeguard our cultural inheritance against forces . . . intent upon subverting it," kills children of "subversive families" (1–2) deemed a threat. By breaking the children's necks and raping women, "all part of an educational process . . . cultural process," he seeks to preserve "loyalty to a free market." Free Trade, which the Minister so smilingly and fundamentally defends along with the Free Market, not only ignores the opposing view (that multinational companies, which come in purportedly to alleviate poverty, employ those they impoverish at wages that trap whole populations in economic slavery) but in *Press Conference* crushes and kills all opposition. Here Pinter dramatizes how fear can allow the forces of death and destruction to remain more powerful than love, unless just love awakens courage to intervene, confront, and reverse injustice. While *Ashes to Ashes* implies why unconfronted fear cannot be ignored or eschewed during peaceful times, *Press Conference* dramatizes the bloodless, bloody consequences.

Pinter, like Sophocles, dramatizes how the worst offenses are committed from within a society, from leaders lacking self-knowledge and a citizenry too paralyzed to act. *Press Conference* locates the lack of knowledge in the Minister's deliberate stifling of free press, as information, education all turn into smiling entertainment, but Pinter nowhere excuses the citizenry's ignorance—of both factual information and the self. The death of Free Press in *Press Conference* becomes the death of freedom itself betokening the death of a society. *Press Conference* dramatizes how, when ethical values are replaced by material profit, core values are lost. This serious entertainment plays through insightful comic wit, introducing us, through our own fear and terror, to our responsibility in any loveless, state-sanctioned destruction.

If we doubt our fascination with crime, consider how we cheer for Roskolnikov in Dostoevsky's *Crime and Punishment* and hope that he eludes the police pounding on the door below although he has just brutally murdered two women in premeditated cold blood. Our hope for his escape, as we also look forward to his capture, makes us imaginary participants, colluding with him and the police. The line in Pinter's work between criminal and cop, aristocrat and commoner, politician and priest, entertainment and war is often fine, sometimes nonexistent. In fact, Pinter repeatedly shows us we are *both* in order to show us that we are also much more. Though we rarely wish to face the fact that we may simultaneously crave and fear disaster, Pinter's recent plays confront and embrace that "unknowingly" of desire as a genius solution, not an either/or but as a *both/and* choice.

III

Just as *Betrayal*'s shifting alliances and reverse structure shifted the direction and form in drama casting all as equally responsible, Pinter's killer comedy *Celebration* sends Western drama in yet another new direction as comedy conjoins with crime to create incongruities both more deeply disturbing and more comically hilarious than any other Pinter play in the past several decades. Instead of killing us with outrage, his comedy lets us die laughing in the slow realization of the complex causes of the characters' deadly crimes and of our kinship with them. *Celebration*'s comedy dramatizes political and global consequences in the least, most private choice and action, as these characters reach an apex among global crimes and capital crimes of the heart no less lethal. Thus, Pinter's comedy dramatizes crime and power as intimate bedfellows. In this play the young Waiter, by innocently yet imaginatively praising the real-life alliance of the powerful in literature, the arts, entertainment, sports, and politics, reveals power's complicity in destruction in any sector it inhabits.

As Lambert and Julie celebrate their wedding anniversary with his brother Matt and her sister Prue in the most expensive restaurant in town, Lambert indicates that Suki is dining at another table with her husband Russell, announcing that he once "fucked her when she was eighteen." Then he invites Suki and her companion Russell to their table. Russell, in banking, sniffing the power these men possess, proposes a business alliance with Matt and Lambert who scarcely hint at their "peacekeeping" guns and drug deals. In the end, Lambert picks up everyone's tab, and all exit except the Waiter who throughout the play offers reminders of power and fame as he interjects recollections of a remarkable grandfather who he claims knew most of the early and mid-twentieth-century luminaries in literature, the arts, sports, crime, and politics—from Yeats, Eliot, Clark Gable, Hedy Lamar, Al Capone, John Dillinger, Stravinsky, Picasso, Don Bradman, the Inkspots and the Three Stooges to Mussolini, Hitler, and Churchill—these three leaders revealed as in bed together—along with his grandfather and the Archduke Ferdinand who together all played cards.

The sexually brutal language of Pinter's recent torturers in works like *One for the Road* assimilates itself into comic dinner table talk in *Celebration*: men and women calling one another *fuckpigs,* men calling each other *cunts*. Recalling Mae West and Lenny Bruce, Pinter's language conducts a subversive guerrilla warfare but to quite deeper ends—not merely to search and destroy but also to delight, enlighten, and inspire. To appreciate just how far Pinter's comedy exceeds his predecessors in revolutionizing drama in intent and delivery is to appreciate how Pinter's comic shocks do more to *disguise* his attack at some most cherished aspects of our vision. The trickster, the huckster, the vaudeville clown so admired in Beckett, all remain in Pinter's celebrants' bag of comic tricks, and he is above nothing to get a laugh in service of disclosing disquieting, unsayable, often terrifying, truths.

However, those moving psychological aspects of his comedy run both with and counter to received practice. Pinter, who knows that laughter engenders laughter, begins like most comic writers with a guaranteed laugh, often a puerile, sexual reference; then, he keeps the laughs rolling. *Celebration* breaks the social "rule" that we laugh *with*, not *at*, others, and it breaks satire's "rule" that we laugh not at evil but at foibles (where *evil* is defined as deliberate human acts of destruction with malicious intent and foibles are character flaws producing minor misdemeanors). Pinter's comedy now has no rules, signaling characters of a different order from his earlier plays, but not so different from us. Insofar as we laugh at them, we abdicate any defense against their danger, any recourse against their weapons of mass destruction we also traffic in, and, laughing with them, we evince our complicity in their war games—literally and metaphorically. When laughter stops at the end of the play, we discover the destruction in their most ordinary acts and choices.

The scatological and sexual slang in *Celebration*, as in many of Pinter's plays, points up the longing for love. From *One for the Road* through *Celebration* men with limited vocabularies call one another *cunts* as an attack or to signal familiar affection. *Cunts* are everywhere in his torture plays, whereas *cocks* are notably absent.[11] While *cunts* and *cocks* still carry a toxic taboo in this country (*cunts* less so in England), both terms, slang for procreative- and pleasure-producing portions of the human anatomy, remain debased and largely debasing compared with the more agile *fuck*.[12] Pinter both heightens and diminishes by overkill the impact of the word *fucked* as slang for the actual generative act. Yet all hilariously illuminate and intensify the erotic: the term's generative value and the love and respect the characters seek but destroy all along the way. In his most desolate, inhuman, and uninhabitable torture landscapes, Pinter deploys *cunt* as a male appellative to underscore lovelessness and to point audiences to the generative necessary to survive and thrive. When Lambert first confesses his deepest secret—that he "once fell in love. And was loved," his wife Julie says, "'Wasn't that me, darling?'" He scoffs, "Who?" as if the idea had never occurred to him (24). Yet the laughter that obliterates his love for his wife punctuates his longing for lost love, engendering the unspoken love that is lacking among all.

Pinter's bawdy language dramatizes and embraces human complexity through ambiguities that spill into the comically incongruous; ultimately, it explores the dangers that exist in unexamined assumptions and resultant actions. Revealed in that rarely acknowledged interface between opposites in the self, comedy lights that space where the erotic meets the destructive, desire butts up against revulsion, normalcy with nightmare, reality with the invented and the imagined. His salacious comedy exposes to audiences how the resultant unacknowledged, unconfronted underside of internal conflict—the rejected, denied, ignored, and discarded—carries an explosive charge of external destructive force. The characters never see that destroying what they cannot claim—love—destroys others and imperceptibly the self. Their freshly comic assaults create a sustained, almost unreleased tension that brilliantly dramatizes how the loveless destruct. In this play nothing seems to happen—except almost every line is edged with a deadly wit designed to destroy in a single stroke a previous speaker and to slash into multiple others. Pinter's comedy remains in the service of exposing evil committed by quite ordinary people propelled by a seemingly benign insecurity.

Fearful insecurity registers in each celebrant's expression of confidence. "They believe in me," says Russell in his opening gambit to his wife Suki, which is echoed by Lambert's crowing, "I know I'm well liked [. . .] deep down they trust me [. . .] they respect me." Like all self-referential statements in all Pinter's work, they signal just the opposite—and that incongruity registers in a laugh of recognition. "Do you know how much money I made last year?" Lambert asks (3), emphasizing that his identity and pride rest in newly amassed wealth announcing itself as blustering fear. In *Celebration* both powerbrokers of the world and grocery clerk bureaucrats who deliver the guns design strategies of destruction in exchange for millions. We join in the "peacekeeping" with those in the club who know the code words and have the cash and savvy to enter and play. Yet our laughter reveals how, when money is equated with the self and power asserted for its own sake and severed from an ethical basis, a pervasive destruction results. Reflexively fighting to sustain power, they are without conscience. As such, they are extremely dangerous, among the most dangerous of all Pinter's characters—until the Minister in *Press Conference* who, curtailing freedom, enslaves the free. Throughout *Celebration,* as in *Press Conference,* Pinter shows us the faces of outright destructors, laughing at their deadly deals in the name of "peacekeeping" and "Free Trade."

Greed and smiling avarice originate in fear. The fear unconfronted that propels Aston in *The Caretaker* to amass a kingdom of junk imprisoning him in his constructed self is little different from Lambert's self constructed by amassing wealth. But where Aston damages only himself and the tramp Davies he expels from his last home, Lambert's destruction, like the Minister's, may be almost limitless. In fact, after *Celebration* it is difficult to take seriously anything that is not also comic. The crime Pinter confronts is far more serious than the cops and killers, cowboys and Indians, and combat warfare of most film, television, and theater. His comedy also reveals our own complicity in crime at the deepest levels of our attitudes, choices, and action. Yet the guaranteed laugh of the unexpected salacious attack provides setups for Pinter's horrifying images that reverse the direction of the joke to the truly terrible, most egregious, terrifying political crimes of our time.

Celebration's opening comedy links our laughter with crime by revealing the incompetence of the major players. The Waiter's "Who's having duck?" is met by Lambert's "The duck's for me" (1); yet, the entrée is immediately claimed by his wife. Lambert's, "What did I order?" discloses the men running the show do not remember their dinner orders, nor does the Waiter. The characters freely associate Lambert's "Osso Bucco" (literally a "bone with a hole,") to "arsehole," setting the ribald comic attack and tone of the rest of the play and defines the characters' deepest values. Lambert's, "[W]hat's the Italian for arsehole?" elicits Prue's, "Julie, Lambert" providing a zeugma that yokes Julie and Lambert to *arsehole* to define them. The comic turns sounding merely like, *Who the fuck's having the duck?* promise the comic conflict's fireworks and violence that proceed from self-absorbed "who-cares?" inattention. The incongruity between the low language in the "best restaurant" that sets the laughs rolling for the rest of the play takes comedy to darker corners than it has gone before. *Celebration*'s very title resonates with the delightfully terrifying dramatic irony of other paradoxically celebratory titles throughout the Pinter canon. Yet as Pinter comically shows us the faces of the criminals fueling war—hot and cold, at home and abroad—he takes us beyond irony.

IV

"Humor does more than grin at misery," says comic writer Melvin Helitzer; "It cuts into a target with a knife so razor thin that no one sees the incision— just the blood" (26). Yet we are so caught off guard by Pinter's razor wit that we feel no wound. For some writers comedy can serve as a substitute for assault (Helitzer 18), but, for Pinter, comedy becomes an assault in itself: at them (the characters) and us (including himself). And where humor maintains the status quo by affirming the values of a targeted audience, Pinter gives us comedy that is an equal-opportunity targeter.[13] Aimed at our received heroic vision that carries the seeds of its own destruction, his comedy everywhere dismantles the status quo in the service of truth.

It is no accident that *Press Conference*'s Minister of Culture becomes Minister of Defense, suppressing and subverting truth, accelerating destruction in the name of preserving education and culture. Pinter marshals the Minister's very weapons against him, turning his cold joke as a comic attack upon him. Because the target of ridicule in Pinter's comedy is so complex, the release also differs profoundly. Targeting attacker and attacked (rarely

wholly praising or condemning) he can say, "I think I write quite affectionate humour" (qtd. in Knowles 180). Yet his comic wit advances by embracing the reverse, "I've actually contradicted myself. I've said laughter is
created by true affection; it's also created by quite the opposite, by a recognition of where we are ugly" (*Various Voices* 62).[14]

Celebration, with its reductive images that perhaps recall the satiric
comic values in Congreve's *Love for Love* or D'Urfey's more blatantly titled
play *Love for Money*, shares Restoration comedy's guiding trinity of power,
sex, and money conjoined by comedy to marriage to expose lies, disguises,
and deception by dissolving them in laughter.[15] For these men to maintain
such bloated power by committing their necessarily unnamed crimes, their
women must be diminished to inconsequence. But the women choose to ca-
pitulate. They endorse the men's moneymaking prowess and equate that
power with love. "I want you to be rich," says Suki to Russell, "so that you
can buy me houses and panties and I'll know that you really love me" (3).
The sexual innuendos in the zinger "panties" ties power to lust, love to justice—here, powerlessness to injustice in their global crimes—but also affirms Suki's dependence upon Russell. The men in *Celebration* steamroll
over their marginalized women, not only because the women do not stand
their ground and use only the same dirty attack tricks the men do but also
because they employ no new strategies, they remain subservient while pro-
claiming the reverse. Were the women not to strike back each time they are
struck—were they to do anything differently, even laugh, they would
change the equation and dynamic of the relationship. They don't. Yet they
all make us laugh until they exit to the world of death and destruction all are
creating.

Julie Lambert provokes the final battle between the sexes impotently
sticking it to their men in the guise of sympathizing with Prue's nose-drip-
pings complaint. In a single stroke she targets their mother-in-law, her sons,
and their own husbands: "All mothers want their sons to be fucked by themselves," but the men top the women to score the final point with assertions
that exhaust the ridiculous and sheer tenacity, namely, by appropriating the
opposition's weapons and then raising it. "How old do you have to be . . . ?"
Lambert asks, "To be fucked by your mother." Matt concludes, "Any age,
mate" (10). "Mate," the lower-class slang, reminds us that all the life mates
lost this round. The freewheeling *fuck* throughout gains greater force at the
end. Where earlier it diminishes the barb into inconsequence to reveal that
our worst crimes transgress not sexual verbiage but assault human minds
and bodies, Pinter enlists *fuck* as our greatest sexual taboo to attack global
crimes of even higher import.

Fucking, comically carries a multiplicity of meanings, but with each
repetition, Pinter, like any poet, shifts the meaning. At the end, *fucking* reverses meaning to become the greatest intensifying adjective that signals veracity. *Fucking*, in Lambert's third mention of love, begins to unravel all ties

to reveal this play's core subtext: love. When Lambert again confesses a poignant remembrance of having once been loved, he says, "I'm talking about love, mate . . . , real fucking love" (25). When Matt protests that he never knew about that, Lambert disowns him as a brother, "You knew nothing about me. You know nothing about me. Who the fuck are you anyway?" (24). *Fuck* again diminished, abdicates its power for truth and love, reverting to an impotent diminisher. Wealth gained in killer "peacekeeping," these men exit in death imagery: "Rest assured," and "Dead right," signaling themselves as unstoppably lethal (33).

As in all Pinter plays, the laughter ends at the abyss where we stand facing ourselves nakedly. Pinter's greatest comic payoff comes when comedy takes us to that edge—and beyond, here, to the mystery of life. The young Waiter concludes: "My grandfather introduced me to the mystery of life and I'm still in the middle of it" (54). Alone on stage in his desolate isolation, the Waiter moves us stunningly to recognize his dangerous inertia as our own. Imprisoned in the restaurant "womb," he cannot leave, he is little different from Rose in *The Room*, Aston or Lambert—from anyone clinging to a place, idea, or vision unexamined. But though he recognizes his imprisonment and wants to escape, he admits, "I can't find the door to get out" (54). Even as the Waiter himself gains a momentary attention and power by association with his grandfather, who he claims consorted intimately with many notable men and women in the early twentieth century, he subtly dramatizes the danger in love that discards the rejected portions of a beloved. Yet when the Waiter touchingly claims his grandfather knew them in their wounds, "where they were isolated, where they were alone, where they fought against savage and pitiless odds" (47), that brutally, lovely line describes the odds that anyone with or without power fights against, finally allowing us sympathy for all these characters who, despite their destructive power, have no shot at such fame or earthly immortality as one icon of film, entertainment, sports, and politics the Waiter catalogs. *Celebration* discovers public people unconsciously embracing destruction. Yet Pinter comically awakens us to their desiring, dreaming, longing for love, revealing that however misguided their attempts to be loved and respected, they invite us to care for them.

V

Pinter's conflict whispers the secret every dramatist must know—that in the reflexive, short-term negative emotions, such as fear and rage, are stronger than love, as they must be for short-term individual survival: to flee or fight attack. But laced through even his deadliest criminal conflicts, Pinter's comedy conveys a more important secret revealing that long term human survival requires a just love. If Pinter deeply feels both outrage and compassion, his comedy as a counterbalance to powerlessness, cynicism, and despair, brings to mind ancient Chinese military strategy that appropriates the best weapon of the enemy to defeat him. *Press Conference* appropriates more than the cold joke; a cold war brought home internally takes aim at the Minister's taking aim at his own people to defeat him. The comic brush strokes in Pinter's plays that force us to witness, even to participate with a nervous laughter in a Minister's or torturer-master's jokes, inescapably raise the question: How can fear transform into courage?

Pinter's sympathy with all his characters, like that quintessential impartial fairness that defines justice itself, allows us, through comedy, to collude with the enemy as we do through our laughter, while recognizing in that collusion our own power for both love and destruction. As he traverses the distance between the poles of comedy and tragedy, conveying a generosity and optimism necessary to action, Pinter's new work pits love and lust with loathing, the familiar with the unexpectedly bizarre, rejection with intimacy, normalcy with nightmare, establishing a dynamic that goes beyond the Hegelian dialectic, beyond rejecting either/or dichotomies to summon what Stuart Brand in *Inventing the Future: at MIT* calls both/and genius solutions, beyond irony. Through the convergence of comedy and criminal conflict, Pinter affirms that I/we are bastard *and* angel. Pinter's comedy and crime partner to display a symmetry, a whole new way of seeing. While his plays may not offer a theory on violent conflict, his comedy dramatizes conflict's hidden causes and profound consequences.

If after Pinter it is difficult to take seriously anything that is not witty, it may be even more difficult to laugh at vacuous, soulless comedy without subtext or at the vision that drives desire and danger. Yet laughter remains essential in Pinter's work—illuminating what prevents change, inspiring transformation. Although Pinter's work is rarely far from crime and the criminal, from his early fearful marginalized outsider seeking equity, parity and power with the more privileged to his recent entrenched and powerful seeking transcendence through the received, heroic vision, his intent is to dramatize their fundamental desire for respect, love, and justice. In their misguided attempts to preserve power, their destroying what they hope to achieve moves us beyond awareness of the causes of destruction. Thus through the conjunction of comedy and crime Pinter seems to have accomplished the opposite of Brechtian Alienation by allowing the audience to feel their complicity even while that felt thought he administers is made palatable by comedy.

Notes

1. The classical element of the heroic quest is defined as confronting a worthy opponent in the face of an opposing fate, against impossible odds to secure the safety and peace of a community. If we have only three choices in life, a choice

of attitude, intention, and action, all are driven in the West by the received heroic vision.

2. I am indebted to comic writer Thomas Jacobs for this insight, in conversation, Cleveland, 17 September 2000. This chapter began as the invited lecture, "Harold Pinter's Comic Vision: The Erotic Ethic," in the Distinguished Speaker's Series at St. Bonaventure University. I wish to thank Carra Stratton, Olga Prentice, Meg Powers, and Professor Donald Savage for careful readings of this extended version; thanks as well to Ros Fielden, Harold Pinter's assistant.

3. Jennifer Mortimer, a childhood friend, observes that Pinter himself never engaged in the destructive powerplays he dramatizes: "Harold wasn't fighting for supremacy. He was just floating to the top because of his genuine interest and love and talents" (Billington 50).

4. Pinter's comedy and conflict dramatize why in a free society it becomes incumbent upon each citizen to assume the heroic quest. To confront the forces of human devastation (a worthy opponent) in order to secure safety and peace in the global community all become our task.

5. Rather than suggest that all truth is relative or unknowable, Pinter's conflicts weigh in on the side of choice. Comedy often exposes those choice moments in a conflict when a character makes a choice that tips the scales toward violence. Pinter's characters' incongruous choices, conflicting judgments, and paradoxical conclusions keep alive the great Pinter puzzles.

6. Consider the dying Andy in *Moonlight* who jokes his blind way to the grave and Deborah in *A Kind of Alaska* who awakens after a twenty year sleep trapped in an aging body. Pinter himself, like his plays that celebrate *homo ludens*, men at play in the very serious play for survival, seems to possess a laughing nature.

7. While more research and writing has appeared on comedy in the past twenty-five years than in all of human history (including such contributors as Aristotle, Socrates, Darwin, Bergson, Wilde, Shaw, Alan Ayckbourn), no one yet has fully charted Pinter's comedy or innovations. Just as it is not possible to be a playwright in the twenty-first century without knowing Pinter's plays, it may not be possible to be a serious playwright without knowing his comedy.

8. As a young man suffering the horrors of war—waking to flames in his garden and bombs flying down his street—he confronted rather than eschewed violence. Pinter's private fascination with film noir crime, with playing villains as a young actor, with writers such as Raymond Chandler, and finally his own writing allowed him to confront and illuminate, often comically, what is most fearful, namely, annihilation. Though Pinter occasionally espouses a doomsday vision, he remains a stunningly well-informed, active champion of human rights around the world, and his plays continue to awaken consciousness, often through horrifying comedy that nevertheless inspires courage.

9. Appropriately, Pinter coupled his first play *The Room* with his recent *Celebration* in its first London and New York productions, principally, one surmises, because both portray characters who, engaged in the same struggle for respect, love, and power, desperately cling to what is familiar.

10. Pinter reserves his commentary for prose—voluminous public and private correspondence, essays, lectures, and speeches on global injustice. Like other best playwrights of the twentieth century, Chekhov and Shaw wrote treatises con-

fronting justice, crime, and imprisonment, and Pinter's commentary, like theirs, informs the private vision in his plays and, as separate from his plays, also allows the plays to avoid didacticism.

11. So is *cocksucker*, the word that landed Lenny Bruce in prison, though a circumlocution to the act in *No Man's Land* as low, soft porn, that builds humor on the way to bigger laughs as two aging, sexless poets, recall in Edwardian discourse a shared woman whose "predilections" went in that direction.

12. Pinter employs *fucking* neither as David Mamet's repetitions, numbing audiences to its toxicity while guaranteeing laughs nor as Lenny Bruce's social commentary against those who condemn sex while condoning violence nor as Mae West's revolt against sexual mores while celebrating sexuality.

13. Helitzer maintains all comedy contains "THREES": a *t*arget, *h*ostility, *r*ealism, *e*xaggeration, *e*motion, and *s*urprise. Superiority and surprise, he maintains, are paramount (17–18). To his credit, Pinter intertwines *e*xaggeration, *e*motion, and *s*urprise to serve astonishing ends; tension and anxiety trigger the momentary release of laughter produced by the *s*urprise, but the surprise almost always reveals values at depth in the vision.

14. Laughter is "very much a question of recognition of our own worst characteristics," Pinter says, and we laugh "When we recognize the ugliness of people, we see the ugliness of ourselves" (*Various* 62).

15. Where Restoration comedy engages us as participants in the dark comedy, it points nowhere. Pinter's puerile, often bawdy, vaudeville musical hall comedy works to displace received meaning at deeper levels at which his comedy works to wrench consciousness to awareness. Because his comedy reaches not for the jugular, but beyond to the heart, it administers a felt/thought made palatable by a comic laughter that exposes terror.

Works Cited

Billington, Michael. *The Life and Work of Harold Pinter.* London: Faber and Faber, 1996.

Helitzer, Melvin. *Comedy Writing Secrets: How to Think Funny, Write Funny, Act Funny and Get Paid for It.* Cincinnati: Writer's Digest, 1999.

Knowles, Ronald. "From London: Harold Pinter 1996–1997 and 1997–1998." *The Pinter Review: Annual Essays, 1997–1998.* Tampa: U of Tampa P, 165–85.

Narveson, Jan. *Moral Issues.* Oxford: Oxford UP, 1983.

Pinter, Harold. *Betrayal.* London: Methuen, 1978; New York: Grove Press 1978;

———. *Celebration.* [Typescript] 1999.

———. *Complete Works: 1.* New York: Grove-Weidenfeld, 1976, 1990.

———. *Complete Works: 2.* New York: Grove-Weidenfeld, 1977, 1990.

———. *Complete Works: 3.* New York: Grove-Weidenfeld, 1978, 1990.

———. *Complete Works: 4.* New York: Grove-Weidenfeld, 1981, 1990.

———. *One for the Road.* Published with "A Play and Its Politics: A Conversation between Harold Pinter and Nick Hern." New York: Grove Press, 1986.

———. *Press Conference* [Typescript] March 2002.

———. *Various Voices.* London: Faber and Faber, 1998.

6
Lost in the Funhouse: Spectacle and Crime in Pinter's Screenplay of Kafka's *The Trial*

ANN C. HALL

The works of Harold Pinter are peopled with the wounded and the criminal, and Pinter's fascination with crime and crime stories is well documented (Gillen, Kane, Kundert-Gibbs). In his early works such as *The Birthday Party* (1958), *The Dumb Waiter* (1959), and *No Man's Land* (1975), hit men and vagrants dominate the stage. At first glance, the characters seem to behave like the Hollywood gangsters they mimic—Pinter admits that films like noir classic *The Killers* were influential to his early writings—but as his dramas unfold, it becomes clear that many of these unsavory types are more virtuous than the society they supposedly undermine.[1] Frequently, Pinter's thugs are not the threats to, but the victims or products of, the status quo. More recent dramas such as *One for the Road* (1985), *Mountain Language* (1988), and *Party Time* (1991) make Pinter's inversion of criminal stereotypes explicit: the imprisoned, the alleged criminals, are, in fact, innocent victims of oppressive governments that enslave them. Even domestic dramas such as *The Lover* (1963), *The Homecoming* (1965), and *A Kind of Alaska* (1982) exhibit at the very least an atmosphere of transgression.

It is no surprise then that Pinter chose to write a screenplay of Kafka's *The Trial* (1993), a novel whose many tentacled judicial system gives new meaning to the phrase "long arm of the law." Pinter has also admitted a long-standing fascination for and indebtedness to Kafka and his works. His first full-length play, *The Birthday Party* (1965), for example, relied heavily on Kafka's *The Trial*.[2] In his study of the relationship between Kafka and Pinter, Raymond Armstrong notes that Kafka serves as the inspiration for Pinter's recent play, *Moonlight*, citing the numerous references to moonlight at the end of *The Trial* (121). And in a celebration of literary influence, not the anxiety outlined by Harold Bloom, Pinter sent a copy of *The Trial* screenplay to Samuel Beckett, his other great inspiration, just before his death in order to "cheer him up" (qtd. in Gussow 144).

And while most do not think of comedy when *The Trial* is mentioned, Pinter's appreciation for Kafka's humor reflects his affinity with and respect for this Czechoslovakian author.[3] Perhaps in Kafka's honor, Pinter's adaptation follows the original very closely. As Frank Gillen notes, Pinter's version remains "extraordinarily faithful to Kafka's text in what he includes, in the order of the events, and even the language itself" (138). Pinter himself argues against a heavy-handed interpretation, one that indicates that the Kafka novel foreshadowed the Holocaust, for example: "Kafka didn't write a prophetic book. He wrote a book based on the Austro-Hungarian Empire, before the First World War. So what you have is an apparently solid structure in every way . . . within which there is a worm eating away . . . I felt it to be a very simple narrative" (qtd. in Billington 349). And given the voluminous critical opinion on the Kafka text, the decision to keep the narrative as clear and simple as possible was probably a wise one, for Pinter's light touch with the original leaves many of the critical conundrums intact.

What is interesting to note, however, is that Pinter's faithfulness to the original has led some to conclude that Pinter offers no interpretation, that he has succeeded in creating a pristine version of Kafka, one that has not been sullied by the critics. Michael Billington, for example, notes that Pinter tried to "strip away layers of interpretation and go back to first base" (349). While I may be overstating the case, it is important to remember the lessons taught to us by the postmodernists in particular, namely, all reading, all adaptations are acts of interpretation. Pinter may not handle the details of the Kafka text in the freewheeling way that Orson Wells adapted the novel to screen, but he has made choices. For example, he rejected the opportunity to work with director Istvan Szabo who wanted to offer an expressionistic interpretation of the novel through film (Billington 348). But by using the camera and film technology, he highlights, as I will demonstrate, the relationship between spectacle and crime in a way the literary medium cannot.[4] K.'s complicated relationship to surveillance and observations, for instance, is clear in the novel. On the one hand, he is crushed by the high level of observation he is subjected to. On the other, he seeks a witness, a transcendent eye, someone or something that is beyond the gaze of the court who will see and protect him. With this complex relationship between crime and speculation intact, Pinter's screenplay wrests the audience from their passive position as spectator and places them in a more uncomfortable one, that of witness and participant. We see that Josef K. is oppressed by his surveillance, but we must also examine our own roles as viewers. By consciously and conspicuously using the technology of film, Pinter makes audiences reconsider their own participation in spectacle and ultimately makes his version of *The Trial* uniquely his, a new work of art.[5]

Before examining the screenplay, it is important to note that the relationship between crime and surveillance is a long-standing one. Michel Foucault in *Discipline and Punish: The Birth of the Prison*, for example, illustrates how that relationship has evolved over the centuries, from medieval to modern times.[5] Up until the eighteenth century, crimes were punished publicly. Communities may not have had the details regarding court cases, but they certainly saw the results through various punishments, among the worst being drawing and quartering, hanging, and the pyre (Foucault 3–7). According to Foucault such spectacles were designed to show subjects the power of their monarchies. The ruling classes had the power and used it swiftly and brutally. Part of the problem with these public executions, however, was that they frequently did not achieve this goal—prisoners might take extended periods of time to die, which would make the governing body appear cruel, not just. Or prisoners might be tempted to rally the crowds against the monarchies with inspiring speeches.

In addition to the uncertainties of public execution, governing bodies also became increasingly uncomfortable in their role as executioners. According to Foucault, punishment became less a case of the ruling class's power and more a case of the government merely bending to a natural or higher law. One of the most noticeable changes as a result of this shift in penal philosophy was the emphasis not on execution but on the trial, the process of justice. Briefly, the attitude toward punishment shifted in the eighteenth and nineteenth centuries from one of retribution to rehabilitation. Prisoners were ill, misdirected. They were social problems and the prisons were the solution.

Surveillance was the newest and most popular way to affect the cure. And this cure was embodied in the prison architecture and philosophy of Jeremy Bentham, the creator of the Panopticon. Simply put, the Panopticon was a building that afforded the greatest opportunity for surveillance possible:

> All that is needed, then, is to place a supervisor in a central tower and to shut up in each cell a madman, a patient, a condemned man, a worker, or a schoolboy. . . . In short, it reverses the principle of the dungeon; or rather of its first three functions—to enclose, to deprive of light, and to hide—it preserves only the first and eliminates the other two. . . . Visibility is a trap. . . . He [the prisoner] is seen, but he does not see. (Foucault 200–1)

The method of control was thought to be so successful that it was used as a model for schools, hospitals, and insane asylums, and many of Bentham's practices remain with us today. The goal of the observatories, of course, was not just incarceration but transformation: criminals would become law-abiding; the ill, well; the mad, sane; and the student, productive. Success would be determined by how successfully the prisoner internalized the external surveillance. As Foucault notes, the prisoner eventually "inscribes in himself the power relation in which he simultaneously plays both roles; he becomes the principle of his own subjection" (202–3). But the method is even more insidious because, as Foucault notes, the tower need not be manned. Bentham's principle of power "should be visible and unverifiable. Visible: the inmate will constantly have before his eyes the tall outline of the central tower from which he is spied upon. Unverifiable: the inmate must never know whether he is being looked at at any moment; but he must be sure that he may always be so" (201). No one needs to watch; the merest hint of supervision is enough to elicit control: the Panopticon "arranges things in such a way that the exercise of power is not added on from the outside, like a rigid constraint, to the functions it invests, but is so subtly present in them as to increase their efficiency by itself increasing its own points of contact" (206). Such effective methods of control, of course, could yield abuse, but as Foucault explains, the Panopticon's creators constructed safeguards against such events by opening the institutions to visitors who would, in effect, guard the guards.

> Modern culture is entirely dependent:
>
> not on spectacle but surveillance . . . it is not that the beautiful totality of the individual is amputated, repressed, altered by our social order, it is rather that the individual is carefully fabricated in it, according to a whole technique of forces and bodies. We are neither in the amphitheater nor on the stage, but in the panoptic machine, invested by its effects of power, which we bring to ourselves since we are part of the mechanism. (217)

And this is precisely the kind of society Pinter creates in his screenplay of *The Trial,* a "spectacular," paranoid house of mirrors. Like the prisoners in the Panopticon, we learn, as Josef K. does, that there are people viewing us at all times, but that there is, in fact, no one in the tower—no ultimate judge, earthly or divine. The ultimate supervisor is absent, but this supervisor, at least in the case of *The Trial,* is created mythically through obfuscation, a confusing hierarchy of judges, legal myths, and court legends. For the creators of the Panopticon, such obfuscation occurs in the criminal justice system in order to make the punishment appear to be the natural response of the society, not the demonstration of power by a ruler (Foucault 73–104). But in the Kafka novel and the Pinter screenplay, the chain of command is deliberately mystified by a legal system determined to keep its citizenry oppressed and by a society that has lost its God, the ultimate guard in the tower. The results, however, are the same—Herr K. is overcome by actual and imagined surveillance; he internalizes the watchful eye, participates in his own objectification, and finally, looks for a "spectacular" protector, finds there is none, and dies "like a dog."

The opening of the screenplay leaves no doubt that K. is being watched. It also very clearly demonstrates that Pinter certainly had at least one eye on *The Trial* as he composed his *Birthday Party.* And without going into great detail, some of the more noticeable similarities are worth mentioning. As in *The Trial*, Pinter's piece begins with young men stalked and subsequently interrogated for some unknown reason by some unknown representatives of some undefined authority. And while the predicaments of both young men are dire, both celebrate their birthdays, and both are more concerned with the disruption of their breakfasts than their situations.[6]

The camera movements during the opening credits underscore the omnipresence of film technology and the surveillance that Pinter's screenplay highlights. The camera moves from the street to Josef K.'s window, thereby imbuing it with transcendent qualities. Pinter's screenplay supports this strategy by introducing K. while he is asleep. We are clearly privy to a high level of observation on K.'s life, but at the same time, we are as much in the dark as he is about the voices that whisper outside his door and the old woman who peers into his room from her window in the apartment across the street. Moments later, we discover that K. is under arrest and in retrospect we see that the camera movements, the whisperings, and his elderly neighbor all have K. as their subject. He is under suspicion and observation, and as the subsequent scenes demonstrate, he will continue to be. When, for example, a second man joins the elderly woman at the window, K. does not see them; but they see him, and we see them watching him. He is under a watch, whether he is aware of it or not, and our perceptions are being directed by the camera, which may or may not provide us with complete information. During a scene with the inspector, yet another person joins the people in the window, and this time K. confronts them, and they immediately move away. K. appears to have succeeded, but our position in the room clearly illustrates that K. may have removed the nosy neighbors, but he is still under our watchful gaze, that of the inspector, and the other men in the room. From this moment on, he is under surveillance, and the Inspector says as much when he informs K. that his bank colleagues, unnoticed by K., are in the room and will accompany him to the bank, ironically to avoid the appearance of impropriety.

One of the more unfortunate deletions in the film from Pinter's screenplay is the encounter K. has with his landlady, Frau Grubach, the prototype of Pinter's Meg in *The Birthday Party*. And though Pinter agreed to the cuts, another level of menace is missing as a result of these deletions. In the novel and the screenplay, Grubach is the "Big Brother" of the rooming house. She knows everything about her tenants, and she warns K. about Frau Burstner, another tenant with whom K. is enamoured. But Grubach is also poor, and she has a nephew who needs a room, so no matter what she may think of K. or how much she may need the money he continues to lend her, it is not difficult to imagine that she would betray him or anyone else in the house if the price were right. Her nephew, Lanz, is just as menacing, but he is only fleetingly mentioned in the film. Burstner warns K. about him, and in the screenplay, Burstner soon disappears after this warning. Her room, then, is taken by another woman who says she is Burstner's roommate, and this woman has also taken up with Lanz. Through these subtle disappearances and appearances, Pinter's screenplay further emphasizes the paranoid world of Kafka's novel through visual cues.

Josef K.'s interest in Frau Burstner, despite the warnings from Frau Grubach, reflects both his ignorance of and disdain for this world. And it is this kind of behavior that leads many critics to conclude that K. is egotistical, guilty of the tragic weakness, pride.[7] Frank Gillen, moreover, links this character flaw to the visual: "through the images of eyes and looking, through dramatizing some of K.'s feelings of superiority to others, his treatment of them as objects, and his lack of concern with anything other than his own fate, Pinter's screenplay shows K. finally as a victim differing only in kind and degree but not in essence from those who destroy him" (147). At this point anyway K. still believes that he can, as an individual, affect changes. One of his first defenses when he is accused, for example, is to find his "identity papers" as if who he is will somehow protect him from accusations. On the one hand, such behavior is profoundly egotistical. On the other hand, it is profoundly ignorant—K. has no idea how pervasive the court's power is.

K. is so secure in his power as an individual that he volunteers to perform the details of his arrest for Frau Burstner. He casts himself into the role of the object-to-be-viewed because he assumes that he can take on or discard the role at will. He does not realize that he is already the object of the court's gaze, and he does not realize that Frau Burstner is not impartial. Burstner, for example, mentions that she is "joining a law firm next month" even though she knows nothing of the law (11–12). While K. is not suspicious, the screenplay suggests that he should be. Her behavior, after all, is consistent with the other court representatives. In a court system, in which image is all, Burstner only reacts to the invasion of privacy when she discovers that her photos have been rearranged. She is clearly part of the system in some way. K., moreover, is so willing to relinquish his power to her, unwilling to gaze at her critically, and continually objectifies himself for her. Burstner, perhaps because of her understanding of the court system, tries to help Josef out of this objectified role. "Look" she tells him, and encourages him to be more aware of his surroundings (14). K. cannot. He buries himself in her neck, kissing her passionately, blind, completely at the mercy of the gaze.

At this point, K.'s behavior may indicate that he has already internalized the gaze of the court. As an accused criminal, he immediately becomes oppressed, an object-to-be-viewed. Further, his unwillingness to "look" could indicate his naïveté, as well. He does not want to take responsibility for his actions; he wants the observing eye to protect and care for him, this time embodied in the maternal figure of Burstner. Kafka's novel makes it clear that K. at one time participated in the role of the viewer, frequenting performances (17), but in the Pinter version, K. is always objectified by a gaze, ours or the court's, and he seems particularly reluctant to acknowledge the court's relationship to spectacle, even though his experiences indicate otherwise. Here, for example, he ignores Burstner's explicit cautions about the culture of surveillance they inhabit.

Once he leaves Burstner, K. enters a judicial version of a funhouse, and Pinter's screenplay makes the most of Josef's absurd situation. He is called to a hearing, but the caller does not give him the time. He takes circuitous routes, with intricate passageways and secret code names. Coincidentally, one of the names he mentions to gain access to the court is Lanz, the same name as Frau Grubach's nephew, the Captain. Here, he may be a plumber, but given the similarity in names, as well as Burstner's warning, Pinter's screenplay is highlighting the omnipresence of the court. Pinter underscores this warning in a comic scene fit for a Marx Brothers movie. When K. knocks on the door of one apartment, people respond from a door several apart- ments away. Nothing is as it appears to be; appearance is all; the court is everywhere and nowhere; these are the truisms of K.'s world and the Pinter screenplay.

When K. finally finds the court, he is shocked—it is chaotic and behind the home of a Washerwoman. The symbolism may be clear to us—the mun- dane is illusory; all is the court—but K. does not make such connections. He assumes that the court is reasonable. When he is told that he is late, he chal- lenges the court, its weaknesses and contradictions. He gains the applause of those he presumes are his well-wishers. Of course, K. has completely misjudged the situation. His speech does nothing to change the absurd and arbitrary nature of the proceedings. In fact, he is viewed as a form of enter- tainment, not the leader of a rebellion. He is merely a performer. If we were tempted to judge K. harshly before this scene, it is difficult to judge him so now. Like us, he has made incorrect assumptions about his situation. To un- derscore this conclusion, Pinter and Kafka interrupt K.'s speech with the public lovemaking of the law student and the Washerwoman. Nothing K. can say will make a change; there are only new diversions. The Magistrate who also lusts after the Washerwoman concludes the scene by telling K. that he has lost all "the advantages that a hearing can afford an arrested man" (21). K. tells them all to go to hell, but his gesture is impotent.

Undaunted and still secure in his belief that he can control his own des- tiny, K. returns in order to view the law books, to "look" for himself, an activity the Washerwoman says is forbidden. K. is clearly objectified, incapable of subjectivity, but he forces his way into the courtroom and he discovers that the books are filled with pornography. Such a choice under- scores the court's ability to objectify people, for pornography is one of the powerful forms of visual oppression available to us. In both the Kafka text and the Pinter screenplay, the law is image, and these images are perverse. In the process of his discussions with the Washerwoman, she attempts to seduce him, but in a truly absurd scene, she is interrupted and transfixed by the Svengali-like presence of the student. Here, Pinter's screenplay highlights the court's powerful ability to objectify through speculation. The Washerwoman is overcome by a gaze, and K., who appears to be viewing the scene and thereby occupying a position of power, is, in fact, being watched by the student, objectified. The student even comments that K. has been given too much freedom (25), thus establishing his knowledge of court proceedings K. does not have access to.

At this point, K.'s future does not look promising. After this scene, he meets the Usher, the husband of the Washerwoman, who tells K. that he could take revenge on the student and Magistrate because he has "nothing to loose" (27). And when the Usher provides K. with a tour of the court offices, K. sees Magritte-like figures lining the hall, devoid of expression and will to live. Those waiting for news of their cases are completely passive, objectified. Initially K. is upset with their docility, but moments later, he is like them, suffocated by the court atmosphere. The Usher, who was helpful, suddenly becomes sadistic and violently throws him down a flight of stairs. K.'s egotism, his assumption that he is somehow different from the other accused, is quickly dispelled.

His pride is further injured when, in the screenplay, K. meets with Fraulein Montag, Burstner's new roommate. In this scene edited from the film, she tells K. to stop trying to contact Burstner: "She knows what this talk would be about and is convinced that it would be in neither her interest nor yours for such a talk to take place" (30). The interchange ends with Captain Lanz ignoring K. and kissing Montag's hand. Unfortunately, the scene does not appear in the film, so K.'s isolation and the growing menace he faces are not as clear. Further, because he is no longer the object of the Captain's gaze, K.'s time as a visual object is dwindling; he is becoming invisible.

And, as the next scene so painfully illustrates, he is really no different from the court representatives. As he is leaving from work, he hears screams of pain. In a closet of the bank, again underscoring the pervasiveness of the court culture, he finds the two warders he complained about being flogged. They, of course, beg him to put a stop to the flogging, but he cannot: "It's my job to flog people I'm told to flog and that's what I'm going to do" (32). K. literally turns a blind eye to the two men, and when asked about the noise by bank colleagues he says that it was just a dog howling (32). The canine imagery is similar to his final line of the screenplay.

The scene, however, is important because here K. no longer attempts to change the system. When faced with the flogger's flawless logic, K. does nothing, like everyone else in the screenplay. He is becoming nothing, and he does nothing. The film, however, does not show the darker side of K.'s apathy, but Pinter's screenplay does. After witnessing the flogging, K. returns home and in a camera shot reminiscent of the opening scene, we see K. on the bed, this time with his eyes wide open. He is still a spectacle, but perhaps not quite such an innocent one as at the beginning of the film. The next morning, he checks the closet and finds the men still being flogged. And rather than attempting to stop the flogging, K. shuts the door and tells one of his clerks to clean out the closet because if they do not, "we're going to be smothered in filth" (33). K., like other members of this culture, is fearful, apathetic, and overwhelmed by the power of the court. Though some would argue that K. has been this way all along, it is difficult to ignore the fact that during his speech to the court about its abuses, he argued for reform, not just for himself but for others who were also victimized by the process. It would appear, then, that K. has undergone a transformation as a result of this process and observation. He is no longer capable of even performing as a subject.

Surprisingly, K. still seems unaware of the court's power and pervasiveness. When his uncle, for example, takes him to Huld, the advocate, he is shocked to find out that people are discussing his case. More disturbing still is the mysterious appearance of a court representative while Huld and he discuss strategy. At this critical moment in his case, his first meeting with his lawyer and the court representative, K. does not stay, perhaps in an attempt to escape the gaze of the court. He leaves the room and is subsequently seduced by Huld's voluptuous caretaker, Leni. Whether he realizes it or not, his escape has led him back to the court, once again. Leni, who seduces all accused men, proclaims triumphantly, "Now you belong to me" (39).

When he returns the next day, he finds that his case, according to Huld, is "moderately cheering" (41). But K. is still under the illusion that he can control the outcome. He tells Huld that he will settle the entire case by writing a "short account" of his life as a defense (41). In no uncertain terms, Huld dismisses this suggestion: "What you say is madness. . . . Absolute madness" (41). Individuals, identity, personality do not matter. K. has been completely objectified by observation as a result of his participation in this absurd justice system. He wishes to tell his own story, but he does not realize that as an accused man there is no story to tell.

In an effort to help K.'s case, Leni sends him to the court painter, Titorelli, who further illustrates the court's relationship to spectacle. Not only is K. subjected to the gaze of Titorelli's prostitutes, Titorelli tells him that there is no real escape from the court, only variations on the level of enslavement. When Titorelli is finished, he shows K. an alternative exit from the studio that leads to the court. Echoing Kafka's text, the screenplay has Titorelli ask the significant question, "Why are you so surprised?" (48).

K. still does not understand the hopelessness of his situation, and he decides to fire his lawyer Huld and make his case without a lawyer. During his visit to Huld, he not only realizes that Leni is as much a part of the court as

Titorelli's prostitutes but he also meets Bloch, an accused man whose trial has been going on for five years. Bloch tells him that the people in the court stood when K. entered because they could tell by the shape of his lips that he was a condemned man: "So we didn't think you were arrogant, we thought you were deluded. And so we felt pity for you" (50). And to a certain extent they are correct. K. is deluded. He expects logic from the court, but in the end, superstition and obfuscation is all there is. What is surprising is that K. take so long to learn this; he firmly clings to a faith in the law and its order, its logic. Despite his arrest with no charge, his discovery that the law books are filled with pornography, and his meeting with Titorelli who tells him there are no full acquittals, K. believes that logical confrontation can change this system. He soon learns that not only has he been deluded about the law but he is also deluded by Leni. The film merely suggests that Bloch and Leni are having an affair, but in Pinter's screenplay, the relationship is made much more explicit. As Huld tells K., he is not different: his relationship with Leni is not special; it is defined by the court:

> She just finds accused men wildly attractive. She can't help running after them. She falls in love with them all and indeed they all seem to fall in love with her. Even that miserable worm Block she finds attractive—just because he's an accused man. (52)

Any illusions Josef K. has about his individuality are shattered during this meeting with Huld, Leni, and Bloch.

To make matters worse, Leni and Huld offer a performance for K. at Bloch's expense in order to create a court morality for K. K. sees not only his future, a life like Bloch's, but he also sees that the court is indomitable; he is powerless to change the system. Deliberate cruelty is all that is in store for him, and though he is shown this spectacle, he is not in any position of power.

Following this performance, K. is called to take a visiting Italian client "sightseeing" at the cathedral, and in the Pinter screenplay, K. once again remains awake, eyes open, on the night before his tour (56). In the cathedral he meets a priest, not an Italian banker, from whom he seeks solace. Despite all the recent evidence to the contrary, Leni, Bloch, Titorelli, and others, K. presumes that the priest is an ally. He also still thinks justice available, something fair and just above the law and the culture he inhabits. The priest is quick to say, "don't delude yourself . . . about the Court. . . . The Court doesn't want anything from you. It receives you when you come and it dismisses you when you go" (60–63). To highlight this point, he tells K. the preface to the Law, a story about a man who seeks the law, is afraid to enter without permission, and realizes, too late, that all he needed to do was ask permission to enter. Before the priest tells the parable, however, he says: "In the writings that preface the Law it says about this delusion" (60). The phrasing is unusual, and it is very easy to read the line as "it says this about delusion," but this wording is much more ambiguous, making the subsequent parable even more difficult to interpret. If the phrase was, "it says this about delusion," it might be easy to interpret the parable as an example of what happens when one is deluded by oneself or someone else, but as it stands, the wording does not offer any interpretive hints to the parable. Is the man who seeks the law blinded by fear? Is the doorkeeper merely waiting for further instructions or a sadist, as K. thinks?

Volumes have been written on this hauntingly ambiguous moment in the novel. What is so refreshing about the Pinter version is that it appears to be as balanced as it is in the novel. Either interpretation could be possible, and either interpretation could lead to unforeseen interpretive consequences. What is striking about this moment in the screenplay is the priest's unwillingness to explain his interpretation of the parable. The only explanation he offers is through the priest who says, "But you've missed the point. The scripture is unalterable" (63). He then tells K. that he means nothing to him. He is, after all, a member of the Court. At the very least, the parable offers a microcosm of the screenplay's entire court system: it is confusing; there are no guides to interpretation, and the ones that are there are impenetrable. At the same time, it is "unalterable," unchanging and powerful. It is, like the symbol of justice, blind and in the balance.

In the final scene, K. is led to his death, and with it comes another array of images regarding spectacle and speculation, objectivity and subjectivity, oppression and power. According to Pinter, in *The Trial*:

> Kafka obviously employs the whole idea of how a bureaucratic system works but he's also looking at something quite different. And that is—I have to use the term—religious identity. One of the captions I would put on *The Trial* is simply: "What kind of game is God playing?" That's what Josef K. is really asking. And the only answer he gets is a pretty brutal one. (qtd. in Billington 349)

This statement is as close to an interpretation that Pinter offers. It is also the one that most influences the final scene and the placement of the viewers' and K.'s gazes. Initially, K. resists his executioners, but after he sees Frau Burstner, he decides to keep his "mind calm and discriminating," in effect, to face death nobly. If this were a Shakespeare play, and if K. were a Lear or Hamlet, the glimpse into the abyss, death, would afford the tragic character a moment, at least, of nobility, insight, and subjectivity. Kafka is no Shakespeare, however. For if we recall Burstner's earlier statements, her poise and serenity are not based on nobility but upon fear and passivity: "I'm never angry with anyone," she tells K. as she is about to show him the means by which the Grubach residence spies on its lodgers (14). Once again K. is viewing himself and his situation incorrectly, but here we cannot fault him entirely, for his desire to make sense of his death and life is a desire we all share. In the Kafka universe, however, such expectations are not only unattainable, they are absurd. Kafka in his novel and Pinter in the screenplay, however, provide another false clue, that leads us and K. to assume there is meaning, there is redemption, there is something above and beyond K.'s petty trial. As K. looks from the rocks to a window, this time he sees a beatific vision, perhaps a glimpse of paradise. Since he is the viewer, it also appears that he is in a position of power. He sees a vision of transcendence, a way out, the ultimate eye in the sky. Pinter's screenplay and Kafka's text do not offer such solace, for at this moment, the vision is interrupted by the peering faces of the two executioners who block K.'s glimpse into paradise. Further, K. is clearly objectified by their gazes. He is a spectacle once again, a "dog" (66).

With this visual image, Pinter communicates the last lines of the Kafka novel and most effectively concludes the screenplay's illustration regarding spectacle, speculation, and crime. K. is not redeemed at the end of the film because there is no transcendent viewer, only film audiences to witness his sufferings. Just as there are no judges in charge of the Court, the trial, there is no divine, transcendent being above the culture of the Court. Instead, there are only human beings oppressing one another and creating through the sum total of their parts, the illusion that there is a God, a final judge, a full and complete acquittal. The culture of the Kafka novel and film, a culture that Pinter captures brilliantly through the emphasis on the visual technology of film, is, in Foucault's words regarding prisons and spectacle, " a machine for altering minds" (125). And Pinter's use of such machinery in his screenplay will, perhaps alter our own.

Notes

1. Michael Billington reports that *The Killers*, both the film and the Hemingway short story, were important to Pinter during his writing of *The Birthday Party*. He also mentions other popular culture influences such as the comedy act of Jewel and Warriss and a 1950s quiz show starring "a bullying Michael Miles" (77). Most important, Billington notes that "the power of the play . . . resides precisely in the way Pinter takes stock ingredients of popular drama and invests them with political resonance" (77). As we will see, Pinter uses a similar technique in this screenplay, which is, as Pinter says, a "nightmare . . . precisely in its ordinariness" (qtd. in Gussow 88).

2. Depending on which interview you believe, Pinter has been reading *The Trial* since he was seventeen (Marks 22), eighteen (Gussow 88), or fifteen ("Pinter's Czech Mate"). Whatever his age, Pinter was profoundly affected. Marks reports that it "determined him to be a writer" (22). And Kafka's influence was great: "*The Trial* seeped into many people's subconscious, including mine. It had an

undeniable influence on my early writing. *The Birthday Party* is a play which owes a lot to Kafka" (Pinter qtd. in Burley).

3. In her essay, "Peopling the Wound," Leslie Kane compellingly demonstrates the Jewish heritage that Kafka and Pinter share, a heritage that is subtly expressed by both authors in *The Trial*: "Although Pinter does not denote the identity of his protagonist as Jewish any more than Kafka does, Josef K.'s numerous stereotypical traits" are, finally, "traditional negative qualifiers of Jewish nature" (150).

4. Pinter's expertise with film and screenplays has been demonstrated through works such as *The French Lieutenant's Woman* (1981), *Turtle Diary* (1985), and *The Comfort of Strangers* (1990). Joanne Klein notes: "like the camera Pinter manipulates not reality, but the mechanisms through which we glimpse it" (qtd. in Gillen 138). And on *The Comfort of Strangers* Katherine Burkman concludes that by consciously using the camera, Pinter foregrounds "its potential for destructiveness (exposing the complicity between film and power)" that "invites us to interrogate our own role as audience" (44). In my own essay on *Mountain Language*, I argue that not only does Pinter bring his stage expertise to the film but he brings his film expertise to the stage. In this case, he employs the filmic technique of the voice over to strengthen the political play.

5. In an essay soon to be published by the Missouri Philological Association, "Discipline, Self-Regulation, and Silence in Pinter's *The Dumb Waiter*," Charles Grimes uses Foucault's work to examine *The Dumb Waiter*. Because he offered me a copy of the essay prior to publication, I took greater care in reading Foucault's discussion of the visible and unverifiable.

6. See my essay on *The Birthday Party* for a greater discussion on the nature of spectacle in that play.

7. In the notes to *The New Trial*, the play he had been working on at the time of his death, Peter Weiss claims that his Josef K., a member of a corporate conglomerate who is shot by a stray bullet at the end of the play, is "neither hero nor victim; he is a marginal figure, exploited for others' purposes and discarded when he is no longer needed. He is *not a tragic figure*" (107; Weiss's italics).

Works Cited

Armstrong, Raymond. *Kafka and Pinter Shadow-Boxing: The Struggle between Father and Son*. New York: St. Martin's P, 1999.

Billington, Michael. *The Life and Work of Harold Pinter*. London: Faber and Faber, 1996.

Burkman, Katherine. "Harold Pinter's Death in Venice: *The Comfort of Strangers*." *The Pinter Review Annual Essays 1992–93*. Ed. Francis Gillen and Steven Gale. Tampa: U of Tampa P, 1993, 38–45.

Burley, Leo. "The Jury Is Still Out on Joseph K." *Independent* (London) 23 Apr., 1993. *Lexis-Nexis*. 24 May 2000.

Foucault, Michel. *Discipline and Punish: The Birth of the Prison*. Trans. Alan Sheridan. New York: Vintage Books, 1995.

Gillen, Francis. "From Novel to Film: Harold Pinter's Adaptation of *The Trial*." *Pinter at Sixty*. Ed. Katherine Burkman and John Kundert-Gibbs. Bloomington: Indiana UP, 1993, 136–48.

Grimes, Charles. "Discipline, Self-Regulation, and Silence in Harold Pinter's *The Dumb Waiter*." *Publications of the Missouri Philological Association* 25 (2000): 92–106.

Gussow, Mel. *Conversations with Harold Pinter*. London: Nick Hern Books, 1994.

Hall, Ann C. "Looking for Mr. Goldberg: Spectacle and Speculation in Harold Pinter's *The Birthday Party*." *The Pinter Review: Collected Essays 1997 and 1998*. Ed. Francis Gillen and Steven Gale. Tampa: U of Tampa P, 1999, 48–56.

———. "Voices in the Dark: The Disembodied Voice in Harold Pinter's *Mountain Language*." *The Pinter Review: Annual Essays 1991*. Ed. Francis Gillen and Steven Gale. Tampa: U of Tampa P, 1991, 17–22.

Kane, Leslie. "Peopling the Wound: Harold Pinter's Screenplay for Kafka's *The Trial*." *Cycnos* 14 (1997): 145–59.

Kundert-Gibbs, John. "I am powerful . . . and I am only the lowest doorkeeper": Power Play in Kafka's *The Trial* and Pinter's *Victoria Station*. *Pinter at Sixty*. Ed. Katherine Burkman and John L. Kundert-Gibbs. Bloomington: Indiana UP, 1993, 148–60.

Marks, Louis. "Producing Pinter." *Pinter at Sixty*. Ed. Katherine Burkman and John L. Kundert-Gibbs. Bloomington: Indiana UP, 1993, 18–26.

"Pinter's Czech Mate." *Times* (London) 26 Feb. 1992. *Lexis-Nexis*. 24 May 2000.

Pinter, Harold. *The Trial*. Boston: Faber and Faber, 1993.

Weiss, Peter. *The New Trial*. Trans. James Rolleston and Kai Evers. Durham, NC: Duke UP, 2001.

7

Lie Detectors: Pinter/Mamet and the Victorian Concept of Crime

IRA B. NADEL

If falsehood like truth had only one face, we would be in better shape.
— MONTAIGNE, *Essays*

No one goes to jail in the plays of Harold Pinter or David Mamet—which is not to say that crime doesn't exist. It's just that it's likely to go unpunished. In Pinter's "comedy of menace," violence, often implied, is never disciplined. The intrusion of Goldberg and McCann in *The Birthday Party*—hit men, avengers—disrupts the boarding-house comedy, bringing threats, abuse, fear, and abduction but they do not pay for their crime. At the end of *The Dumb Waiter,* Ben pulls his gun on Gus, but no shot is fired. In *The Caretaker,* crime and criminal behavior occur but while Mick directs his violence at Davies and then a Buddha, which he smashes against a wall, his aggression receives no check. The onstage violence of *The Room*—Bert violently beating Riley—again occurs with no penalty. In Pinter the perpetrators of these acts remain free.[1]

Mamet's stage criminals display similar freedom from punishment: much of American *Buffalo* is spent planning a crime that doesn't occur. Threats replace actual violence, although Bobby is roughed up and Teach, in frustration, destroys Donny's junk shop. But since no crime has been committed, no punishment is needed. In *Glengarry Glen Ross,* there are numerous deceptions and misrepresentations and even a burglary of the real estate office by the misled Shelly Levene; his punishment, however, remains unspecified. In *Oleanna,* violence is almost enacted but at the last moment, John puts down the chair he raises to hit Carol at the play's conclusion, while his punishment is administrative and based on questionable premises. Carol, his accuser, appears to go free.

Only in the screenplays of Pinter and Mamet does punishment, with cruelty, become more pronounced. In *The Comfort of Strangers* Pinter provides detailed on-screen violence from posters calling for the castration of rapists to the lust murder of the handsome Colin by slitting his throat. Mamet provides a similar degree of violence as punishment in *The Untouchables,* with Al Capone clubbing one of his defectors with a baseball bat, and running to murder in *Hoffa,* extended in *Homicide* and *Spanish Prisoner*—although a number of these moments are tricks, such as the attempt to extort $6,000 by the gambler who pulls a gun during the poker game at the opening of *House of Games.* The frightened psychiatrist, Margaret Ford, realizes, at the last moment, however, that it is not real. It's a setup, a typical Mamet ploy. But from his first film, *The Postman Always Rings Twice,* through his latest, *Heist,* Mamet, like Pinter, feels freer to portray physical crime and punishment in film than on the stage.[2]

An exception, however, to crime as physical violence in their screenplays is the foray of Pinter and Mamet into the Victorian and Edwardian periods. *The French Lieutenant's Woman,* directed by Karel Reisz, and *The Winslow Boy,* directed by Mamet, alternately reveal a more attenuated, nonviolent portrayal of crime at the same time that they document its punishment. They also direct their outrage at a specific crime that threatens the morality of the period, namely, lying. But before either playwright could revise his representation of crime from the violent to the moral and record, as well as rationalize, punishment, he had to adapt the original work to the new genre (film) while incorporating attitudes generated by the historical specificity of the period.

I

Attracted to works that feature the Victorian or late Victorian period, Pinter and Mamet first had to refashion their source-texts for the screen. Pinter faced a formidable challenge: in the film he had to somehow balance the curious stereoscopic element of Fowles's novel, which presented both the Victorian and modern times. He also had to condense the lengthy descriptive passages, historical digressions, character analysis, and distracting minor characters into a visual drama. His solution was (pun intended) novel. He decided to frame the Victorian story within a modern love affair between the two actors who play the roles of Charles and Sarah in the film.[3] Named Mike and Anna, the two actors border the story of the two fictional characters, although where the Victorian story in the film has a happy ending— Charles locates Sarah after three years of searching and they go off together—Anna, the American actress, leaves Mike when the filming is completed. In this manner, Pinter accommodates the choice of endings, one positive and one negative, that Fowles provided in his novel.

Fowles found Pinter's solution to the problem of transferring his novel to the screen brilliant because he had the independence of mind to free the film from the novel. In a "Foreword" to the screenplay, Fowles explained that the greatest gift a screenwriter can provide for a director is "not so much a version 'faithful' to the book as a version faithful to the very different production capability (and relation with the audience) of the cinema" (xii).[4] Few directors or screenwriters in the ten years between the initial effort to film the novel and when Karel Reisz began to shoot the script (May 1980) were bold enough to free themselves from the novel. Pinter, however, did and the result was an imaginative treatment of the story, reducing what Fowles acknowledged as his "over-plotted book" to a clear story by *adding* another story to it.

Mamet did not face such a problem when he adapted Terrence Rattigan's successful 1946 play based on the actual legal case of George Archer-Shee, asked to leave the Royal Naval College at Osborne for allegedly stealing a postal order, an incident that occurred in 1908. The public issue of clearing the young man's name was debated in the House of Commons, so inflammatory was the situation. The remarkable thing about Rattigan's play, which he wrote after Anatole de Grunwald, screenwriter, and Anthony "Puffin" Asquith, the film director, turned down Rattigan's proposal for a film about the event, is that he succeeded in creating a drama without the presence of a single courtroom scene. The four-act play was an immediate success, playing the Lyric Theatre in the West End of London for more than a year and recording 476 performances (Wansell 160). Alexander Korda, noted British film producer, quickly bought the film rights and by 1948 the film was released, directed by Asquith with a screenplay by de Grunwald adapted from Rattigan's play.

Mamet has long been fascinated by courtroom dramas, beginning with his early, Academy Award–nominated screenplay, *The Verdict*. The dramatic setup of a courtroom is a natural theater where protagonist, antagonist, and chorus (the jury) are fixtures. *The Verdict* showed how carefully one can manipulate the situation to sustain drama until the final few moments. But ironically, Rattigan's *The Winslow Boy* intentionally avoided a courtroom scene; more important was the theme of injustice and victimization, which was equally central to Mamet and his interests. Three other attractions of Rattigan's play were its well-made quality, its logical development, and its precise language, which have long characterized Mamet's best work, features partly drawn from the example of Pinter. Another attraction for Mamet was the play's rendering of Edwardian England, evoking its Victorian inheritance. Mamet for some time had been attracted to this period, reading and rereading a set of Victorian novelists including Thackeray, Trollope, and George Eliot; a quote from Trollope's *He Knew He Was Right* is the epigram to Mamet's *On Directing Film* and he often quotes Kipling from memory. A violated world of order searching to restore its balance is a frequent theme in Mamet's own work, which Victorian fiction constantly explores. Rattigan, who sets his play over a two year period preceding World War I, captures the world of Edwardian England that Mamet evokes through his detailed 1912 setting.

But if the period is late Edwardian, the attitudes are Victorian, marked by class awareness, gender differences, social hierarchies (and embarrassments), proper moral behavior, and highly fixed attitudes. Re-creating these features required the authenticity of time and place to validate the authority of moral law confirmed at the end of the play and film by a biblical sense of "right," not "justice," a distinction reiterated by the successful barrister, Sir Robert Morton, in the closing lines of the work. Underlining this dimension of the conflict is a question that has absorbed Mamet for some time, one that crosses principle with the selfish interests of the individual: "when does a fight for justice become an arrogant pursuit of personal rectitude . . . at what point does one give up the fight for an abstract principle?" (qte. in James 23–24). Contradicting the high principle of Sir Robert is the seemingly personal pursuit of Arthur Winslow to clear his son's and his family's name, although he shares Sir Robert's determination to triumph. In a line Mamet added to Rattigan's script, Sir Robert declares, "It's only important to *win*," repeating a mantra of Mamet's father, a Chicago labor lawyer, often repeated at the dinner table (*WB* 165).

For Mamet, the issue was not restructuring but condensing the original four-act play to 99 minutes of drama, while creating a single, seamless film. "Someone once said, 'the better the play the worse the movie it's going to make' so a lot of my work here has been lifting passages of narration that can be better explained through montage and by dramatizing the purely narrative," Mamet explained to an interviewer on the set (qtd. in James 23). He elegantly achieves this in visual, as well as verbal, terms, confirming his understanding of the period as much as the formal properties of the two genres, drama and film, that must be divided in order to fulfill the expectations of each.

Surprisingly, Mamet keeps much of the original language intact and introduces none of his characteristic profanities. A comparison of the screenplay with the drama finds extraordinary similarities of expression. To cite one passage from the end of the play, Mamet quotes Rattigan almost exactly when he has Sir Robert explain to Catherine Winslow: "To fight a case on emotional grounds, Miss Winslow, is the surest way to lose it. Emotions cloud the issue. Cold, clear logic wins the day" (*WB* 208). Rattigan writes "to fight a case on emotional grounds, Miss Winslow, is the surest way to lose it. Emotions muddy the issue. Cold, clear logic—and buckets of it—should be the lawyer's only equipment" (176). Mamet values the precision of Rattigan's language, editing and updating only selective expressions in the play-text.

The only major changes Mamet makes to the play in his condensation of Rattigan are structural, where, for cinematic impact, he alters the order of action. Mamet's movie opens with the Winslows returning from Sunday church; Rattigan's play begins with the surprising return of the dismissed

Ronnie Winslow being greeted by the housemaid and then shows him alone almost tearing up a letter to his father about his "sacking." Mamet does not embellish the play but pares it down to its essentials. Through the visual texture of the film, he makes the most impact, the images equalling the seriousness of the theme. Such cinematic technique as camera angles, period detail and sound maintain the stately pace of the drama. Mamet's respect for the play is evident throughout the film, the first Mamet directed from material he hadn't written.

Pinter dealt with two matters: how to restructure his source-text while maintaining the original's Victorian/modern linkage without sacrificing the fundamental Victorian emphasis of the novel. He solved the problem by adding a new story to Fowles. Mamet faced one issue: how to condense a well-plotted play with rhetorically effective language into a tightly focused, visual drama to establish tension through what we see and hear. Emerging from these issues was the similar treatment of crime and, as their adaptations show, for Pinter and Mamet it is a question of morality not violence, dishonor not murder.

II

Both *The French Lieutenant's Woman* and *The Winslow Boy* adopt a Victorian attitude toward crime defined as a moral rather than physical act involving the violation of a social order disrupted by a lie. Deception, deceit, betrayal, and dishonor are the operative concepts, with punishment a powerful public rather than legal act. Reproducing the Victorian /Edwardian worlds in their films meant that social rather than judicial punishment was more effective. Consequently, in *The French Lieutenant's Woman* Charles loses his reputation and credibility as a gentleman and is shown to be an outcast, although one whose passions have been fulfilled. In *The Winslow Boy*, punishment through admission of wrong is "visited upon" those institutions (the Admiralty and the Crown) that threatened to ruin the individual. Eliot Ness may have needed a machine gun to fight crime in Mamet's *The Untouchables* but Sir Robert Morton, the heroic barrister and MP in *The Winslow Boy*, needs only words.

The breakdown of the moral order and its consequences, rather than blood on the floor, long occupied each playwright, equally affronted by betrayal through language and the failure of justice. Mick in *The Caretaker* makes this clear when he indicts Davies: "Every word you speak is open to any number of different interpretations. Most of what you say is lies" (73). The frustrated Teach shares this view. At the end of *American Buffalo,* he angrily voices the creed of those for whom words fail to find backing through deeds: "There Is No Right And Wrong. The World is Lies" he exclaims (103). Violating the sanctity of language eliminates trust and destroys a world. Deceit is a social/ moral crime that is its own punishment.

A Short History of Nineteenth-Century Lying

The morality of the Victorian period privileged honesty, making its transgression through lying a crime. For the Victorians, lying was the most threatening of acts, partly because it was the most difficult to deny while potentially causing the most harm. Differing from a secret in that "every lie stands in need of justification, all secrets do not," lies nevertheless can be defended in certain exceptional cases—perhaps to deceive an enemy or maintain domestic peace (Bok, *Secrets* xv). "All civility depends on little lies" one social critic has recently argued (Gopnik 86).[5] But lying can also coerce people into acting against their will, although in our period, lying, it has been argued, is "neither inherently moral nor immoral," merely "inextricable parts of our relationships with ourselves and with other people" (Ford 283). Hannah Arendt went so far as to argue that our ability to lie confirms the existence of human freedom, affirming a view expressed by a sixteenth-century writer: "never to lie admits of no imagining" (Arendt 250; Ingannevole in Barnes 3).

The history of lying in the nineteenth century begins with its cavalier treatment by Byron, reflecting a Regency point of view. In *Don Juan* he writes,

> And after all, what is a lie? 'Tis but
> The truth in masquerade, and I defy
> Historians, heroes, lawyers, priests to put
> A fact without some leaven of a lie.
> (Canto XI, St. 37, 406)

Celebrated as the necessary fiction to make a fact palatable, lying became an imaginative staple of the Romantics' diet, which even Blake through his criticism, upheld: "A truth that's told with bad intent/ Beats all the lies you can invent" (586). This Aristotelian view—"falsehood is in itself base and reprehensible, and truth noble and praiseworthy" (241)—quickly assumes a powerful moral authority by the time of Kant who declares "by a lie a man throws away and, as it were, annihilates his dignity as a man" (qtd. in Bok, *Lying* 32).

The Victorians were quick to accept this view, testing if not exploiting it repeatedly in their fiction. The disreputable Mr. Jingle in Dickens's *Pickwick Papers,* for example, is one of numerous deceivers, although a few are permitted redemption: Rochester, who lies to Jane Eyre about his married state while Bertha, the mad woman in the attic, languishes upstairs, is allowed to marry Jane but only *after* he purges and maims himself through fire in his effort to rescue his detested wife. Becky Sharpe, however, is not permitted such a reversal of fortune: caught lying to her husband Rawdon about her relationship with Lord Steyne in *Vanity Fair,* she suffers banishment to foreign lands and the loss of her son. In Dickens's *Our Mutual Friend*, the Lammles lie to each other about their supposed wealth only to find out that they are both virtually penniless. In George Eliot's *Romola*, Tito Melema lies to Tessa who believes they are legally married when, in fact, he has married Romola whom he soon betrays, as he does others. In Anthony Trollope's *The Way We Live Now,* lying defines almost every action of the financier Augustus Melmotte, who misrepresents the origins of his money, his stock schemes, and his importance. The collapse of his American railway scheme leads to the ruin of many and his suicide. Trollope's earlier *Orley Farm* similarly turns on a lie by Lady Mason and the forgery of a signature on a codicil to a will. The price of lying remained high.

Lies equally imperiled nonfiction writers. Carlyle in his life of *Frederick the Great* branded the eighteenth century the "lying century" while Ruskin analyses true and false lies in *Modern Painters,* soon linking them to issues of honest or dishonest visual representation. Purpose, he argued, was the main distinction between honorable and base lying. Tennyson, however, contained the purest statement on the most detrimental type of lie when he wrote, "A lie which is half a truth is ever the blackest of lies" (II: 600). Yet Browning could make a liar a hero. In "Mr. Sludge, 'The Medium,'" his hero declares "there's a real love of a lie,/ Liars find readymade for lies they make/ As hand for glove, or tongue for sugar-plum" (871). By the time of Samuel Butler, the admonition not to lie was being reconsidered. In his notebooks, Butler wrote, "Truth consists not in never lying but in knowing when to lie and when not to do so," later extended to the view that "if a man is not a good, sound, honest, capable liar, there is no truth in him" (248). Anticipating Wilde in tone if not concept, Butler adds, "I do not mind lying, but I hate inaccuracy." Even Robert Louis Stevenson could see the ambiguities attached to lying: "it is possible to avoid falsehood and yet not tell the truth," adding that "the cruellest lies are often told in silence" (79, 81).

By the end of the century some, like Nietzsche, believed that "the powerful always lie," a cynical or perhaps candid view of those in control (204). But others, like Wilde, believed that lying, "as an art, a science and a social pleasure," had deteriorated so far that he had to write its epitaph in his satiric dialogue, "The Decay of Lying" (293). In that work, Vivian laments the collapse of lying, which has become no more than misrepresentation. The liar, he argues, has been the only true hero who "with his frank, fearless statements, his superb irresponsibility, his healthy, natural disdain of proof of any kind" used to be the epitome of elegance: "After all, what is a fine lie? Simply that which is its own evidence. If a man is sufficiently unimaginative to produce evidence in support of a lie, he might just as well speak the truth at once" (292). Literature has virtually collapsed: "ancient historians gave us delightful fiction in the form of fact; the modern novelist presents us with dull facts under the guise of fiction" (293). Wilde published the essay in 1889 and by the turn of the century lying came back, at least as a necessary strategy to preserve a reputation if not a memory. In Henry Arthur Jones's 1897 play, *The Liars,* the need to lie in a hypocritical world is a prerequisite for survival, confirmed by Conrad at the end of *Heart of Darkness* (1902) when Marlowe tells the Intended that the final words on Kurtz's lips was her name; this of course, is not true.

Victorian variations of the lying theme include those characters who tell the truth when others know they are lying: Franklin Blake in Wilkie Collins's *The Moonstone* denies taking the jewel, although he has been seen committing the crime by Rachel Verinder. By the end of the novel, however, it is proven that he was under the influence of opium and had no recollection that he had removed the diamond. For the Victorians and Edwardians, the consequence of lying is criminal because it challenges, if not overturns, the moral order. But sometimes it goes undetected. Inspector Bucket or Sherlock Holmes always got their man (or woman) but many a liar has gone free. Lying, unless under oath, is not, of course, a criminal offense, but its impact has often had major ramifications on the lives of many nineteenth century characters.

Unlike the amoral universe of their plays, Pinter and Mamet found that the Victorian and Edwardian worlds they presented had definite rights and wrongs—or at least believed they did. Replacing the world of relative ethics—Richard Roma in *Glengarry* declares, "I do those things which seem correct to me *today*"—is a society based on inherited cultural and religious concepts of right behavior and moral action (49). Its ethics were clear and the immorality of lying unquestioned. Pinter and Mamet could not avoid the clarity of morality and likely welcomed it. In *The French Lieutenant's Woman*, Pinter emphasizes the way lying permeates both the Victorian and the modern periods, although in the former it is unacceptable and in the latter taken for granted. Sarah lies to Charles, telling him that she is the French lieutenant's whore, although she never had a sexual liaison with him. Nevertheless, she allows the story to circulate giving lie to her fiction while maligning her reputation in Lyme at the same time it provides her with notoriety. Only when Charles has sex with her does he discover she is a virgin, disproving her "story." Confronted with what he discovers, she admits she lied to him and to society (71–72). She cannot explain why she did it, although there is a suggestion that with such a tale she has gained a certain caché.

Charles then lies to Ernestina when, in the grip of his love for Sarah, he tells her he is unworthy of marriage because he has been interested only in her fortune. But Ernestina immediately knows he is lying and he confesses—only to offer another lie, slightly closer to the truth: he states that an earlier attachment to a woman he knew some years ago in London is not over and he must break off his engagement with her (75–76). Charles purposively does not tell Ernestina about Sarah, his lie an attempt to protect her from further hurt. The exposure of his affair occurs, however, when he is pressured into signing a confession of guilt in the presence of Ernestina's father and a set of lawyers.

What Charles has done, taken another woman while engaged to Ernestina, is understood as a criminal act. His friend Dr. Grogan makes this clear: when Grogan asks Charles if he intends to marry the "other woman," Charles answers, "That is my deepest wish." Grogan then bursts out with "You have committed a crime. It will fester in you all your life" (79). The crime is threefold: involvement with the unpredictable French Lieutenant's woman, violation of the moral pact established though his engagement with Ernestina, and confirmation of his total dissolution through a life devoted to an immoral woman. The *confessio delicti* Charles signs admits his criminality, acknowledging that he broke the engagement to marry Ernestina through his own "criminal selfishness and lust" and that his liaison has been "clandestine." This is a public form of punishment. As a consequence of his behavior, his dishonourable actions have meant the forfeiture of his "right to be considered a gentleman" (87).

Lies equally define the relationship of Mike and Anna who hide their affair from Mike's wife, Sonia, and Anna's boyfriend, David. Constant deception is the only way the affair can exist, although their own self-deception about their love is the greater lie. When on the set of the film in Dorset during the shooting of *The French Lieutenant's Woman*, Mike and Anna appear to maintain their love quite easily. But back in London, the watchful glare of Mike's wife and Anna's boyfriend forces it into hiding. The Sunday lunch party Mike and Sonia hold at their London home for the film's cast brings Mike and Anna publicly together, but in the painful and awkward presence of their significant others.[6] Their punishment will be their ultimate separation at the end of the film.

The power of passion ironically determines Pinter's choice of a romantic ending for the Victorian portion of *The French Lieutenant's Woman*: after three years of searching following his renunciation of Ernestina, Charles rediscovers Sarah. By contrast, Anna leaves Mike and chooses to return to David and America. Mike is left alone at the hotel window in the final scene. Ironically, love lives with the Victorians who will not accept lies but dies with the moderns who accept lying as a matter of course.

Lies and the question of truth are at the center of Rattigan's play, which, after its successful premiere on the stage in 1946, was adapted into a 1948 movie that starred Robert Donat, Margaret Leighton, and Cedric Hardwicke. Mamet, in fact, saw the film in Chicago as a youngster and discovered the play about 1979, when he was doing some revisions for an off-Broadway production of J.B. Priestly's *The Dangerous Corner*, becoming excited by its reconstruction of the late Victorian period and exact

language. What appealed to him was its "drama of manners" and its emphasis on fighting for what one believes is right (qtd. in Graham 17). It takes
courage to challenge the Admiralty and the Crown, who have supported the
accusations by the Naval College that young Ronnie Winslow stole the
postal order. The social cost is high: the family's finances shrink, the father's health deteriorates, the elder son must leave Oxford because of the
expense, and the daughter, Catherine, loses her fiancé because of the unfa-
vorable publicity and her suffragette ideas. Yet their commitment to the
truth and belief in the "Winslow Boy" that he *is* telling the truth displays
their heroism.

Punishment in the film takes the shape of the public embarrassment of
the First Lord of the Admiralty in Parliament and, subsequently, the commander, chief petty officer, and other officials of the Naval College. Underscoring the defeat of the government is the Attorney General's statement on
behalf of the Admiralty declaring Ronnie Winslow's innocence. The victory
belongs to the people as much as to the Winslows, which Arthur Winslow
emphasizes when he addresses the press at the end. The triumph, he declares, is not his, nor his family's, but the people's—a victory "over despotism," which he suddenly alters to the less pretentious statement, "'Thank
God We Beat 'Em'" (205).

For Mamet, whose characters are often shady figures for whom the
truth is malleable and lying frequently a means to an end, the clarity of
morality in *The Winslow Boy* was a welcomed change, although he had previously written several upright characters, notably Eliot Ness in Brian De-
Palma's *The Untouchables* and Gino, the honest Italian who refuses to lie
but still convinces a mob boss that he is *il capo di capo* in *Things Change,* a
film Mamet cowrote and directed.

In *The Winslow Boy,* it is bureaucracy, in the form of the Admiralty and
the government, who believe in the lie, not the family, nor the public. Interestingly, we see no one who believes the charges. The first words of the film
are Arthur Winslow's: "He's a good man" (which in the play occurs after the
opening scene of the returned Ronnie Winslow meeting the housekeeper;
107). They set the moral tone of the work, although the reference is ambiguous: the pronoun might refer to Ronnie Winslow, the boy, and it might not.
The conversation quickly reveals that the allusion is not to Ronnie but to the
preacher the family has just heard at church. Five lines later, Grace
Winslow, Ronnie's mother, prefigures the theme of the film when she asks,
"what's the use in being good if you're inaudible?" (107). This suggests the
intense and vocal defense the family will mount against the accusations that
young Ronnie Winslow stole a postal order for five shillings and forged the
signature of another student to cash it.

In the first of two inquisitions, after his father reads the letter turning
him out of the Naval Academy, Ronnie Winslow is told to speak the truth:

"if you tell me a lie, I shall know it, because a lie between you and me can't be hidden. I shall know it, Ronnie" (134).[7] When asked if he stole the order, Ronnie denies it. The second inquisition is more dramatic and is the high point of Rattigan's play and Mamet's film. The scene takes place in Sir Robert Morton's chambers at a hastily called meeting. Sir Robert, in fact, is to dine at Devonshire House and is glamorously shown donning his evening wear while the Winslow's straggle in (the 1948 movie has Sir Robert visit the Winslow home in cape and top hat for this meeting.). With everyone present, he begins to cross-examine the boy in an effort to determine the truth; depending on the outcome of the discussion, Sir Robert will decide whether or not to take the case. He quickly confuses young Ronnie Winslow, who despite his bewilderment, consistently denies the charges of forgery and theft, although he reveals that there is an unaccounted for twenty-five minutes in the locker room in which he could have easily taken the postal order of his friend, Charles Elliot.

Getting Ronnie to admit that he had practiced forging Elliot's signature was not difficult, nor the admission that Ronnie went to the locker room. Sir Robert then summarizes the reasons why Ronnie would have forged the signature and cashed the five shilling order, while Ronnie emphatically shouts that he is not "a forger, a liar, nor a thief" (163). Sir Robert seems convinced he is all three—or so it seems to the family and the audience. But then, with a marvellously understated flourish that Mamet copies from Rattigan's play, he has Sir Robert, now about to depart, abruptly turn to the family lawyer of the Winslows and declare, "Send all of his files here." "But, but, will you need them now?" the startled solicitor asks. Crisply, Sir Robert replies: "Oh, yes, the boy is plainly innocent. I accept the brief" (164). This *coup de théâtre,* which brought down the second act curtain in Rattigan's play, also brought forth applause from the audience: the unexpected reversal and precision of Sir Robert's action caught everyone but the playwright off-guard. The moment has precisely the sharpness and directness valued by Mamet and Pinter.[8]

How did Sir Robert know Ronnie told the truth? The mystery is revealed nine scenes later in Mamet's film when, in response to Catherine Winslow's question concerning what happened in the examination to make you sure he was innocent, Sir Robert explains: Ronnie made far too many damaging admissions that a guilty person would have worked to cover up; he failed to fall into a trap he set and then did not escape through a loophole he also outlined (176). The only remaining question was the unaccounted for twenty-five minutes. What happened during that period? The ever suave Sir Robert teases Catherine: she should have guessed what happened because she, too, indulges in this "crime"—smoking (176–77).

At the end of the film, right triumphs over justice in a speech underscoring the moral center of the screenplay. Hasn't justice been achieved, Catherine asks Sir Robert? "No. Not justice. Right. Easy to do Justice—very hard to do right," he states, explaining no more (209). Mamet also says no more, preferring the economy of statement to the distraction of explanations. To overexplain is to undermine the power of the scene, a principle Pinter made clear several years earlier in an interview concerning his screenplay for Joseph Losey's film, *Accident*: "it is the mystery that fascinates me: what happens between the words . . . when no words are spoken." "In this film," he continued, "everything happens, nothing is explained" (qtd. in Gale 242). Mamet's view is similar. In his short study, *On Directing Film,* Mamet writes, "you always want to tell the story in cuts. Which is to say through a juxtaposition of images that are basically uninflected" (2). Mamet elaborates this in *True and False*, his guide to acting: "Great drama, on stage or off, is not the performance of deeds with great emotion, but the performance of great deeds with no emotion whatever" (13).[9] Rattigan, however, felt the need to explain fully and has a further sentence in the play defending Sir Robert's emotionalism in court: "Unfortunately, while the appeal of justice is intellectual, the appeal of right appears for some odd reason to induce tears in court. That is my answer and excuse" (177).

Ironically, both Pinter and Mamet mitigate the punishment of their protagonists. There are costs to the reestablishment of the truth, to be sure, but there is not really much discipline directed to the offenders or sympathy to the victims. In *The French Lieutenant's Woman*, Ernestina suffers social embarrassment because Charles jilts her while her father seems to suffer more as the subject of gossip. Charles is temporarily humiliated by the scene in the lawyer's office when he signs the *confessio delicti,* the public pronouncement of his misbehavior, a broader but temporary form of punishment. His suffering, however, is more psychological, although limited only to the three years of searching for Sarah; interestingly, he has lost status but not income. When he finds Sarah, they unite after a momentary rejection and romantically disappear, gliding across a lake in a boat in the evening. Even Mike, who loses Anna at the end of the film, seems more heartbroken than "punished" for his affair as Anna drives off with seeming indifference into the night and back to her companion, David. Guilt for any of these actions is negligible. Nevertheless, the mores of the age demand some gesture of punishment.

In *The Winslow Boy* punishment is generic rather than individual. The family as a whole suffers but the government is punished or, rather, publicly censured. Arthur's finances diminish, his health deteriorates, his eldest son must leave Oxford and Catherine's fiancé decamps (she will find solace only in the suffragette cause and in flirting with Sir Robert). But publicly and personally, the family has triumphed. It is the government who must offer the apology and admit they were wrong in their accusations. In both films, lying is undone, deceit rejected, and honesty reasserted. There is no need for extensive punishment because the lies have either been exposed or expunged. But while the Admiralty and government have been reprimanded through the trial and their public admission of error, there is no suggestion that the Admiralty will ever change its ways.

III

Lying is offensive because it betrays language and invalidates morality. This is what outrages Pinter and Mamet. The Victorian and Edwardian periods shared this outlook and confirmed their own urgency for the truth that Galvin neatly summarizes in *The Verdict* when he tells Laura "we become tired of hearing people lie" (119). Pinter and Mamet both agree with Mamet's statement that "the theater affords an opportunity uniquely suited for communicating and inspiring ethical behavior." And when an actor deviates from the "through-line" of a piece, "he creates in himself the habit of moral turpitude; and the *play*, which is a strict lesson in ethics, is given the lie" (*Restaurants* 26, 25). *The French Lieutenant's Woman* and *The Winslow Boy* embody similar views.

Pinter and Mamet are lie detectors who challenge language as a sign of cultural and moral decay. Ernestina knows immediately that Charles is lying when he offers his lame excuse for ending their engagement. His manner and his words betray him. Conversely, Sir Robert accepts the truth of what Ronnie Winslow tells him because of his language; its simplicity, directness, and consistency confirm that the young boy is telling the truth, logically balancing Arthur Winslow's instinctive belief that his son has always told him the truth. Neither Sir Robert nor Arthur Winslow need further proof and while they may doubt the overall success of the case, they never question the honesty of young Ronnie.

By contrast, Charles uses lies to manipulate and even benefit his position, allowing lies to grow, even when they are misplaced. Ernestina, in her anger, assumes Charles's new love, the cause of their breakup, is married. He does not correct her but when he says, "I came to tell you the truth" and that this is "the most terrible decision of my life," she accuses him of lying (76). Charles persists in using lies for his own benefit, even late in the film when he tries to, and succeeds, in accusing Sarah of lying about her love for him. He expresses his anger at her apparent unconcern by flinging her to the ground as he leaves after accusing her of making a mockery "of love, of all human feeling;" she rejects his statement and asks his forgiveness of her deception of him (101). Her fall and injury force him to reconsider his charges and he conveniently renounces the lie he instigated (that she did not love him). Ironically, his forgiving her of a lie *he* actually set up convinces Sarah of the truthfulness of their love, although she seems unaware of his pattern of using lies for his benefit.

The victory of right rather than justice connects both works. The triumph of love, deeply felt, passionately touched, overrides the convenient and the conventional in marriage. Passion, not the purse, controls human behavior, although Charles must sacrifice his reputation in the process. Yet, he recovers some degree of self-esteem and triumphs by the end in winning Sarah. A similar victory occurs in *The Winslow Boy*. Despite last minute temptations to end the court fight—Arthur Winslow realizes that John Watherstone will refuse to marry Catherine unless the Winslows end their challenge to the Admiralty—the family persists with the case. Perhaps the only sacrifice or "punishment" in the film of note is Sir Robert's decision to turn down the offer of an important judicial post in the government in favor of continuing with *Winslow vs. Rex* (198).

When word arrives that they have won, first with Violet, the housekeeper, and then Sir Robert, Arthur Winslow accedes to the demands of the press at his door to make a statement, but with Sir Robert's sarcastic but truthful answer to the question, "what shall I say?" ringing in his ears: "whatever you say will have little bearing on what they write" (205). The film closes with a sharp but revealing exchange between Sir Robert and Catherine that contains unacted sexual overtones (added by Mamet) that may or may not continue. In a world without lies, romance may thrive.

Crime in both films is not a physical but a moral violation of the social order, a transgression in keeping with the tone and tenor of the times. Reflecting a late-nineteenth-century morality that, on one hand, reverted to lying as a means to deflect the harshness of the truth and, on the other, constructed a lie to mask the truth, Pinter and Mamet share the view that while lying is hardly ever defensible, it is a natural response to preserving the status quo or resolving a threatening situation.[10] But because it is morally unacceptable, it must also be punished.

What did Pinter and Mamet find dramatically powerful about lying as a crime? Why didn't they tailor their adaptations to reflect the kind of criminal life they had portrayed in their own work on the stage and screen? The answers may lie in their confirmation that the Victorian and Edwardian periods shared their own outrage against deceit while acknowledging its existence. Additionally, their source-texts provided an alternative to the amoral worlds found in their own work. Instead of the menacing and often violent nature of crime seen or reported in *The Room* or *Ashes to Ashes*, in *American Buffalo* or *Homicide*, *The French Lieutenant's Woman* and *The Winslow Boy* allowed Pinter and Mamet to substitute morality for violence, ethics for action. And the lie became the answer Pinter and Mamet offered to the question, "what is a crime?"

Notes

1. Pinter's filmscript for Joseph Losey's movie *Accident* neatly illustrates this: the car crash that precipitates the action occurs off-screen. We hear the noise and witness the aftermath but do not see the violence.

2. *Homicide,* for example, bookends its story with violence, first with the violent attack in the police station on Gold, the Jewish detective, by a murderer in a holding cell who seizes his pistol and then at the end with the brutal battle between Gold and Randolph, the cop killer. The murder of the candy store owner, Mrs. Klein, and then the death of Gold's partner, Sullivan, in a gun fight are further moments of on-screen violence. Such scenes are balanced by Gold's visit to the elegant but sedate apartment of the son of the murdered Mrs. Klein and the scene in the Jewish library where a librarian and Chassidic student assist him in understanding the Kabbalistic implications of some of the clues he has pieced together.

3. The solution was not Pinter's but the director's, Karl Reisz. Pinter, however, thought through the structure of the new framing story and wrote the script incorporating both Mike and Anna, as well as Charles and Sarah. See Pinter in Michael Billington, *The Life and Work of Harold Pinter* (London: Faber and Faber, 1996), 272–73.

4. For a negative view of Pinter's method see Sarah Lorsch, "Pinter Fails Fowles: Narration in *The French Lieutenant's Woman,*" *Literature Film Quarterly* 16 (1988): 144–54. Lorsch's critique is that Pinter's double narrative shows the greater similarity between the Victorian and modern periods; Fowles, she argues, stresses the reverse. On differences between the screenplay and the actual film, see Peter J. Conradi, "*The French Lieutenant's Woman*: Novel, Screenplay, Film," *Critical Quarterly* 24 (1982): 41–57.

5. The most useful analytical study of lying from a literary and cultural perspective is J.A. Barnes, *A Pack of Lies, Towards a Sociology of Lying* (Cambridge: Cambridge UP, 1994). For a literary/ linguistic discussion of "the most important pun in the language," lie/lie (to misrepresent and to lie down) see Christopher Ricks, "Lies," *Critical Quarterly* 2 (1975): 121–42.

6. Tom Stoppard develops this as the opening gambit of *The Real Thing*, his 1982 play in which we learn in the second scene that the playwright Henry is having an affair with the actress Annie while he remains married to Charlotte. Max is Annie's husband who is acting in a play by Henry starring Henry's wife, Charlotte.

7. Mamet has almost an identical passage in *The Verdict* when Galvin speaks to Laura: "Now tell me the truth. Because you cannot lie to me." *The Verdict,* unpublished screenplay, 37.

8. In his movie, Mamet places the moment in scene 39–40, just past the midpoint; there are seventy-four scenes in the film.

   The Mamet-Pinter relationship originated in the mid-1970s. In several interviews, Mamet has attributed his early use of the sketch and blackout, developed in *Sexual Perversity in Chicago,* to similar work by Pinter, notably his *A Night Out* and *Revue Sketches.* Their friendship solidified in the early 1980s when Mamet sent Pinter a draft of *Glengarry Glen Ross* for comment; Pinter liked it immensely and forwarded it the National for production. Mamet, in gratitude, dedicated the work to him. Pinter directed the 1993 premiere of *Oleanna* at the Royal Court Theatre, London. There is also a link to Rattigan: in the mid-1960s, Pinter was among the then younger playwrights who advocated Rattigan's work, which had gone out of favor. Both Rattigan and Pinter celebrate the unspoken, although in the former it represents suppressed emotion, in the latter, usually a veiled threat. For details on the Rattigan-Pinter connection, see Geoffrey Wansell, *Terence Rattigan: A Biography* (1995), passim.

9. In the "Preface" to *On Directing Film*, Mamet asserts that "a good writer gets better only by learning to *cut*, to remove the ornamental, the descriptive, the narrative and *especially* the deeply felt and meaningful" (xv).

10. Mamet develops this idea in *The Cryptogram* when Del is caught telling lies about the knife he supposedly received from Robert. This becomes an act of betrayal not a slip of memory. On the nature of deception and the unravelling of lies in the play see Leslie Kane, *Weasels and Wisemen, Ethics and Ethnicity in the Work of David Mamet* (New York: St. Martin's Press, 1999), 203–12.

Works Cited

Arendt, Hannah. *Between Past and Present*. New York: Viking, 1968.

Aristotle, *Nicomachean Ethics*. Trans. H. Rackham. 2nd ed. London: Heinemann, 1947.

Barnes, J. A. *A Pack of Lies: Towards a Sociology of Lying*. Cambridge: Cambridge UP, 1994.

Billington, Michael. *The Life and Work of Harold Pinter.* London: Faber and Faber, 1996.

Blake, William. "Auguries of Innocence." *The Poems of William Blake*. Ed. W. H. Stevenson, text by David V. Erdman. London: Longman, 1971.

Bok, Sisella. *Lying: Moral Choice in Public and Private Life*. New York: Quartet Books, 1986.

––––––. *Secrets: On the Ethics of Concealment and Revelation*. New York: Pantheon, 1982.

Browning, Robert. "Mr. Sludge the Medium." *Poetical Works, 1833–1864*. Ed. Ian Jack. Oxford: Oxford UP, 1970.

Butler, Samuel. "Truth and Convenience." *Notebooks*. Ed. Henry Festing Jones. London: A.C. Fifield, 1912.

Byron, Lord. *Don Juan*. Ed. T.G. Steffan, et al. New Haven: Yale UP, 1982.

Conradi, Peter J. "*The French Lieutenant's Woman*: Novel, Screenplay, Film" *Critical Quarterly* 24 (1982): 41–57.

Ford, Charles V. *Lies! Lies! Lies!*. Washington, DC: American Psychiatric Press, 1996.

Fowles, John. Foreword. *The French Lieutenant's Woman: A Screenplay*. By Harold Pinter. Boston: Little Brown, 1981. i–xv.

Gale, Steven F. *Butter's Going Up*. Durham, NC: Duke UP, 1977.

Gopnik, Adam. "What's Cooking." *New Yorker* 4 Sept. 2000, 86.

Graham, Reneé. "Mamet with Manners." *Boston Globe,* 2 May 1999, N17.

James, Nick. "Suspicion," *Sight and Sound* 8 (Oct. 1998): 10.

Kane, Leslie. *Weasels and Wisemen: Ethics and Ethnicity in the Work of David Mamet*. New York: St. Martin's Press, 1999.

Mamet, David. *American Buffalo*. New York: Grove Press, 1996.

——. *Glengarry Glen Ross*. New York: Grove Press, 1984.

——. *On Directing Film*. New York: Penguin, 1992.

——. *True and False, Heresy and Common Sense for the Actor*. New York: Vintage, 1999.

——. *The Verdict*. unpub. screenplay

——. *The Winslow Boy. The Spanish Prisoner and The Winslow Boy: Two Screenplays*. New York: Vintage, 1999.

——. *Writing in Restaurants*. New York: Viking, 1987.

Nietzsche, Frederich. *Beyond Good and Evil*. Trans. Walter Kaufman, et al. New York: Random House, 1967.

Pinter, Harold. *The Caretaker*. Rev. ed. London: Methuen, 1963.

——. *The French Lieutenant's Woman: A Screenplay*. Boston: Little Brown, 1981.

Rattigan, Terrence. *The Winslow Boy. Plays: One*. Intr. Anthony Curtis. London: Methuen, 1999.

Ricks, Christopher. "Lies." *Critical Inquiry* 2 (1975): 121–42.

Stevenson, Robert Louis. "Truth of Intercourse." *Virginibus Puerisque*. London: Kegan Paul, 1881.

Tennyson, Alfred Lord. "The Grandmother." *The Poems of Tennyson in Three Volumes*. Ed. Christopher Ricks. 2nd ed. London: Longmans, 1987.

Wansell, Geoffrey. *Terrence Rattigan*. London: Fourth Estate, 1995.

Wilde, Oscar. "The Decay of Lying." *The Artist as Critic*. Ed. Richard Ellmann. New York: Vintage B, 1970, 290–320.

8

Gradations of Criminality
in the Plays of David Mamet

KIMBALL KING

In many, perhaps the majority, of Mamet's works the behavior of his protagonists may seem "criminal" in that it is cruel or exploitative, a clear violation of personal obligations or an attack on values that sustain human
communities. Plays such as *Sexual Perversity in Chicago* (1974), *The Water
Engine* (1977), *The Woods* (1977), *Speed-the-Plow* (1988), or *Oleanna*
(1993) contain numerous personal betrayals, invasions of privacy, and violations of conventional ethics; yet, they stop short of criminal punishable offenses. The young couple who assault each other physically in *The Woods*
are more clearly co-conspirators than, say, the female student who is physically attacked by her professor in the final scene of *Oleanna*. In both cases,
however, audiences are made uncomfortable by their unwitting participation
in socially unacceptable violence, often surprised to learn they can drop
their civilized masks and enjoy the physical retaliation that erupts as a result
of verbal sparring. In other plays, the line is crossed between ethically re-
pugnant but legal actions and overly antisocial, prosecutable acts.

The protagonist of *Edmond* (1982) slashes a pimp and kills a prostitute.
And a year later in *Glengarry Glen Ross* (1983) an office burglary has dire
consequences and depicts the breaking of laws. Overt physical violence is
always regarded as deplorable in Mamet's plays, which are sensitive to ethical issues and dramatize the conflict between individual needs and the demands of community. It is never clear whether the individual in the
community will survive this conflict. From *American Buffalo* in 1975 onward Mamet permits us to observe the fragmentation of modern communities, especially the urban worlds, and the sexism and racism that threatens a
fragile social fabric. When the laws of society are literally transgressed, by
murder, burglary, rape, or unwarranted physical assaults, he forces his audience to confront the ultimate moral and ethical issues that can sustain or
wreck a civilization. While his dialogue and settings preserve a sense of

contemporary life, their psychological impact is more surreal. Mamet the craftsman and philosopher dares to name the "crimes" of modern life, that actions have consequences and that while moral boundaries are easily transgressed, personal satisfaction remains evasive and unpunished crimes lead to a wasteland, not a Utopia.

Socially irresponsible behavior may be amusingly described in Mamet's dialogue but it is not rewarded. The young "studs" in *Sexual Perversity in Chicago* may be rivals in real or imagined sexual conquests but their puerile boasts and desires result in their being deprived of genuine intimacy with another. Similarly, *Edmond*'s protagonist is punished for his racist and homophobic attitudes when he becomes the sex slave of a black man after he is sent to prison. And while the greedy proprietors of the corrupt real estate firm in *Glengarry Glen Ross* are free to accumulate wealth at the play's end, protected from petty theft by the law that punishes desperate underlings for criminal behavior, they sit precariously on the top of a crumbling financial pyramid. In a later play, Bobby Gould and his partner in *Speed-the-Plow* preserve their high salaries and "insider" status in the cynical film industry at the expense of their personal integrity and self-esteem. Such characters reflect the fact that Western society in the twentieth century and at the beginning of the twentieth-first century has, for the most part, adapted to a laissez-faire morality, situation ethics, and a refusal on the part of many artists to assert rules for social behavior. Mamet may be alone among major American playwrights to reveal the shallowness and futility of ethical systems that permit personal, and often self-serving, interpretations of acceptable human behavior. His literary predecessors, Arthur Miller in the United States and George Bernard Shaw, Tom Stoppard, and others in Great Britain, did not hesitate to identify actions they considered immoral nor fail to show how language could be shaped to conceal the truth or to make a pragmatic "bending" of moral codes acceptable to ordinary people.

Superficially, Mamet appears to share ethical concerns with these playwrights. For example, a possessive uncle's betrayal of two young immigrants to the immigration authorities in Miller's *A View from the Bridge* parallels the betrayal of the real estate salesmen by a corrupt coworker in *Glengarry Glen Ross*. And Shaw's Professor Higgins and Dr. Pickering wager that they can transform a flower girl into a duchess in Shaw's *Pygmalion*, anticipating the bet between two Hollywood would-be moguls that one of them could seduce "the temp" in Mamet's *Speed-the-Plow*. Similarly, Archie in Stoppard's *Jumpers* argues that there is no such thing as "good" or "bad," only how you "feel" about it. He is as unconcerned with the murdered Professor Mcfee as Edmond is with the prospect of killing a pimp and a prostitute. Nevertheless, Mamet presents evidence of right and wrong in every one of his artistic endeavors, clarifying civilization's dependence on identifiable moral laws.

Yet, it seems that in a reassessment of Mamet's major plays and the enormous body of critical response to his work that has been generated in the past two decades, the presence of Mamet's gradations of criminality is less apparent than the irrelevancy of these gradations. The failures of American society are most frequently attributed to images of capitalism run amok and the self-congratulatory language of support, which encourages situation ethics and relativistic morality. As long as there are no moral absolutes, no inviolate ten commandments of behavior, each character deludes himself or herself into believing that what is best for one individual is applicable to others. Nearly all of Mamet's plays, novels, and screenplays reveal these same patterns, but the stage plays especially illustrate this contention. *Edmond, Glengarry Glen Ross,* and *Speed-the-Plow* each capture a special aspect of Mamet's assertion in relation to criminality. *Edmond* deals with the conflict between conventional domestic life and the assumed liberation of the individual. *Glengarry Glen Ross* depicts the essential role of the business ethic in shaping American values, and *Speed-the-Plow* is concerned with the manufacture and sale of images to promulgate both the mock-existential pose of American individualists and the triumph of commercial values over such pretenses.

In the first play, Edmond, a trendy 1980s spouse, leaves his wife in order, he says, "to find myself" (17). His first act of self-assertion involves a quest for sexual release; however, the bar girl whom he hopes to take to bed not only charges a high fee for personal access but is obliged to share her profits with the bartender, bar owner, and virtually a whole chain of entrepreneurs, which make her accessibility beyond the price Edmond is willing to pay. An encounter with a peep-show performer is no more satisfactory. Separated by a plexiglass wall, Edmond must pay for the illusion of sexual contact, all the while bitterly complaining that he would like to remove the unwanted barrier. When he finally locates a prostitute he finds he must barter first with her pimp, who wants his percentage of the money Edmond has agreed to pay her. Enraged, Edmond slashes the pimp with what he euphemistically refers to as his "survival knife."

Later, imploring the prostitute to admit that she is actually a waitress and not the "actress" she says she is (ironic because Edmond is hardly the modern Don Quixote figure he would claim to be), he ends his argument by killing her. Soon imprisoned, he is forced to become the sex slave of a black criminal. Unlike Mamet's *Edmond*, Albee's *Zoo Story*, in which a similarly alienated middle-class male is driven to an atavistic act of violence (albeit defending himself against Jerry, a deranged self-proclaimed prophet), there is no suggestion that Edmond, like Peter in Albee's play, has learned from his experience, or that he will demonstrate greater tolerance in the future or perhaps even enter into a discipleship to continue an idealistic vision such as Jerry's. Still, Edmond accepts the "justice" of his new subservient role and expresses an odd affection for the man who molests him sexually, just as Peter in the *Zoo Story* remains to defend his seat on the park bench because of his implicit, possibly sexual, attraction to the dangerous, suicidal Jerry.

Edmond and *Glengarry Glen Ross* are plays that Jon Tuttle has compared philosophically to Joseph Conrad's *Heart of Darkness* (157), and C.W.E. Bigsby has selected Christopher Lasch's *The Culture of Narcissism* to help explain Mamet's underlying purposes in *Edmond* (Bigsby 101). Both studies clarify important issues, of course. From resemblances to Bertolt Brecht and Edward Bond, Arthur Miller and Eugene O'Neill (as well as to Conrad and Lasch—and, perhaps, Tom Stoppard), Mamet may have drawn on a series of literary predecessors and contemporaries, or, at least, he may have explored social issues that also intrigued them. All of the writers whom he resembles share an overriding passion for moral definition. Ultimately we must ask if Mamet's characters have been overtaken by their own atavistic impulses, even as they might have attempted to avoid a descent into their personal hells, if they are driven by the relentless injustice of capitalism and the spectre of universal greed, or if extreme individualism—perhaps as a byproduct of capitalistic self-interest—has doomed them to solipsistic despair. The one point of agreement between the Marxists and Freudians and latter-day cultural anthropologists is that Mamet has created a bleak, corrupt backdrop for his floundering and generally despairing characters. Tuttle has said that perhaps a "deconstructionist reading" might find elements of hope in the absence of any positive redemptive signs, preferring himself to believe that Mamet shows how easily man reverts to his most bestial instincts (168). Without insisting that the portrayal of evil necessarily implies the existence of some sort of good, it is still possible to see signs of what, for lack of a better term, we might call "goodness" in Mamet's plays. If mankind is made up entirely of actors playing roles that are stereotypes of corruption, they might, given different roles to play, be capable of altruistic impulses. Yet how does one audition for better roles in Mamet's universe? In Mamet-land every human transaction seems to be attached to a price. One can purchase companionship, sex, the material goods that others possess; but the traditional conception of a friendship in a functioning community with its requirements of loyalty, forgiveness, and compassion implies a kind of bonding of neighbor to neighbor that seems tragically absent in the affluent milieu of the late twentieth century.

In *Glengarry Glen Ross* a Chicago real estate firm attempts to sell essentially worthless tracts of land in Florida to petty entrepreneurs, who like the early pioneers, according to Mamet, wanted "something for nothing" (qtd. in Bigsby 111). Set upon an emblematic American pyramid model, where the top salesperson receives a Cadillac and the less successful ones are fired, the firm distributes the names of probable customers (so-called top leads) to the currently successful sales staff, while assigning the names of proven "deadbeats" to less adequate personnel, thereby insuring their doom. Eventually one of the salesmen past his prime, Shelly Levene, robs the company safe for "good leads," which he proposes to sell to a real estate competitor. Yet Levene is no more despicable than the arrogant top salesman, Ricky Roma, or the firm's owners, Mitch and Murray, who never appear but apparently keep the lion's share of profits generated by their underlings. By feigning the values of friendship, family, and personal loyalty all the salesmen hope to seduce potential "marks" into buying their bogus product. The mixture of lies and self-deceptions in each sales pitch reveals perversions of language and communication, although it also evokes a wistful longing for a world in which ethical exchanges might yet be possible.

Tony J. Stafford in "Visions of a Promised Land" stops short of an allegorical reading of *Glengarry Glen Ross* but he does offer the intriguing suggestion that Levene, Moss, and Aaronow are older Jewish men who might be identified with Old Testament figures and have been attracted to the real estate business partly by their personal searches for a "promised land" (192). Ricky Roma, Mitch, and Murray are more likely to be gentiles, associated both with conquering Rome (in Roma's case) and latter-day Christian entrepreneurial types (193). However, the frequent allusions to Old Testament figures and the motif of land for sale imply, Stafford believes, that "the division of the conflict into old versus new, age versus youth, previous values versus current vales and spiritual beliefs versus material beliefs, gives a sense of historical perspective wherein the ancient traditions have been replaced with a modern day religion based on greed, deceit and spiritual bankruptcy" (194). Similarly, in her 1999 study of Mamet, *Weasels and Wisemen*, Leslie Kane concurs that the playwright uses allusion to such archetypal biblical characters as Moses, Aaron, and the Levites "as a link between ancient and modern worlds, values, aspirations and spirituality" (61). Yet it is clear that a callous business consortium has, in a sense, replaced ancient Judaic concepts of community and moral obligations. As a result the characters in *Glengarry Glen Ross* are caught in a moral dilemma, trapped between their desire to possess the land or gain from its sale and their longing for old value systems.

In much the same way, Arthur Miller reveals the very early breakdown of community in *Death of a Salesman* (1949) and the disturbing onslaught on family ties caused by a burgeoning materialism. Unlike the late legendary Dave Singleman, a salesman whose funeral was attended by hundreds of people, Willy's mourners include only his wife, sons, and neighbor, Charlie, whose son, unlike Willy's boys, is not dysfunctional, becoming, in fact, a successful attorney. Willy's encouragement of the boys to cultivate "false" values of popularity and personal attractiveness has probably not harmed them as much as his dependence on their achieving financial success as a means of justifying his own value as a father and person. At least in

Miller's play, the audience is allowed to focus on the protagonist's neurotic response to material pressures. In the world of *Glengarry*, the frantic salesmen appear to live outside the supports of a family life, except perhaps when Shelly Levene alludes to his daughter's fragile health, with a mumbling, ambiguous plea, "John: My daughter . . ." (Mamet 62). Twice his imprecations fall on his boss John Williamson's deaf ears. Whether we consider breaking into a company safe to steal profitable leads as a justifiable response to administrative oppression or not, we recognize that a law has been broken and that punishment, in some degree, will be meted out. Mamet insists that laws exist to preserve order in the world and that at some level crimes will always be punished. Mitch and Murray may escape, for the moment, the mundane punishments that an office robbery may entail but the audience is reminded that a day of reckoning comes to all transgressors.

In *Speed-the-Plow* (1988), however, which Mamet wrote five years after *Glengarry Glen Ross*, no actual law is broken, unless we consider a possible case of sexual harassment by an employer. The corrupt Hollywood milieu of *Speed-the-Plow* corresponds, though, to a Chicago real estate company's ruthlessness in *Glengarry Glen Ross*, and the cruelty and sexism of its male protagonists are extreme. Bobby Gould and his colleagues are as rapacious and destructive as any of Mamet's characters, but their marauding violates the "spirit" of the law rather then the "word" of the law and hence is not punishable in an earthly court. "Criminality" at last is not merely a disregard for the community's legal system but an assault on its core values of mutual respect and protection of the weak. In this play, Bobby Gould is a recently promoted head of movie production and Charlie Fox is his assistant producer. Reasonably comfortable with a project to film, "Doug Brown: A Buddy Film," which is sure to make the studio a profit and preserve Gould's and Fox's jobs, the two Hollywood moguls are confronted by a temporary secretary, Karen, who has read a compelling book about radiation and who proposes that the studio produce an intelligent, environmentally correct film for a change. Mamet by implication raises the issue of whether Hollywood satisfies the already established needs of its audiences or inculcates in them a desire for mindless violence and sentimental pieties. Gould bets Fox five hundred dollars that he can seduce Karen. In turn he is nearly seduced into producing her film preference until Fox recalls him to his materialistic senses. Karen's virtue and her intellectual project are both sacrificed, and production of a new buddy film is imminent. As Kane has noted, Gould is motivated both "by fear and his desire to do good" but is rescued (if we subscribe to the Hollywood view) by Fox, who "brings about a change in time—thereby saving his own life and career and that of his friend" (*David Mamet* 96)—from, presumably, his higher (but weaker) impulses.

Although the protagonists of *Speed-the-Plow* find it necessary to succumb to prevailing values in a corrupt society, Mamet demonstrates his belief in the possibility of altruistic behavior and moral choice while emphasizing the dark side of his characters' natures. For example, in *Edmond* any observer of Edmond's world recognizes his and his wife's neglectful attitude toward marital responsibilities, as well as the self-absorption and irresponsibility of contemporary men and women in general, which lead to their casual acceptance of sexual immorality and outbursts of violence. One longs for the kind word, tender gesture, and unselfish commitment. Similarly the deceived customers of relentless predators in *Glengarry Glen Ross* are vulnerable because they are greedy, guilty, or unsure of their value as human beings. Salesmen *and* victims are products of the same materialistic social construction. Finally in *Speed-the-Plow* one must not overlook public complicity in the acceptance of "bad taste," no-content movies and literature, the sexist presumptions of so-called buddy films, and the obsession with adventure over moral definition. In every case Mamet exposes society's immorality and by implication challenges us to alter a system that makes the dysfunctional possible.

In addition to these plays, two recent Mamet screenplays seem particularly relevant to the subject of criminality, *The Spanish Prisoner* (1998) and *The Winslow Boy* (1999), both featuring Mamet's wife, Rebecca Pigeon, as the leading female protagonist. The first of these films, *The Spanish Prisoner*, is set in contemporary America and some off-shore islands of the Caribbean and focuses on a computer software inventor who wants to be paid fairly for his invention, which has been named "the Process." The plot centers on a "con game," in which corrupt business practices lure the characters into criminal actions. The second film, *The Winslow Boy*, presents Mamet's adaptation of a 1947 play about British justice by Terence Rattigan. Here a fourteen-year-old English schoolboy is expelled from school for supposedly forging a postal money order. No one believes in his innocence except his own family and a conservative lawyer with what turns out to be an undeserved reputation for self-aggrandizement. In both *The Spanish Prisoner* and *The Winslow Boy* criminality is defeated and the more virtuous characters are vindicated.

The title of *The Spanish Prisoner* refers to a "con game" in which a supposedly wealthy person befriends an emotionally and financially needy person, exploiting and framing him or her at the same time. For a person to be "conned" he or she must be to some extent vulnerable to greed, easy money, or undeserved prestige. In a rather confusing plot, which includes the presence of the F.B.I. seeking to capture the con-artists, the computer-nerd hero Joe Ross avoids being conned and killed by his corrupt employers. Once again big business is seen as the source of corruption, and an unwillingness to pay a deserving employee fairly unleashes a series of violent events. With Mamet's devotion to natural speech, there is some crude dialogue, and yet the movie is rated PG and the characters' conversations sound almost decorous when compared to those in *Glengarry Glen Ross*. The protagonist learns, nearly too late, that the seemingly honest and financially disinterested secretary whom he befriends is an integral part of the con, willing in fact to order his execution. Ross, a semi-honest man, with far more altruistic qualities than bad ones, has no family or established social circle. His one tenuous connection with humanity is a disloyal, even treacherous girlfriend. In many ways he recalls Kafka's justly paranoid "Joseph K." Mamet appears to be warning us once more that disengagement may at first create the illusion of personal freedom but leads us closer to a moral abyss. James Bernardinelli, reviewing the film, argues that "the current business climate rewards those who act ruthlessly and punishes those who hold to a code of ethics" (4). Ross is mockingly referred to as a "Boy Scout," as if the values of that organization are inappropriate in the 1990s, but it is with the "Boy Scout" in Ross that the audience identifies. On the other hand, *The Winslow Boy*, based on an actual case in England in which a family sued to secure the honor of its young son, might seem to be an unlikely vehicle to elucidate the author's views on criminality. Yet it comes closer than many of his works to directly expressing his ethical system. The film follows Rattigan's plot and dialogue closely, clearly asserting the principle of honor as an absolute. There is a subtle difference in that neither the boy's mother nor his sister in the original work had such clear feminist leanings, yet as Rattigan based his play on a real-life criminal case, it is possible that the actual mother and sister were more assertive, as Mamet presents them in the movie. Another more significant change rests on the altered sequence of events from play to film. In the play an unexplained gap in time that the son refuses to account for might have contributed to the skepticism of the boy's accusers, for Rattigan reveals only at his play's conclusion that the boy had lingered in the locker room after dinner for an illegal smoke, which he is afraid to admit. Wisely, Mamet's movie explains this secret to us in an early scene since the breaking of school rules by smoking is a mild infraction in the present world of drugs and violence that has intruded into so many twentieth-century secondary schools. In both play and film the Winslow family sense of honor is so great that the father, in particular, is willing to inflict hardships on each of its members by pursuing a costly legal defense. His elder son is forced to leave University and his daughter's affluent fiancé backs out of his engagement. There is even talk that the family's loyal servant—and emblem of their middle-class status—might be sacked. Fortunately, Sir Robert Morton, a skillful barrister, exposes a forgery and other evidence that had been unfairly used to incriminate the boy. Triumphantly Morton tells the Winslow's daughter that the jury reached not only a "just" decision but a "right" one. The distinction is significant. In a world governed by principle, and to some extent by moral absolutes, "right" and "wrong" can be clearly defined.

Bernardinelli believes that *The Winslow Boy* asks two principal questions of its viewers: "At what point does a 'quest for justice' turn into an exercise in pride and self interest" and "How does what's right differ from what justice demands" (7)? Rattigan, writing in 1939, clearly believed that the senior Winslow's defense of his family's honor—and social position—was heroic. Mrs. Winslow, as played by Gemma Jones in the Mamet film, questions the autocratic nature of her husband's decisions concerning the lawsuit and demands that he consider personal vanity as a motive for his zealotry. The preservation of community, Mamet may be arguing, could be related to maintaining a degree of status while justice under the law must concern itself with the maintenance of civilization. "What is right" seems to represent a more personal, possibly metaphysical privileging of truth.

The values of justice, land, and community in Mamet's plays are linked inevitably to his use of violence and criminal behavior. Anne Dean, writing in 1990, makes an astute comparison of English playwright Edward Bond's work with Mamet's. She suggests that while Bond uses "the most appalling violence to emphasize his political points," Mamet utilizes "obscene language as a means of pointing to the spiritual malaise that he considers endemic to the United States" (35). While anyone would agree that Mamet's stage dialogue is patently obscene, it might be argued that his plays contain as much violent behavior as Bond's. Bond has often found himself in the position of defending violence in his plays, as he did when British censors threatened to close down *Saved* because it contained the notorious scene where a baby in a carriage was being stoned by young toughs. In the preface to his play, *Lear*, here appropriating the title of Shakespeare's masterpiece (which surely contains as much violence as any contemporary play), Bond writes: "I write about violence as naturally as Jane Austen wrote about manners. Violence shapes and obsesses our society and if we do not stop being violent we have no future. People who do not want writers to write about violence want to stop them writing about us and our time. It would be immoral not to write about violence" (qtd. in Dean 36).

Both Bond and Mamet lament the collapse of communities where human life is no longer treated with any dignity or respect. And they appear to share the belief that corruption starts at the top, rather than the bottom of society. For example, Mamet once told Matthew Roudané that "the hierarchical business system tends to corrupt. It becomes legitimate for those in the business world to accept petty crime; the effect on the little guy is that he turns to crime, and petty crime goes punished; major crimes go unpunished" (qtd. in Roudané 75). And he told Richard Gottlieb that there was essentially no difference between the *lumpenproletariat* and stockbroker and corporate lawyers because "at a certain point vicious behavior becomes laudable" (qtd. in Mc-Intire-Strasburg 8).

While a critical comparison between the works of Edward Bond and of David Mamet might be expected, a comparison between Tom Stoppard's work and Mamet's seems more tentative. Yet Stoppard, in plays such as *Jumpers*, posits a conflict between those who embrace situation ethics and moral relativity, such as Archie, the psychiatrist/acrobat who challenges George, a "mossy" professor who defends moral absolutes. Similarly, Mamet taunts us with a series of incidents that would at first glance appear to endorse a relativistic position. For example, lying to customers is seen as an entirely appropriate role for a salesman in *Glengarry Glen Ross*. Yet stealing "leads" out of a company safe is perceived as a criminal act by all the corrupted and corrupting salesmen. The audience reaction adds an additional moral twist. Since the entire real estate operation that the salesmen labor for is exploitive and dishonest, robbing it seems "just," rather than "criminal." This particular business *deserves* to be robbed, the audience reasons. Corruption in Mamet's world is so pervasive that any audience observing aspects of it begins to question preconceived concepts of right and wrong, especially since in the particular world Mamet has described the moral and the immoral choices are never clear-cut opposites. Dorothy Moore, the female protagonist in Stoppard's *Jumpers*, questions whether the Ten Commandments are equally applicable to life on the moon, say, as well as on the earth. Similarly, Mamet's mise-en-scènes are often "moonscapes" reflecting life as most of us know it on earth, forcing us to question whether anything we have considered at some time is real or actually an illusion.

Not only Stoppard but also George Bernard Shaw share some philosophical turf with Mamet. To place a bet on the fate of another person constitutes an immoral denial of his or her individuality and worth, and yet both Mamet and Shaw have presented situations that most audiences accept without question. Seldom are there complaints about the inhumanity of Professor Higgins and his friend Pickering, wagering that Higgins can or cannot turn Eliza Doolittle into a counterfeit duchess. Similarly in *Speed-the-Plow*, Bobby Gould's bet that he can seduce his secretary is made more acceptable to audiences by our implicit understanding of Hollywood's corruption. What so-called nice girl expects to influence an unscrupulous movie producer with intellectual arguments? There is an assumption that one's morality is best preserved by staying away from Hollywood rather than by attempting to reform it. Shaw's *Pygmalion* (an underrated play whose virtues perhaps have been unfairly tainted by its having been successfully adapted to musical form) strongly expresses Shaw's belief in the wickedness of the affluent who meddle in the lives of the poor. But Shaw was able to amuse the upper-middle-class and upper-class people he was satirizing to the point at which they could, with an unconscious act of denial, refuse to see their own duplicity but bask happily in the knowledge that they were "linguistically" superior to others. Shaw's play concerns the debasement of language because pronunciation is considered more important than content—the way one says things matters more than what one says.

In *Pygmalion*'s most comic—and brilliant—scene, the former flower girl, Eliza, who has been instructed in phonetics by Professor Higgins, is given a "test-run" at a tea given by his mother. Although Eliza has learned to pronounce words perfectly, she reveals in her conversation the tawdry realities of working-class British life. Her comments shock and amuse Mrs. Eynsford-Hill and her son, Freddy, respectively; but neither is troubled by Eliza's disclosures about her disreputable family because her mastery of an upper-class accent nullifies her crude reflections on life. An audience responds with hysterical laughter to this incongruity, but I believe that Shaw subversively intends to show that any amused audience is vulnerable to placing more emphasis on the way something sounds than on what it means. Higgins and his mother realize the truths Eliza is communicating about her life; the Eynsford-Hills do not.

Similarly, Mamet is able to show in *Glengarry* and other plays that language, often comic in its deliberate vagueness or transparent insincerity, is used to confuse, to mislead, or to preach conventional pieties that most of the characters know to be false. Bigsby has gone so far as to say that the only moment of "honesty" in the play occurs when a character "refuses to name his accomplice" and remains silent. Bigsby adds, "There is evidentially an honesty in this silence which is not there in speech" (116). But Bigsby may also have been seduced by the moral relativity of *Glengarry*'s world. It is true that a character's refusal to expose an accomplice reveals unexpected principle, but it is not, in fact, evidence of his "honesty." Differing from Shaw (yet like him in his exposé of hypocrisy), Mamet attempts to show that what is not said is more important than actual utterance.

In her interview with Gregory Mosher, Kane and the director of *Glengarry Glen Ross* both note the unsentimental nature of Mamet's works (*David Mamet* 240). Most British playwrights I've observed share Mamet's distaste for sentimentality. Even the relatively light-hearted Alan Ayckbourn will not allow his audiences to resort to a sentimental acceptance of life, as do the American audiences of, say, Neil Simon. Thus, in Ayckbourn's *A Small Family Business*, an English family, struggling to maintain its middle-class prosperity, has sustained its private company through increasingly corrupt and illegal machinations. Nevertheless, it appears to have preserved the tenuous bonds between family members, and they are seated at the conclusion of the play in a more-or-less celebratory dinner. Yet as the audience watches what might otherwise be a tender moment, the open set reveals a missing daughter in an upstairs bathroom injecting heroin into her arm.

In Mamet's works, criminality begins with a failure to use language to convey meaning. The clever use of words to obfuscate and mislead by the salesmen of Glengarry, the inability of Edmond to connect with others, including his wife of several years, and the mastery of "Hollywood Speak" in

Speed-the-Plow, as well as the failure of the naive inventor in *The Water Engine* to protect himself, his sister, or his invention, as he is verbally outsmarted by a corrupt and ultimately criminal "establishment," all indicate that innocence is equated with extreme vulnerability and that success in a capitalistic free enterprise society is equated, in the playwright's view, with diversionary linguistic tactics or the ability to sustain conversational dominance. Even the choric effect of the chain letter in *The Water Engine* emphasizes that within the pyramid structure of capitalism only those at the top of the chain have an infinitesimal chance of success.

At the beginning of the new millennium there is a great deal of talk about public standards for distinguishing between what is "inappropriate" behavior and what is clearly illegal behavior. Most people regard moral issues with the infamous "shades of gray" mentality, proving themselves to be moral relativists. The court system is designed to recognize differing degrees of guilt and to determine what is felonious as opposed to misdemeanor behavior. What has evolved as a predictable courtroom measurement of human error, however, is not necessarily aligned with Mamet's personal assessment of guilt or innocence. His methods for evaluating gradations of criminality are based on his notion of the individual's relationship to his or her community and the validity, in Mamet's eyes, of that community's moral standards.

The breakdown of a sense of community in Mamet's plays parallels a breakdown in language; no one can communicate higher thoughts or noble sentiments. This perversion of language precedes a comparable perversion of human values. Thus, the salesmen in *Glengarry Glen Ross* use language primarily to deceive clients about worthless real estate. Seducers in *Speed-the-Plow* and *Sexual Perversity in Chicago* falsify their emotions and mislead the objects of their lust with false promises. Similarly, in *Edmond*, the protagonist kills a pimp and a prostitute because he lacks the verbal skills to reason with his victims, just as he has been unable to engage a subway passenger in a conversation about her hat, which reminded him of his mother's. Lacking either the intention or the means to communicate true feelings, Mamet's characters seem unable to construct a moral universe.

Given Mamet's belief that society has been corrupted by misleading social and economic goals, one does not expect justice to prevail. Yet in the silences of certain characters (Aaronow in *Glengarry*, who at first refuses to state his accomplice's name) and in the disturbing absence of just consequences being meted out to immoral men, Mamet implies that a better system is possible, even if it is presently suppressed. It might be exaggeration to suggest a sense of hope exists in Mamet's works. Yet at least the map of his world (alluding to his friend and admirer, David Hare's play) includes a utopia, even if by definition Utopia is a nonexistent state.

A person who accepts our present form of government and judicial system might well conclude that shoplifting or petty crimes are less threatening to the social order than breaking and entering or armed robbery, that ruthless seduction is a less serious assault on an individual than a rape, and that an accidental killing or an act of self-defense is more defensible than premeditated murder. It is not certain that Mamet would agree to list such crimes in an escalating order of gravity. The need for situation ethics may suggest to him that the rules that regulate contemporary society are suited only to a game he refuses to play. Edmond's killing of a pimp and a prostitute, Bobby Gould's seduction of his secretary, and Shelly Levene's theft of the real estate "A-list" may not represent a hierarchy of criminal behavior but may be almost equally representative of responses to a greed-driven world, which fails to provide affection for those who crave it or opportunities for principled behavior to those who aspire to it.

Recently, Mamet has used the medium of film to counter the atmosphere of despair in his stage plays. Although Mamet encountered the image-making of Hollywood as early as 1980 when he wrote the screenplay for a revival of *The Postman Always Rings Twice* (1981), his two recent screenplays may indicate that, unlike the fictive Bobby Gould, he is capable of writing serious works for the movies, which may, in fact, sound an alarm for more wholesome values. *The Spanish Prisoner* and *The Winslow Boy* emphasize the dangers and temptations of resisting "criminality" or the appearance of participation in it; but, they also prove that with courage and some luck total absorption into a decadent culture may be avoided.

For Mamet, then, the only antidote to a life of ubiquitous crime and deception is the creation of a community based on truth, loyalty, and a concern for the welfare of others. Such a community would be free of destructive personal competition, delusionary justification, and atavistic self-interest. Presently we bully people, dominate them, or accede to them with words; we invent a rhetoric that ascribes the highest motives to lust, greed, or the quest for power; we mask an impoverished personal philosophy with the jargon of an irresponsible existentialism, consoling modern therapies or pious defenses of mechanistic economic systems. So-called family values are equated with bigotry, privilege, and the protection of wealth. And feelings of personal loyalty are preempted by canned sentiments of buzzwords that permit what's believable to mask what's true. If, however, we can abandon our central American myth, which Mamet asserts is the desire "to get something for nothing," Mamet's work implies that we might yet create communities of promise.

Works Cited

Bernardinelli, James. "The Spanish Prisoner." 7 Aug. 1999. <http://movie-reviews.colossus.net/movies/s/spanish.html>.

———. "The Winslow Boy." 7 Aug. 1999. <http://movie-reviews.colossus.net/movies/w/winslow.html>.

Dean, Anne. *David Mamet: Language as Dramatic Action*. Rutherford, NJ: Farleigh Dickinson UP, 1990.

Kane, Leslie, ed. *David Mamet: A Casebook*. New York: Garland, 1996.

———. *Weasels and Wisemen: Ethics and Ethnicity in the Works of David Mamet*. New York: St. Martin's, 1999.

Mamet, David. *Edmond*. New York: Grove Press, 1983.

———. *Glengarry Glen Ross*. London: Methuen, 1984.

Mc-Intire-Strasburg, Jeff. Rev. of *The Spanish Prisoner. The David Mamet Review* 5 (Fall 1998): 7–8.

Roudané, Matthew C. "Something Out of Nothing." *Studies in American Drama, 1945–Present* 1 (1986): 73–81.

Stafford, Tony J. *David Mamet's Glengarry Glen Ross: Text and Performance*. Ed. Leslie Kane. New York: Garland, 1996. 185–94.

Tuttle, Jon. *Glengarry Glen Ross: Text and Performance*. Kane. 157–83.

9

Melville's *The Confidence Man* and His Descendants in David Mamet's Work

BARRY GOLDENSOHN

Stanley Kaufmann, in a lecture at Skidmore College about Mamet's *House of Games*, suggested that its concern with con men, betrayal, and trust in American life might well stem from Herman Melville's *The Confidence Man*. This essay is merely an elaboration of that suggestion. When I spoke to Kaufmann after the lecture to draw him out on the subject he said that it was merely a hunch, and that he hadn't read the novel for, he guessed, fifty years. I was interested because the novel was a favorite of mine. I taught it for many years in a hobby horse seminar at Goddard College called "Irony," and as a student in the 1960s, David Mamet took the seminar.

When I spoke to him about Kaufmann's lecture I asked him whether he'd read *The Confidence Man*, and he said "of course" with the right amount of bluster, in the tone of a student being quizzed by a teacher. And I never doubted his answer. Despite his picture of his Goddard years in his essay "Sex Camp" (in *Make Believe Town*) as a brainless bedroom romp, he was a highly disciplined, brilliant student, and the sexual revolution was not hidden away in northern Vermont.

In speaking of the con man as a literary figure we cannot dismiss him as a marginal criminal oddity. By the customary modern morality we take public and private fraud for granted and are more inclined to be horrified by crimes of violence. Our images of the depth of moral depravity are shaped by Hitler, Pol Pot, Stalin, and the organized production of death, in what Camus called the *univers concentrationaire*. However, in the moral world of Aquinas and Dante, the lowest circles of hell are reserved for frauds, betrayers of the spirit and of God, crimes they considered much more grave than acts of violence, which are merely sins against man. When one has one's eyes on threats to the integrity of a culture and its spiritual values, one need not be a Thomist to place in your visionary Hell panderers, seducers, flatterers, simoniacs, sorcerers, barrators, hypocrites, thieves, counselors of fraud, sewers of discord, and falsifiers (the descending scheme of Dante's *mal-bolges*.) And the very worst, traitors to their kin, country, guests, and lords temporal and spiritual, are placed in the depths of hell. This set of values is not a moral inversion or a bizarre theology or merely a provocative literary device, but a severe and often caustic view of the human condition and the social world.

Now, let us consider the moral world that Melville deals with in *The Confidence Man*. I am going to offer here a reading of the novel that focuses on the elements that would be useful to a brilliant undergraduate like Mamet with a highly developed sense of satiric comedy and with a fundamental commitment to theater.

The narrative point of view in the novel is not the customary omniscient third person narrator. It is, in fact, subtly variable, moving from a wry and witty observer to a kind of subtle, deliberate moral obtuseness that refuses to recognize or judge what seems to be obvious to the reader. There is a minimum of description of setting or scene. Often the details invite allegorical reading. The action takes place on April Fool's Day on a Mississippi river boat, the *Fidele*, which, like the *Ship of Fools* (it's called that, at one point) contains a cross section of American types just like the infantry platoon or the flight crew of a World War II movie. It announces that this is your country, the particular setting in which you are fated to deal with your universal confusions. (The international crew of the *Pequod* in *Moby Dick* dramatizes different theological problems dealing with different issues.)

The novel consists largely of a series of dialogues in which a man in many disguises, running from a crippled "negro" (as he's called) to a suave cosmopolitan, who argues for the need to be given the confidence of his interlocutors, as an act of faith both in him and in mankind and in divine *caritas*. Formally, *The Confidence Man* is a virtuoso stunt in which we never enter the mind of the central character, who is in every scene. We hear him talk and see him act, but we never learn what he is thinking or see him changing disguises. A new character appears, as from nowhere, and we can only surmise from the general direction of his talk that it is the same man. Description of action and setting serves almost entirely as stage setting and stage direction, and the novel's symbolic bearings are carried largely by dialogue. In other words, its method is primarily dramatic. The con game, the exchange of confidence, enters the dialogue as a form of high-spirited intellectual comedy. It is all very Christian and very philosophical. We do not have to look too hard, in the wake of contemporary Christmas, to see the debasement of the spiritual for commercial purposes, but it had an especially bitter edge in the first half of the nineteenth century when the language of radical Calvinism, and of the messianic hope of the new world and its institutions, of the New Jerusalem, were current and living language and the promise of America, the New Land (1).

Faith in God and Man were under a severe test in the wilderness, in the unstable and unfamiliar new world where messianic and salvationist hope and the pastoral ethical teachings of Christianity struggled with the language of daily life and commerce.

This is a country, Melville reminds us, with multiple and dubious currencies and coins issued by states in and out of the Union, and by private banks, as well as the central government, and with a wild and unregulated brokerage. To call it freewheeling simply reminds us of how contemporary it seems, and how similar to the world of *Glengarry Glen Ross*. What could one trust? It was an explosive mixture in which the language of the spirit is put under more stress than language or the spirit can bear. And the faith in this language of Christian teachings was matched in loftiness and purity of spirit by Emerson and the Transcendentalists and their faith in a beneficent nature. This often boundless spiritual optimism of Christians and Transcendentalists is the butt of the searching and extravagant intellectual comedy that delights in its absurd clash with the cruelty of the natural world and the selfishness of natural man, to put it into the traditional theological language that was still part of the current debate in Melville's day. And this spiritual optimism abounded as well in the ideology of the world of commerce. Melville enters the lists as the ironist and sophisticate in the community of the faithful—of the pious. This ironic posture is not unlike Jonathan Swift among the *enthusiasts* and *projectors*, and Melville uses these words of Swift repeatedly. A savage indignation at folly and duplicity, recorded through the orders and disorders of language, unites Mamet, Melville, and Swift.

What happens in the novel? Almost nothing. In his first guise (and some critics doubt that it is the confidence man, but most don't) he appears as a deaf mute, a true fleecy lamb of god, who raises up alongside the poster that warns of the con man his chalk slate that reads: "Charity thinketh no evil," "Charity suffereth long and is kind," "Charity endureth all things," "Charity believeth all things," "Charity never faileth." And after this gospel series, as an anticlimax, "His aspect was at once gentle and jaded" (6–7). This phrase is offered by the narrator with a seeming unawareness of its contradictoriness: a disingenuous voice that we again know from Swift.

It is hard to do justice to the complex and delicious texture of the novel, and this deaf mute is compared in a dazzling sequence to Christ, Caspar Hauser, Manco Capac (from Incan mythology), Vishnu, Joseph Smith, the mooncalf and Jacob dreaming at Luz: figures of divinity and insanity, saintly fools, prophets and gods in one breath. A dangerous and heretical list when assembled in one figure. We are reminded this is the dawn of comparative religion, cultural anthropology, *The Golden Bough,* and the half-century of Marx's and Nietzsche's perspectives on Christianity.

Our central character is frequently compared to the devil, and if we believed the novel to be a strict allegory as some scholars argue (though none argue that it is a coherent one), the moral scheme would be simple. However it is not a strict allegory, though it contains many allegorical passages. It is a mixed form, like *Moby Dick*, and the *Satyricon* and *Gargantua and Pantagruel* and *Gulliver's Travels*. On the level of narrative, he's a con man, but a very petty one. As the crippled slave, Black Guinea, he catches pennies in his mouth, and he engages in complex disguises as representatives of various charities—the Seminole Widows and Orphans Fund—the inventor of the Protean Chair that relaxes all infirmities by its flexibility, including infirmities of the tormented conscience, as a naturopath herb doctor, as a representative of the Philosophical Intelligence Office who sells young boys as laborers and servants, defending them from the imputation that boys are naturally troublesome.

Through all of this his profits are minuscule—a dollar or three, a shave on credit, and so forth. His triumphs are the granting of confidence in him, not the money. He is an artist, a con artist on one hand, but clearly aimed at a spiritual goal of getting people to learn to trust in the utterly untrustworthy. He is a theological trickster, more like Puck leading to trouble than the devil leading to ruin and damnation. This aspect of the novel is theological satire.

Few of these are easy conquests, and his triumphs are against worthy antagonists. One truth-speaker sees through the early disguises. A man on a wooden leg recognizes the crippled slave as a fraud and is beaten for speaking the truth by a Methodist minister. A Missourian, a backwoodsman named Pitch—which is black and which things stick to—has massive and eloquent doubts about the benign intentions of nature and the spiritual primacy of confidence. However, these are overcome when he is finally sold a boy by the con man in the guise of the representative of the Philosophical Intelligence Office who has the disingenuous devious innocence of the Special Prosecutor of the Clintons.

The final incarnation (and the word suggests his theological bearings) of the confidence man is Frank Goodman referred to in the last half of the novel as "the Cosmopolitan." This frank, good man is extravagantly dressed in a costume referred to as motley, the colors of the fool and clown, and spends the time from nightfall to midnight, when April Fool's Day ends and the novel closes, in conversation with another con man—whom he recognizes instantly as such—named Charlie Noble, and with two figures who are thinly disguised versions of Emerson and Thoreau. He then cadges a free shave from the barber, whose "No Trust" sign opened the novel, and the night concludes with his encounter with an old man reading the Bible, who reassures him about the Christian provenance of trust. He ushers the old man back to his stateroom and the novel ends with the teasing sentence: "Something further may follow of this Masquerade" (350).

In all of these encounters the main subject of discussion is the appeal for confidence by the confidence man, the giving of it as an act of faith in

God and Man. He marshals on his side the language of Christian faith, brotherly love, and a banal, genial, complacent, humane civility, anticipating George Babbit. He says: "irony is so unjust; never could abide irony; something Satanic about irony. God defend me from Irony, and Satire, his bosom friend." To which Pitch responds, "A right knave's prayer, and a right fool's, too" (192–93).

Yet Pitch, though generally acute in his suspicions, is a hyperbolic crank, and Melville artfully, and with telling irony, manipulates the reader onto the side of the con man. This is true again when he opposes the rigorously selfish individualism and faith in nature's invisible hand mixed evilly with spiritual purism, of the Emerson and Thoreau figures. Sounding reasonable and appealing, he says, "never a sound judgment without charity. When man judges man, charity is less a bounty from our mercy than just allowance for the insensible lee-way of human fallibility" (221). If this is the serpent and the devil—and there are many references connecting him to both—he has his charms that are generous and humane, opposed to an extreme severity. But then theology reminds us that no one would be tempted by a repellent devil. And again, his con jobs are done for very little profit. The trickster—shape-changer—is the more plausible model for this character. He is a virtuoso abuser of confidence, and the goal—at times complex and elusive—is to attack the commercial use and abuse of the language of the spirit, in which confidence becomes both the test of wholesome spirituality and the requirement of the swindle. Melville transforms the Swiftian device of a double ingenue comedy—that we see in the debates between Gulliver and his Houyhnhnm master—into the discussion of truth among liars and faith among the faithless. In the novel there is something of the impulse of Serrano's "Piss Christ," which conflates anger at the abuse of God with anger at God.

What is there in this novel useful to a young dramatist? The dialogue's formal eloquence is too ornate, programmatic, and playful to have been useful to one caught up with dramatic realism. Likewise, the figure of the trickster and his enterprise are entirely too mythic for a realist. It is in the impact of Melville's central themes, the drama of trust and betrayal, the impact of fraud and misplaced faith on American capitalist society that we can see the influence of this novel on Mamet. In an early work like *American Buffalo,* confidence takes the form of an ongoing discussion of who can be trusted, and it is located in the heart of the American Way: theft as a business proposition, in which the thief, or would-be thief, is an agent of free enterprise, where the individual should be free "to embark on any fucking course he sees fit. . . . In order to secure his honest chance to make a profit" (221). This sounds less like the con man than like Mark Winsome, the radical individualist who is a parody of Emerson. The nature of friendship forms the debate between the cosmopolitan and the Thoreau figure, Egbert, who maintains that money or any practical consideration belong outside the pure and spiritual bond of friendship. He is portrayed as a fanatic and monster and refuses on this ground to loan money to a friend in dire need. This, comically twisted, informs the bitter ravings of Teach: "We're talking about money for chrissake, huh? We're talking about cards. Friendship is friendship, and a wonderful thing, and I am all for it . . . but lets keep it separate huh, let's keep the two apart, and maybe we can deal with each other like some human beings" (162).

The chaotic manuscript of *Lone Canoe*, a play of the *American Buffalo* years, is a choral meditation on complex betrayal of trust and loyalty to culture, family, and tribe, between two nineteenth-century explorers. The issue here is not criminality but inauthenticity, fraud, and betrayal. It seems unfair to speak of it in detail because it has never been prepared for production or publication. But it does bear, in these respects, on issues of confidence and trust.

Edmond is a play in which the character's senseless act of murder is prepared for by a series of scenes of con games and fraud, peep shows, and three-card monte. He makes a desperate, brutal lunge toward seeing things as they really are. Some version of "things are not always what they seem" is a signature line for a Mamet play, and breaking through the barriers of deception to the difficult truth is the dramatic thrust that drives Edmond through brutality to acceptance of a genuine human contact that is reached through shame and degradation.

The language of confidence and trust is at the center of both *Glengarry Glen Ross* and *House of Games*. In the former, we are shown confidence and betrayal—in the capitalist war of all against all—at the heart of the American enterprise. In the latter, we see a gang operating a "big con"—some of the procedures of which may have been derived from David Maurer's book of the same name—in which a psychologist, Margaret Ford (played by Lindsay Crouse), is swindled by a con man, Mike (played by Joe Mantegna). When she realizes what is going on, she confronts him with the comment: "You folks were going to con me out of my money." He replies, as a good capitalist: "It's only business. It's the American Way." In a grotesque satiric turn, the psychologist grants herself permission, with help from an older therapist friend, to murder the con man who seduced her. She says: "You raped me. You took me under false pretenses. You used me." His answer, hilariously, is "We live in an imperfect world" (2). In both cases the rules of the game—the modern one of self-fulfilling psychological health (she can't help her patients and thinks of therapy as a con game) and the ancient one of the con game—permit one to get away with murder, figuratively and literally.

In *Homicide*, we see the betrayal of Bob Gold (played again by Mantegna), particularly bitter and intimate, since Mamet at the time was exploring his connection to Judaism with a passion. Like all Jews (a dangerous phrase) Mamet is outraged by crimes against his people. *The Old Religion*, a novel about the 1914 lynching of Leo Frank, framed for a rape and murder, ends: "They covered his head, and they ripped his pants off and castrated him and hung him from the tree. A photographer took a picture showing the mob, one boy grinning at the camera, the body hanging, the legs covered by a blanket tied around the waist. The photo, reproduced as a postcard, was sold for many years in stores throughout the South" (194). However all Mamet's passions are complex and self-reflexive, as becomes an instinctive ironist. Loyalty is never simple. Gold, as the homicide detective assigned to the case of a murdered Jewish storekeeper, is persuaded by her rich and powerful Jewish family that the murder was done by neo-Nazis, through an incredibly elaborate series of deceptions designed to appeal to his rootlessness as a Diaspora Jew. He is systematically misinformed by a sham librarian and lured to a sham meeting of Zionist heroes. He is persuaded by them to blow up the headquarters (in a Lionel train store) of the Nazi group, and then he is blackmailed by photos of himself emerging from the store to get information from an evidence folder in the police files that the group needs. This folder is professionally sacred and to reveal it is a profound betrayal of his work. In the course of this run-around he shows up late for an assignment to trap a killer, in which he has a crucial role as the "con man" hostage negotiator, and his partner is killed. He gets seriously wounded himself, and this defection gets him expelled from the group of homicide detectives, the community that he truly belongs to. So much for confidence.

These questions lead irresistibly to issues of truth and falsity, and *True and False*, Mamet's discussion of honest method for the actor, begins with the following paragraph:

> My closest friends, my intimate companions, have always been actors. My beloved wife is an actor. My extended family consists of the actors I have grown up, worked, lived and aged with. I have been, for many years, part of various theatre companies, any one of which in its healthy state more nearly resembles a perfect community than any other group I have encountered. (3)

That actors, like con men, are impersonators, raises no problem here. The language suggests a framework of love and trust and "perfect community" and how genuine, heartfelt, sincere, *not* fraudulent, these values are. For all the concern throughout the book with the art of impersonation, the goal is truth, and it concludes with the following:

> The well-made play, scene, design, direction, the good performance, must be *true*. The simple truth may stem from a natural disposition, or come from years of arduous study—it's nobody's business but your own.

>   The blandishments of fame, money, and security are great. Some-
> times they have to be quieted, sometimes they have to be compromised
> with—just as in any other sphere of life.
>   What is true, what is false, what is, finally, important?
>   It is not a sign of ignorance not to know the answers. But there is
> great merit in facing the questions. (127)

This is the language of the moral realist with a sense of how difficult it is to
achieve our values and not that of a bitter idealist who rails at man's defec-
tions from the absolute. Truth remains as the problem that the truth-seeker is
committed to pursue. For which reason, we must not accept as a moral conclusion, Del's outburst in *The Cryptogram*, amid the pain of lifelong betrayals of intimate friends: "Oh, if we could speak the truth, do you see? For one
instant. Then we would be free" (54). Despite the echo, this cannot be read as
an affirmation of the promise of salvation in the Gospel of John. Del is driven
away. And as every student of drama knows, the truth is just as likely to force
your Queen-mother-wife to kill herself, you to blind yourself with her brooch,
and then to drive you into exile, as it is to set you free. The redeeming comfortable possession of, and utterance of, the truth is not a safe bet.

The step from this suggestion of dark Sophoclean irony to *Wag the Dog*
is not as great as it appears. Underneath the brilliant satire on the operators
of the media delusion-mill in American politics is another, dark, Swiftian vision of our tragic susceptibility to illusion, to being well deceived. And the
film is conducted with Swiftian extravagance and gaiety. As film satire, it
belongs in the rare company of *Doctor Strangelove* with which it shares a
dizzying mixture of plausible verisimilitude pushed to horrifying absurdity.
(This is about a con job on a global scale and the "real" world of politics-in-
the-media refused to be outdone by the film's extravagant farce. I accused
David of "producing" the Monica Lewinsky scandal to promote the film and
he refused to deny it.)

We can see through this film that it is not only in the figure of the confidence man but also in the ongoing debate about trust, confidence, truth, falsity, deceit, and manipulation that we see the connection between Melville's
novel and all of Mamet's plays and films.

Notes

1. As evidence that this was not a remote, defunct or merely abstract tradition, I
   should put on record that I went to a college in a dumpy little town in northern
   Ohio that was founded in 1833—fifteen years before the publication of *The Confidence Man*—as "A new Jerusalem, a city without sin in the wilderness." The divine spirit was in its full presence there. The college's president in its formative
   years, Charles Grandison Finney, a very successful evangelist, who was pronounced by the Whitman disciple R. M. Bucke, to possess the "Cosmic Con-

sciousness"—the spiritual flood of Universal Divinity—along with Whitman, Jesus, Mohammed, Francis Bacon (the author of plays falsely attributed to a common man of the theater), and a few select others.

2. Quotations from David Mamet's *House of Games* were transcribed from the film.

Works Cited

Mamet, David. *Cryptogram*. London: Methuen, 1995.

———. *American Buffalo* in *Plays: One*. London: Methuen,1994.

———. *The Old Religion*. New York: Free Press, 1997.

———. *True and False*. New York: Pantheon, 1997.

Melville, Herman. *The Confidence Man*. Ed. Bruce Franklin. New York: Bobbs-Merrill, 1967.

10
Fantasy Crimes/Fictional Lives: *Lakeboat*

ANNE M. DEAN

To the men who work on David Mamet's *Lakeboat*,[1] their ability to construct a fictional world that results in a mutually understood dreamlife is as essential as breathing to their daily survival. Without such a safety net, their lives would be intolerable, and so they collectively invest in an elaborate network of fantasies through which they try to bolster their flagging egos and carve a shared moment of mutually "lived" experience—even though that experience has almost certainly never actually taken place.

Storytelling as a means of survival is powerfully depicted in *Lakeboat*; in the same way that the salesmen in *Glengarry Glen Ross* rely and depend upon seducing their clients (and each other) with a potent verbal broth of carefully rehearsed and meticulously constructed narrative, the men who work on the lakeboat are addicted to fiction. In the vaguely surreal world they inhabit, time is dislocated and reality is subordinated to the development of a continuous fictional representation about past events, the sole purpose of which is to distract them from the tedium of their daily lot.

The characters themselves turn crime into art, each of them authors of their own elaborate "screenplay." Although almost certainly lacking the sangfroid and ruthlessness needed to be felons in real life, they endlessly concoct fantasies concerning criminal activity, preferably of the most violent and lurid kind. The macho lifestyles of their celluloid heroes are tried on for size, their dialogue adapted for everyday use on board ship, and their strutting physical attributes both craved and copied, albeit in a considerably watered-down form. This is a world of B-movie clichés and melodramatic twists, where hard-as-nails he-men perform fantastic feats of strength and bravery—and always live to see another day. Key words and phrases appropriated from the movies offer the seamen the sensation of legitimacy as "real" men, and they brag about past brutal exploits, proudly airing their dismissive (and often cruel) attitudes to women. But with little (if anything) of substance at the heart of all this hot air, they remain isolated, unloved, and afraid of what reality might have in store for them.

And so they tell each other tall stories or confabulate tales about those they know—or barely know—into wildly exaggerated tales of violence and murder. In psychiatric nomenclature, "confabulation" means literally to replace the gaps left by a disorder of the memory with imaginary remembered experiences consistently believed to be true. Mamet's seamen seize upon fiction to fill the emptiness in their lives and, in so doing, become confabulists by choice and design. They *want* to be criminals or, at least, have about them the cachet, the notoriety and dark sexual promise of underworld deeds. They spill out their favourite mock-criminal tales, which they love to recount with great relish alongside those of (scarcely credible) rapacious sex and (more believable) epic drunkenness. They wish they *had* been through the mill—at least vicariously—and that their experiences had taken them to Shanghai's heart of darkness or the deepest, anaconda-infested waters of Africa. In fact, they've almost certainly never been further than Lake Michigan, on whose grey waters the play is set.

Mundane events are recast into thrilling adventures; a virtually pointless and mind-numbing existence is reconstituted into tales of on-the-edge abandon, and passionless lives metamorphose into a series of rich and gamey adventures, full of fast-paced and dangerous exploits, often at the cusp of a juicy crime. The scenes these men conjure are redolent of seedy encounters in the kinds of booze-drenched, drug-fueled joints remembered from countless potboilers; hot, breathless, sweaty exchanges occurring in darkened dives as they lean against the bar, coolly swigging tequila and fondling the lustful and fractious whores. All they lack is a soundtrack by Tom Waits. All of this has a very 1940s or 1950s feel about it, conjuring up a vision of the likes of Orson Wells and Ava Gardner exchanging glances in a steamy, tropical hothouse. It is tempting to conjecture how the seamen might have reacted to the contemporary ultraviolent cinema of Quentin Tarantino, whose films teem with the antics of hired assassins and drug dealers and their women, not to mention the most obscene and scabrous language. Surely here they would find rich pickings to feed their imaginations: pulp fiction indeed.

Mamet has always been interested in storytelling and what this can mean for different people. *Lakeboat* is perhaps one of his most perfectly wrought creations in this regard, describing as it does the vacuum in which his seamen exist, together with the fragile mesh of their fantasy worlds, which serve not only to pass the time but also to provide them with a reason for living. Drawn to spurious disclosure and creativity by desperate boredom, their fantasies enable them to validate their very existence. Although an early effort, it is one of Mamet's very best plays: candid, funny, and raw, it has the salty hurt of reality in its short, superbly written and deftly constructed scenes.

This play follows very much the lines of the classic fairy tale: many tribulations and hazards strewn along the way toward that much-needed happy ending. Such tales are able to affect us in various ways through their arousal of our emotions, and they affect our responses to the story's various strands. They make us feel elated or upset, incite us to anger or assuage our fears, and thereby manipulate us into identifying subconsciously with the protagonist, so that we listen to the "story" nonjudgmentally.

It is interesting to apply this thesis to the men on Mamet's lakeboat who use language in a very similar way: they collectively will a simple story of a missing colleague, Guigliani, into a wildly implausible tale of violent robbery involving prostitutes, the Mob—even G-Men. In a strange kind of way, they too seek to create a world where everything is predictable and has a happy ending, even if en route the most salacious and violent notes imaginable are struck.

From the very first scene, the seeds are sewn to engender morbid interest among the men in Guigliani's fate. The Pierman tells Dale that a "slut" (18) had approached Guigliani, persuaded him to leave the bar with her, and had then attacked him (scene 1, 18). After more detailed exposition of Guigliani's supposed misadventure, Dale can't resist probing into the more salacious possibilities of the story:

> DALE: And he didn't even get laid . . . did he?
> PIERMAN: Fuck no, she rolled him first. Then she left.
> DALE: Bitch.
> PIERMAN: So, he stumbles back to the gate, drunk and sobbing . . .
> DALE: Nothing to be ashamed of . . .
> PIERMAN: The guards won't let him in! I mean he's bleeding, he's dirty . . .
> DALE: You didn't tell me he was bleeding.
> PIERMAN: It was understood . . .
>
> (scene 1, 18,19)

Even at this early stage, Mamet imbues the proceedings with the bleak humor that underscores every exchange in the play and, as usual, demonstrates his ability to capture the non sequiturs and absurdities of ordinary demotic conversation. Dale empathizes with Guigliani; after all, he is a young man himself who could feasibly suffer the same fate. This is demonstrated by his observation, quickly followed by a concerned query, about Guigliani's success (or otherwise) in having sexual intercourse with the prostitute: "And he didn't even get laid . . . did he?" (18). The implication is that, if he did "get laid," at least *something* good would have come out of the incident—and Dale's own longing for such sexual exploits is clear. At this stage, he is unaware that the fabricating of such florid tales out of ordinary events is commonplace on board ship.

In his assertion that Guigliani's return to the gate "drunk and sobbing" (19) was "Nothing to be ashamed of . . ." (19), Dale again empathizes and casts himself in the other man's role; in similar circumstances, he himself would probably cry and would not wish the world to think such an act as shameful or unmanly. The lines immediately following neatly sum up the consensual fictional undercurrent that Mamet creates, which begins in this scene and extends throughout the work. Dale is somewhat shocked (but also secretly thrilled and excited) to learn that Guigliani's injuries had been severe enough for blood to be spilled: "You didn't tell me he was bleeding," to which the Pierman responds with deadpan patience: "It was understood" (19).

Thus Guigliani's reported injuries veer through the play in Mametian Chinese whispers from relatively mild to almost fatal, just as in Curtis Hanson's film *LA Confidential*. In one scene, the violence supposedly inflicted by a Mexican gang on some police officers escalates from reports of a mere rough and tumble to demands for violent reprisal after one officer is (untruthfully) said to have lost an eye and another is almost mortally injured. All know they are feeding a lie, but their shared desire to alleviate the awful, stultifying boredom and satisfy violent wish-fulfilment serves to spur each other on to new heights of creativity is rife and must be sated.

The seamen's creative (in every sense of the word) theories about an unseen character's fate are promulgated with the punchiest conviction, though finally demolished in the wonderfully low-beat ending when the humdrum truth is revealed. Their reaction when, finally, it emerges that one of their favorite stories has no truth in it is very telling. Far from trying to find alternative ways of continuing the tale or to dream up reasons why the disappointing denouement may not in fact be true, the seamen quickly (and with a too-ready air of indifference) accept the fact that a particular chapter is over. Almost without missing a beat, they adopt a casual air intended to convey the fact that their interest in the matter has been terminated: "What the hell. . . ." To hide their disappointment at such an indifferent outcome, and to continue with the unspoken understanding of the need for a narrative sublife between themselves and their fellow fantasists, they shed their disappointment like a snakeskin. They know that another opportunity for invention will soon arise; just under the surface, one can almost hear them gearing up for the next instalment that will fill their days and their dream existence.

A good example of this occurs at the end of the play when Guigliani is merely found to have literally "missed the boat" through oversleeping, and Fred, Joe, and Dale mull over this extremely unexciting turn of events. Again, it is interesting to note that, even here, a story is being reported secondhand. Joe has heard about the "truth" of Guigliani's disappearance from another source, though there is still no certainty about what *really* happened:

JOE: . . . Skippy said he said his aunt died, but he thinks the *real* reason is 'cause he overslept.

FRED: . . . sonofabitch . . .
JOE: Well, I'll be glad to have him back.

(scene 28, 211)

Thus, even this "evidence" is based on an unsubstantiated rumor. After days of speculation and invention, a plausibly mundane reason for Guigliani's disappearance is finally revealed, even though this may or may not be the truth. But, for the anecdote-hungry seamen, it will do for now. To hide their disappointment at the revelation of this unexciting conclusion to days of speculation and invention, the men verbally bind themselves together (along with their absent fellow lakeshoreman) into a macho brotherhood, where Guigliani's "misdeed" is gamely forgiven, and he is lauded as a pal, a "sonofabitch" (111), one of their own, whom they will be pleased to have back on board.

In *Lakeboat*, Mamet draws on his student days when, during a college vacation, he spent some time as a steward on a cargo boat on Lake Michigan. He clearly intends his own experiences to be portrayed through the character of Dale, a young Jewish student with an open and inquiring mind, eager to learn about and share in the darkly mysterious world of the lakeboat. Mamet is not the first writer to capitalize on his own experience of working on a cargo boat—Eugene O'Neill did something similar in *Bound East for Cardiff* and *The Long Voyage Home*; clearly, all-male, hermetic environments provide rich fodder for a writer's imagination. To add to the already heady and intense atmosphere on board, there also exists an undertow of homoeroticism that Mamet's seamen seek to allay by adapting an aura of excessive manliness lest they be viewed as anything other than the most hard-bitten *hombres*.

As a result, no softness either in language or behavior is permitted, though there *are* occasionally some touching examples of the gruff support and sympathy that is extended to Joe when he dares to air one of his many anxieties, even though such fears are invariably masked as casual inquiries. It is only Joe, one of the longest-serving and oldest crew members on the ship, who divulges to Dale probably the only genuinely true words spoken in the play, relating to his secret sensitivity and longing for some beauty in his life. It would be quite unthinkable for Joe to relate such thoughts to anyone else on board—his vulnerability would be regarded as weakness and he would become an all-too-easy target for their jibes—but Dale's youth and combination of naïveté and student-like demeanor prompt him to disclosure.

On board the lakeboat, knowledge is power and the "truth" is despatched only to those who can be impressed or coerced. Each man chooses his audience carefully, mentally running his stories through a filter so that he recounts only what is essential to his purpose. Thus, when Fred seeks to demonstrate to Dale his manly grit, he succinctly delineates the seen-it-all nonchalance adopted by himself and the rest of the crew:

FRED: Now the main thing about the boats . . . is that you don't get any pussy. You got that? . . . Except when we tie up. . . . This is why everyone says "fuck" all the time. . . . They say "fuck" in direct proportion to how bored they are. Huh?

(scene 10, 51–52)

Mamet neatly articulates much of the essence of *Lakeboat* in this one short piece of dialogue; a man who feels himself superior to another tells him "the way it is" on board ship, and in so doing hints at his sexual prowess once on shore. Fred endeavors to impress the new boy with his macho insouciance and sardonic humor. Although Dale is clearly no idiot, Fred does not hesitate to patronize him. *He* is a man; Dale is a boy. To Fred, Dale is young—and new—enough to have to endure such condescension, he therefore wastes no time in giving him the benefit of his "vast" knowledge of the mores and truth of life on the lake. Convinced that he alone knows the score and what life is all about, Fred is able to explain—with some dark humor—how unrewarding (and frustrating) their existence can be, and why the seamen's discourse is filled with obscenity. They swear and cuss because they are "real" men doing "real" men's work, their frustration being aired in direct proportion to their loneliness and lack of sexual gratification. In such a society, Dale has everything to learn and nothing to offer.

In their appropriation of the handed-down clichés and banalities of already debased forms of communication, Mamet's seamen also bring to mind James Joyce's *Dubliners*. As Barbara Hardy observes, the Irishmen

move through their nights and days, telling stories to themselves and to each other. However mean their existence, however thin their feelings, however numb their reflections, they are never so paralysed as to be incapable of narrative. Their language and symbolism may be feeble, secondhand or banal, but the form, function and individuality of their stories prove that they are imagined as imaginative. They tell over the past and sketch out the future. They exchange overt or covert confessions, pleas and defences . . . many of them are capable of fervent and energetic lies, dreams, projects, boasts, anecdotes, reminiscences, aspirations, fantasies, confidences and disclosures (206).[2]

Joyce, like Mamet, allows us to "encounter the poor in spirit by letting them speak and think for themselves. In scrupulously avoiding a contrast between his style and theirs . . . he teaches us not to condescend (208)." Similarly, while their verbal savagery may appal us, Mamet ensures that we remain aware of his lakeshoremen's humanity. These characters are vulnerable and afraid, at sea both literally and emotionally, and the baseness of their chosen fictional lives can be understood as a necessary reaction against the truth—a yawning emptiness that terrifies them.

A particularly striking stage-picture encapsulating Mamet's central thesis occurred in Aaron Mullen's superb London premiere of the play at the Lyric Studio in 1998. Here, Fred, macho-man supreme, stood erect center stage in an assumed position of pure aggression, as though he was on set in a film, flexing his oily biceps and squaring his shoulders to a bank of movie cameras—performing alone, to himself, in his own spotlight. Fred casts himself in his own personalized gangster movie as a seen-it-all, done-it-all hard man, cynical and unafraid. His stories are denuded versions of already rough-edged B-movie scripts, the pulpiest of pulp fiction, and his speech is littered with non sequiturs absorbed and reconstituted as his own original thoughts over years of moviegoing. In his mind, he is ur-criminal, the original, the best, the strongest, and the meanest.

It is worth studying his main soliloquy in some detail, since it neatly encapsulates the raison d'être of the play. Here is a perfect example of Mamet's ability to convey, via the brutish and inarticulate speech of one character, the essence of the men's loneliness and desperation. Fred concocts a wholly imagined tale of violence designed to increase his own standing as the toughest guy on board ship, and also to demonstrate his absolute understanding of the kind of world he describes:

> FRED: Mugged. Yeah. Poor son of a bitch. In East Chicago. That's a lousy town. By some whore, no less. . . . Maybe the Maf got him. . . . Maybe the whore, huh? Not that they care for the few C's they took. But you know how they are. You can't get behind. Unless it was the Outfit. Or some freak occurrence. It was probably some Outfit guys got him. Assuming he was into them. It doesn't look like he just got rolled. Beat the living fuck out of him. Left him for dead. Huh? Can you feature it? Flies in his face. Fucking ear stuck to the sidewalk with blood. Ruptured man, he'll never perform again. Ribs, back. The *back*. Hit him in the back. Left him for *dead*.
> (scene 11, 57–58)

Fred's account of Guigliani's supposed attack veers from his being mugged and drugged "By some whore, no less" (the certainty of this statement is rather striking in the circumstances) to being left for dead by "the Outfit" (57). The staccato sentences are intended to convey urgency and drama, and to delineate both Fred's tough-guy compassion for and knowledge of his fallen crony.

His assertion in the opening lines that Guigliani was brought down by a whore in East Chicago (cited as a "lousy town"; one wonders if Fred has ever even been there) is quickly qualified when he decides this story is insufficiently spicy and suggests, rather than asserts, that "Maybe the Maf got him" (57). But he then realizes that in bringing in as exotic a group as the Mob he may have gone too far and strained credibility; quickly thinking on his feet, he negates this by first throwing doubt on it and reverts to citing a treacherous whore as the probable culprit. An unknown and sinister group of faceless heavies, "the Outfit" from whom money can be borrowed is then brought into his increasingly florid tale.

Fred then wavers again in case his melodrama begins to sound too unlikely, and he mentions the possibility of a "freak occurrence" (57) but this comparatively boring and unexciting notion is rapidly swept aside as he really hits his stride in his return to the ruthless and psychopathic behavior of the Outfit. Fred's description of Guigliani's condition after the assault builds into a crescendo of blood thirsty, almost lip-smacking excess: he states that Guigliani was so badly hurt that it didn't seem as though he "just got rolled" (57).

According to Fred (who in no way could have witnessed any such thing), Guigliani's injuries were simply too extensive—not to mention as gory as Fred could possibly make them. He was "left . . . for dead," bloody and so seriously "ruptured" (58) (a sly, confiding reference to the man's destroyed potent masculinity bound to cause a vicarious and fearful *frisson* in the listener) that the implication is that a man like one of them, a *working* man, would no longer be capable of functioning as a sexual athlete. Fred allows the imagined momentary horror of such a concept to sink in for the fullest effect.

He then goes for the linguistic kill, laying on the melodrama and graphically picturing with great, sweaty relish a bloodied ear "stuck to the sidewalk" and flies buzzing round the man's face—literally, "left for dead." Fred's account of the grievous nature of the assault reaches its apotheosis in his repetition of the word "back": "Ribs, back. The back. Hit him in the back" (58). The inference is that Guigliani's attackers were nothing more than cowards, who would hit a man from behind, the only way they could hope to bring down one as tough and well versed in violence and self-protection as the heroic Guigliani and, by implication, a man like Fred himself.

According to Fred's account, Guigliani has moved from being the victim of a mugging (and drugging) by a vicious whore, suffering serious physical injuries of an almost unspeakable nature, on to death itself in the reference to flies making the most of his tragic demise; in Fred's imaginings, Guigliani has finally fled this life and joined the dead heroes who have bit the celluloid dust after a monumental struggle to survive. All things to all men who speak of him, Guigliani has assumed legendary status: a titan laid low by malevolent forces who, through their sadistic venality, have sapped his strength and taken his life.

Later in the play, the Fireman romantically adds his own version of Guigliani's disappearance; he just cannot fathom how a man of such strength and sheer survivalist *nous* could have been "taken" by his assailants. His only conclusion is that "they" must have drugged him or, in an appallingly unmanly act of cowardice, attacked him from the rear (scene 23, 92). Through sheer repetition, the story achieves more credence.

That this follows shortly after one of several lengthy exchanges between Fred and Stan concerning the action film hero Jonnie Fast's supertoughness and his place in the pantheon of the all-time hard men of cinema is no accident. By inference, Guigliani has *become* the "real-life" equivalent of Fast. There is an extraordinary exchange between Fred and Stan as they linguistically circle each other with assertions of which movie star is the meanest. In Fred's opinion, there is no question: he tells Stan that Fast is simply "the strongest guy in ten years" (scene 17, 72). The sarcastic ferocity in Fred's response is notable:

> STAN: I agree with you one hundred percent. He is strong, this Fast. He's probably the strongest guy I've ever seen. I can't think of anything that would be stronger than he is. Unless maybe a pile of shit." (scene 17, 72–73).

To underline—and undermine—Fred's assertion, he goes on to cite Jerry Lewis as one of the all-time tough guys and, subsequently, sarcastically remarks that even Shirley Temple could have disarmed him. He goes on to remind Fred, who believes Fast is "stark" that "The man is not stark. He's no fucking good. That's why he didn't take five fucking guys in that barroom using only one pool cue" (73).

This ever more highly charged exchange about a series of movie scenes being relayed as though they had really happened carries on in similar vein, with Stan naming Clint Eastwood and Lee Van Cleef as being obviously tougher than Jonnie Fast. For these men, defending their cinematic idols becomes personal. It is impossible for them to accept any such criticism, since their own reputations as men to be reckoned with are resultantly threatened, and they bear the same significance as a direct attack on their masculine pride. Similarly, to denigrate the behavior and ability of an action hero serves to bolster the "critic's" self-confidence; in so doing, he compares his own prowess as a hard man and elevates himself above a character whose whole existence is based both on his brawn and his ability to outwit and outfight his opponents.

But soon after, Stan appears to have joined the ranks of those for whom Jonnie Fast is the hard man par excellence. Just what has changed his mind is unclear, unless the growing speculation about Guigliani's fate, and the crew's willingness to blur the "experiences" of the actor and their fellow lakeshoreman has made him rethink his opinion of the celluloid hard man. As he explains to Collins, in one memorable movie scene Fast is confronted with serious trouble and has to tackle at least eight assailants. In this sequence, he never draws his gun; he fights each man off until only one remains—hidden from Fast's sight behind the bar (scene 22, 91). That Stan cannot emphasize enough Fast's fantastic ability to vanquish his assailants when they attack him from behind is surely his ironic riposte to Fred's account of Guigliani's attack earlier in the play—Guigliani, while tough, was nonetheless attacked from the rear—Fast would never allow such a thing to happen, or, if such an attack did take place, he would be ready to take on his attackers. Stan's monologue is rattled out at full speed, and he narrates the filmic event as though it had really happened and he was witness to it. The short, stabbing sentences pile one on the other, as Stan builds the tension, recounting the scene in all its lurid glamour and improbability.

One can almost feel Stan's excitement recounting the "event" as he strives to imbue every word with thrilling import. As he recounts the tale of the fight scene, even when Fast is at a seeming disadvantage, with his back to the bar, thinking that one of his adversaries is already dead, his amazingly rapid reflexes enable him to react and kill the man. The adrenaline that pumps through every syllable of Stan's tale indicates his total immersion in a posturing macho dream of readiness (and willingness) to engage in the most violent activities, to take on and overcome any assailant, to meet all eventualities and take life's challenges on the chin. The reality of the men's banal existence in a metaphysical void provides a very poor counterpoint to such grandiose exploits.

There is a great deal of fear in this play: fear of humiliation and of showing any sensitivity in case it is misinterpreted as weakness. It is imperative that these men appear hard-boiled and resilient enough to compete in such a testosterone-fuelled world, and they must strive to verbally match their colleagues in wildly competitive games of one-upmanship. To fail in any way would be unthinkable, but such fears can nonetheless be felt throughout the work, simmering just beneath the surface.

The most fearful of all is perhaps Joe, the biggest—and saddest—of the seamen who has lived a half-life for too many years, denying his true feelings in an effort to fit in and be accepted by his peers. His words convey a lifetime of lost opportunities, aspirations not pursued and ambitions curtailed. He tells the young recruit Dale of his one-time dream of being a ballet dancer and his desire to catch a graceful ballerina in mid-flight in his strong arms. That Joe yearns to express his feminine (though still strong) self via something as pure and lovely as this provides a wonderfully ironic counterpoint to Stan's description of the violent ballet danced by arch-hero Jonnie Fast as, with supremely choreographed movements, he decimates his assailants with an equal share of viciousness and style (scene 22, 91).

Joe's yearning for softness and beauty is constantly juxtaposed with a reinforcement of his masculinity and strength, which ultimately ring pathetically hollow. A hefty, well-built man, his physical size has helped him survive thus far, but the pretense is killing him: he does not know how much longer he can hold onto the lies, and so he lives literally on the very edge of potential disaster. Much later, he actually confides to Dale that he has often been terrified, lives in dread of illness and of dying, and has even considered suicide, lying on his bed with a gun pointing into his mouth. However, as with all his plans, at the last moment he lost his nerve and did not act.

Joe is consumed with terror at the uncertainty of his lot; out on the murky waters of Lake Michigan, everything is frightening, and has an unnerving sense of incompleteness about it. With contrived nonchalance, Joe interjects his fears into mundane conversations, carefully avoiding the remotest suggestion that he feels any anxiety at all. However, his colleagues on board instinctively recognize Joe's fretting, and, sometimes with a rather touching kindness and subtlety, try to assuage his fears. For example in scene 18, Joe casually, "idly" inquires how long a man would survive if he fell into the water: Collins, the Second Mate, responds with a mixture of dead-pan humor, "You planning a swim?" (76) and reassurance, "they'd have a helicopter here in a half-hour" (77). Similarly, in scene 24 Joe wonders what would happen on board ship if a man were seriously hurt (i.e., if his leg were chopped off [96]). Dale listens sympathetically and suggests that Joe ask the Steward if morphine is readily available. Joe declines, but he goes on to tell him that he feels unwell, and describes his various symptoms. When Dale suggests that he should see a doctor, Joe again declines because he is afraid of what the doctor might tell him. Throughout this exchange, Dale is both caring and supportive; here, and elsewhere, the two men build up the most touching relationship in the play.

Mamet's understanding of a fearful isolation camouflaged through language replete with bullish bravado is powerfully depicted in these scenes. Joe, of all the characters in this play, is emotionally and spiritually disabled and, in their desperate boredom, the seamen convey a sense of absurdity and pointlessness so profound it is almost tangible. One of Mamet's most Beckettian works, *Lakeboat* is shot through with a mainly unspoken (except by Joe) but nonetheless terrible fear of dying. The often stychomythic quality of the exchanges, demotically humorous but nonetheless embodying a fundamental sense of despair, frequently recalls the exchanges between Vladimir and Estragon in Beckett's *Waiting for Godot*. The underlying, usually black, vein of humor surfaces frequently in *Lakeboat*. Even at his most desperate, Joe tries to make light of his anxieties by attempts at barbed cynicism; his fearful queries are usually quickly followed with what he hopes will be taken as a dismissive and ironic speculation on, for example, how long a man could last if he did fall into the water: "I guess the big problem wouldn't be the drowning as much as the boredom . . ." (scene 18, 77).

Mamet often utilizes neat wordplay when his characters want to express the difference between what they see as the outright truth and limitless imagination. For example, in another of a long line of discussions concerning Guigliani's possible fate, Fred and the Fireman make the following observations:

FIREMAN: . . . Things. He knew things.
FRED: Yeah?
FIREMAN: Surer'n hell, that kid. He'd let on like he didn't know, but he knew. I know when they know. I can see it. And that kid's been around. The cops, they don't like that they find out, they don't sit still. They know. . . . I think he was on the run. He had friends. . . . He was no cheap talker, that kid. Talk is cheap.
FRED: You think it was the G, huh?
FIREMAN: I think what I think. That's all I know.

(scene 23, 94, 95)

From beginning to end, this sublimely absurd exchange depends on the fecundity of the Fireman's imagination; his assertions of what he thinks and what he knows become interchangeable. Clearly, nothing is certain. He whips up Fred's curiosity by mysteriously alluding to the "things" that Guigliani knew, "things" which imply trouble with the police, "things" which may even have led to his being "on the run" (95). In the Fireman's overheated melodrama, Guigliani becomes a notorious and dangerous man, one who knew too much for his own good. Quite what he knew remains a mystery, but it was obviously important enough to send the police into overdrive. The Fireman's all-knowing, if ironic closing comment: "I think what I think. That's all I know" (95) is breathtaking in its simplicity. What he thinks and what he actually knows are obviously two very different things.

Throughout the play, Mamet cleverly orchestrates the men's ever-changing impression of Guigliani, whose demeanor, capabilities, and general toughness alter numerous times throughout the play. At first, he is described as the "new kid" (scene 1, 17), an innocent who is so naive he makes the mistake of "flashing the wad every chance he gets" (18) whereas as the action progresses, he is recast as a tower of strength, a tough and sea-soned man of the world, whose downfall has only been possible since it was orchestrated by cowards who attacked him from the rear. For some, literally, Guigliani has become the Jonnie Fast of the lakeboat—as well as being one who knows more than is good for him. He can be capable of anything and, indeed, of *being* anything, it being dependent on the mood of the individual telling the story.

Full of lurid and violent tales, *Lakeboat* is a work suffused with tales of brutality and spurious felonies, although it does not contain a single criminal act within it, and no real crime is ever committed. Its characters are, literally, all talk. The *idea* of (vicariously enjoyed) crime, violence, and thuggish sexuality is a powerful aphrodisiac, and it allows them to endure their predicament with stoicism and dark humor. Without their imaginary worlds, their lives would be as dead as those who would dare to take on celluloid heroes like the much-feared Jonnie Fast.

Thus, Mamet's seamen strive to fight off incipient and all-encompassing boredom through their wish-fulfilling stories of mock-criminality. They turn themselves into the characters who people their stories and vie for supremacy and the upper hand as the spinner of the most fantastic yarn on board. But these are not merely the salty tales told by endless seafarers; in *Lakeboat*, their stories take the place of life itself. Each man turns imaginary crime into his own art form, and each constructs with commendable creativity a parallel universe that teems with danger and horror but which, at the same time, can be molded to insure that even the most frightening nightmares have a happy ending.

Notes

1. Although *Lakeboat* had its world premiere at the Goodman Theatre, Chicago, in 1982 under the direction of Gregory Mosher, its first British production was not staged until 1998. Directed by Aaron Mullen at the Lyric Studio, Hammersmith, the production featured Jim Dunk, Simon Harris, and Jon Welch.
2. See, in particular, Mamet's remarks in "Radio Drama."

Works Cited

Hardy, Barbara. *Tellers and Listeners: The Narrative Imagination.* London: The Athlone Press, 1975.

Mamet, David. *Lakeboat.* New York: Grove Press, 1981.

———. "Radio Drama." *Writing in Restaurants.* New York: Viking Penguin, 1987, 12–18.

11

David Mamet's *House of Games* and the Allegory of Performance

ELIZABETH KLAVER

David Mamet had already written numerous plays and screenplays before writing and directing the film *House of Games*, released in 1987. Like other drama coming out of the absurdist tradition (Beckett, Ionesco, Albee), Mamet's works have a serious concern with theatrical and narrative structures, with semiotic systems and their generative and deconstructive impulses. Even though plays such as *American Buffalo, Sexual Perversity in Chicago,* and *Glengarry Glen Ross* are known for their use of hard-hitting, vernacular language, they and especially *House of Games* take up many other textual issues beyond the ones raised by language alone. Based on the idea of a sting operation, *House of Games* subverts realism as we usually understand the genre by examining the functioning of the performative sign and continually forcing a retrospective reinterpretation of the "already played." Exposing its own structure as the generation of a cinematic text out of intertexts, as well as out of writing and rewriting, interpreting and misinterpreting processes, the film demonstrates how the performative sign becomes ever more enmeshed in the artifice of hyperrealism.

The film's title immediately indicates the extent of ironic re-presentation going on in *House of Games*. As Marina deBellagente LaPalma points out, the words "'house' and 'game' are basic tropes or narrative generators" (57). Acting as a three-dimensional site, the film names a locus for games such as poker and pool, which appears in the text as the "House of Games," and it also names itself as a place for related but more dangerous kinds of games—theatrical, narrative, and performative. Certainly, it is a testament to the film's ingenuity that most viewers do not recognize the title as a "tell" to textual forces at work and are thereby both involved in and victimized by its game-playing machinery.

Margaret, the psychiatrist and main character of the film, epitomizes this readerly naïveté when she first enters the "House of Games" and is invited by Mike, the con artist, to sit down at the poker table. Asked to participate in the decoding of the Vegas man's "tells," the gestures that unconsciously reveal information about his cards, Margaret unwittingly becomes the main character in a performance, complete with the semiotic play of languages, actors, and properties necessary to bringing a detailed, realistic, dramatic work to life—or in this case, to the screen. In fact, the poker game can be seen as an axis for the textual problematics many of Mamet's plays explore. In terms of verbal language, the plays often create ritualized, poetic voice as seen in the dialogue between the two old men, Emil and George, of *The Duck Variations*:

> EMIL: It's not cheap.
> GEORGE: I said it was cheap?
> EMIL: Even a small boat.
> GEORGE: I know it's not cheap.
> EMIL: Even a very small boat is expensive. (76)

This brief example shows a poetic form being constructed out of the repetition of the words "cheap" and "boat" and out of the basic two-beat meter. As the fourteen variations are built, sometimes in a coherent language and sometimes not, the play becomes a series of narratives that speculates on the life of the duck. C.W.E. Bigsby observes, though, that the poetic cadence implies a harmony with life that the two old men do not feel, since their intent appears to be the building of verbal barricades between themselves and a world that includes loss, irrelevance, and decline (*Mamet* 28, 33).

Similarly, the language of characters in plays such as *Sexual Perversity in Chicago* and *American Buffalo* is used as a way of deflecting intimacy and important concerns. As in *The Duck Variations*, dialogue between two characters has a poetic, ritualistic ring:

> BERNIE: Nineteen, twenty.
> DANNY: You're talking about a girl.
> BERNIE: Damn right.
> DANNY: You're telling me about some underage stuff.
> BERNIE: She don't gotta be but eighteen.
> . . . .
> BERNIE: Had to punch in at twenty, twenty-five easy.
> *(Sexual Perversity* 10)

In the process of producing a macho account of a one-night stand, Bernie's so-called factual narrative is already springing leaks in the continual revision of the woman's age. As he works himself up into a ludicrously violent, pornographic story, it becomes clear that the language primarily acts to conceal and to deny depth among the characters (Bigsby, *Critical Introduction* 261). In a later scene when Joan responds negatively to his pickup line, Bernie reacts in the following way: "So just who the fuck do you think you are, God's gift to Women? I mean where do you fucking get off with this shit. You don't want to get come on to, go enroll in a convent" (20). Bernie wields violent language as a weapon against the sneaking suspicion, symbolized by Joan, that he cannot score with women.

Whereas the language of Emil and George becomes at most bitter and fretful, as in Bernie's case the language of Teach (*American Buffalo*) is used both to hide concerns like the fear of betrayal and to lash out as well. In Teach, the most vulnerable character in *American Buffalo*, pain lies just below the most volatile, linguistic surface. Feeling cheated by Ruthie and Grace, Teach rants: "They treat me like an asshole, they *are* an asshole. (*Pause.*) The only way to teach these people is to kill them" (12). Later, when he begins to suspect Bobby of betrayal, Teach goes into a violent fit:

> TEACH: My Whole Cocksucking Life. (*Teach picks up the dead-pig sticker and starts trashing the junkstore.*) The Whole Entire World. There Is No Law. There Is No Right And Wrong. The World Is Lies. There Is No Friendship. Every Fucking Thing. (*Pause.*) Every God Forsaken Thing. (82)

While Bernie relies on language alone, Teach combines physical violence with verbal, bringing together the properties of the stage with the spoken language in a unified, semiotic assault on those he suspects of doing him harm.

The poker game in *House of Games* combines all of these linguistic and semiotic functions. The gambling scene is full of poetic speech; indeed, Mamet observes in *Writing in Restaurants* that playing poker has given him the insight "that all things have a rhythm" (94), a poetic aesthetic that is surely captured in the dialogue among Mike, the Vegas man, and the rest of the card players. As in *The Duck Variations* and *Sexual Perversity*, this scene is not only ritualized but also combines two very distinctive types of verbal language, one highly aggressive used by Mike and the other poetic and softly threatening used by the Vegas man:

> MIKE: You "call . . ." you only "call . . ."?
> . . . .
> AL (*throwing in his hand*): I can't stand it. South.
> VEGAS MAN: South Street Seaport the man says. He Can't Stand the Heat. He can't stand it.
> . . . .
> MIKE: I know what the goddamn bet is.
> . . . .
> VEGAS MAN: The man can't *play*, he should stay *away*. (18–19)

Neither the violently aggressive nor the poetically menacing language in this scene is being used to cover uncomfortable "truths" about character or the reality of the social or natural world. Rather, they are being used as performance, as linguistic structures that cover, distract, and deflect attention from the more important semiotic system in play—the cards.

In fact, the languages in this scene are designed precisely along the lines of the performative sign—both to hide and to uncover. Mike's aggressive attacks—"You sonofabitch. . . . I think you're bluffing pal, I think you're trying to *buy* it" (19)—do not result from frustration and therefore do not reveal his hand through a loss of self-control; instead, they are part of a staged action that not only distracts attention from his hand but also attempts to lull the Vegas man into a false sense of security so that he will let down his guard and fiddle with his ring. The semiotics of this gesture would indicate to Mike that the Vegas man is bluffing and thereby reveal important information about his hand. At the same time, though, since he has settled into a fortress of ritualized poetry that also hides his hand, the Vegas man stands impervious to Mike's violent parries and tries to threaten quietly Mike's composure.

At least, this is what the card game looks like at first. Only two types of semiosis, the verbal language and the language of the cards, appear to be in play, generating the scene out of a process of collision and concealment be- . tween these sign structures. The viewer is allowed to watch them at work and to feel the tension produced as the performative sign goes about its business of disguise and revelation. Nevertheless, other semiotic apparatuses lie beneath the poker game, making the signs of language and cards also work to distract attention from a whole set of theatrical devices ranging from properties to actors to costumes to gestures. This situation becomes apparent at the moment of climactic conflict when the Vegas man pulls out his gun. Rather than uniting physical violence with verbal as Teach has done, the carefully constructed illusion of the poker game falls apart. The stage directions indicate: "*Angle—Point of view. Very tight on the revolver, the muzzle end is leaking little drops of water*" (23). The realism of the scene both for Margaret and the viewer is revealed as artifice, the product of a theatrical play among semiotic forces once working in harmony but now undercut by the exposure of one rogue sign, the gun revealed as a harmless property.

With Margaret's realization that the poker game is a performance, a confidence game directed at her, the scene collapses into a backstage examination of the con men as actors and playwrights. Although they have written a highly realistic script, complete with all the details necessary for fourth-wall illusion, they have had to work with an unknown, Margaret as an "actor" whose reactions, within the role they have defined for her, may direct the outcome in unpredictable ways. The self-doubt involved in this lack of control is encoded in the script as complications with the gun: the con men cannot use a real, loaded gun because it is always too dangerous in a theatrical venue, especially when much of the script is being written as they go along. Mike claims that the squirt gun would have worked if it had not been filled with water. George (the Vegas man), on the other hand, argues that an empty gun is no threat at all.

The discussion between the two con men begins an examination of the performative sign that will continue throughout the film, with this particular scene indicating several of its characteristics. In any dramatic form, including film, that attempts realism on some level, the stage properties have to *look* as realistic as possible yet be entirely harmless. Mike can accept this fact but George cannot. The gun also inscribes the theatricality of the performative sign itself. It tries to conceal itself as a stage property, yet reveal itself as an element within the world of the play; this function is itself inscribed within its ontology. The revelation of the gun as a harmless property merely foregrounds that aspect of the performative sign that realistic genre makes every effort to conceal. As well, the inability of the performative sign to represent something fully, in this case both a weapon and a dangerous intent, is ironically exposed because the squirt gun, coming as an element from the open range of possible signifiers for the sign, opens up the sign to "representing" much more than semiotic denotation or connotation can control.

Thus, the unmasking of the poker game as artifice also changes the function of the various semiotic systems at work in the scene. Those verbal languages used by Mike and the Vegas man, as well as the language of the cards, the semiosis of the properties including the gun, of the con men as actors, of their costumes and gestures and of the back room setting, now appear as weapons directed against Margaret. The poker scene illustrates that in Mamet's world languages of any kind operate less as a means of communication and more as a means of extortion. As Mamet claims in an interview with David Savran: "All of us are trying all the time to create the best setting and the best expression we can, not to communicate our wishes to each other, but to *achieve* our wishes *from* each other" (qtd. in Savran 137). And the attempt to achieve wishes from another through a linguistic onslaught occurs pointedly in another of Mamet's plays, *Glengarry Glen Ross*.

In this work, real estate salesmen not only attack each other and the audience with abusive language but they use linguistic techniques similar to the con artist's. They spin fictions out of language not to engage in communication but to extract money. One scene in particular illustrates the kind of theatricality these men are capable of when it comes to protecting a sale. Seeing his client coming to cancel a contract, Roma says to his partner, Levene: "You're a client. I just sold you five waterfront Glengarry Farms. I rub my head, throw me the cue 'Kenilworth'" (78). This scene operates as a reversal of the poker game in *House of Games*. In *Glengarry Glen Ross*, the audience is warned beforehand of its fictional nature and therefore watches it as an accessory; in *House of Games*, on the contrary, we experience the poker scene as victim.

The correlation of the con artist, whether as a "true bad man" or as a salesman, to the writer should be clear by now. As Dennis Carroll, Bigsby, and numerous reviewers have observed, the spinners of fiction and drama within Mamet's plays weave the same sorts of illusions as the writer. But rather than follow the long-standing convention of postulating the writer as a messenger of truth, Mamet's works subvert the very idea that the writer can be trustworthy. In the deconstruction of the poker game, we witness the postmodern writer rewriting the writer as con artist.

In fact, the collapse of the poker game, which presents the con men as untrustworthy writers, prompts the viewer into retrospectively reinterpreting the previous scenes. How far back in the film does this particular confidence game go? With such an elaborately staged piece moving into action, the con men surely could not have been waiting in the "House of Games" for just anybody to show up. Does Billy Hahn offer the bait by threatening to kill himself over a $25,000 gambling debt? Does Mike already understand Margaret well enough to devise a script so seductive she will insert herself into it without hesitation? In other words, the poker game seems to "script" backward, making the most spontaneous moment of the film so far, the leaking gun, challenge the illusions of spontaneity that have preceded it.

Is the leaking gun, though, really such a spontaneous deconstruction? As Margaret becomes involved with Mike she enters the script of a second confidence game—a master con—that eventually bilks her of $80,000. Like her, most viewers and readers do not realize that these later events are actually an allegory of the poker game, a reenactment of the already played, that will eventually produce the same denouement. Indeed, the master con is a clinic of the confidence game. As in the poker game, Mike gives Margaret his confidence, and she responds by giving him something in return—her trust. As David Denby notes, "we long to trust the people telling us a story" (101), so that both the character and the viewer fall into a trusting relationship with the fictionalizer. And, as in *Glengarry Glen Ross*, for the first part of the master con we are also in the position of accessory rather than victim, finding ourselves on the side of the con artist and privy to the backstage construction of what appears to be the performance. Mike keeps both Margaret and the viewer updated on the progress of the operation: "Who said it was phoney money? . . . We're showing the guy eighty thousand real dollars" (47–48). When he gives his confidence to the businessman by agreeing to accept $30,000 in collateral, Mike appears to play strictly by the rules.

If there is any kind of suspicion that a sting is being marshaled against Margaret as it was in the poker game, it is effectively deflected by the revelation of the businessman's "true" role. When Margaret sees his gun and overhears his conversation with the police on the two-way radio, the businessman part of the operation falls apart, not as the poker game did with the revelation of its writtenness but because an alternate script, a sting devised by the police, appears to be intruding into the con men's "play." As far as Margaret is concerned, the con men will certainly lose, and she cannot afford to star in a police drama. A struggle takes place and, so it seems, a capital offense.

It is interesting that the appearance of a gun again causes a confidence game to fall apart. This time, its unexpected intrusion into Mike's script of the businessman sting seems to enact the danger first broached in the poker game when real, loaded guns turn up in a performance, especially one that has a large element of anarchy about it. As we will eventually discover, though, the gun in this scene actually functions as an effective, realistic sign, able to conceal itself as a stage property within the performance and relegate to the background its harmless nature. This sort of realism fosters the misinterpretation that the real world is intruding into and deconstructing the fiction of the businessman sting. However, Mike and Joey will turn out not to be bumbling fools at all but consummate actors, playwrights, and scenographers.

Margaret has so thoroughly trusted Mike she does not recognize that the collision of intertexts in the businessman/police story is generating a single, all-encompassing performance. The master con has not, so far, deconstructed, since the collapse of the businessman part of the operation has already been written into the larger swindle directed against her. However, the breakdown of the master con begins to occur when Margaret recognizes the red Cadillac Billy Hahn is driving as the same car she had stolen in order to make the getaway. A stolen vehicle that has been involved in the murder of a policeman would have to be abandoned. Only a stage property *posing* as a stolen vehicle could be used again once its initial role was over.

The realism of recent scenes now unravels. The vision of the world that Margaret had accepted as "true" collapses. Revisiting the "House of Games," she comes upon the characters of the master con now in their everyday roles, and she overhears them dividing up her money and discussing their performances. As in the poker game, the semiotics of the master con turn out to have been directed against her in an elaborately staged artifice that included sets, costumes, and actors. Joey and Mike relate how they had dressed the hotel suite, strewing it with small properties such as cigars, money, and a pocket knife; rented two policeman's uniforms; and played convincing roles as the businessman/policeman, the hotel guest, Joey the fatherly con, and Mike the romantic lover and confidant.

As in the deconstruction of the poker game, the revelation of the businessman sting as part of a larger swindle causes a retrospective reinterpretation not only of recent events but of all contacts with the con men. For the viewer, as well, the entire film up to this point must now again be reread.

Certainly, Billy Hahn's suicide threat is now definitely exposed as a lure. One must even wonder about the opening scene in which the young woman on the street asks Margaret for her autograph: was that Margaret's first meeting with the con artist, the first effort on their part to make physical contact with the author of *Driven*, a popular book on the kinds of compulsive behavior that Mike recognizes in Margaret and uses against her? Explaining how he knew Margaret would fall for the game, Mike says, "the broad's an *addict* . . ." (61).

In fact, the poker game and the problematics of the performative sign that it demonstrated must also again be reread in the light of this new script. Was the collapse of the earlier performance also a part of the larger script? Was the gun filled with water not because the Vegas man had some rude notion of "realism" but because "realism" was meant to collapse? In fact, now Joey, not George (the Vegas man), admits to filling the gun with water. The "businessman" responds, "it's what you pay for, it's realism" (61), a comment that suggests two alternate and incompatible interpretations: either "realism" means that the squirt gun had to be filled with water since the nature of the signifier is seen as dictating the sign's content or the deconstruction of "realism" was the "realism" they were going for. Either they had planned to take Margaret for $6,000 in the poker game and, failing in the attempt, then devised the master con, or they had planned the collapse of the poker game from the beginning in order to seduce her into the more complex and lucrative structure.

Interestingly, as in the poker game, it is a collapse in semiotics that brings down the larger performance of the master con, and results from the inability once again of the performative sign to maintain itself. The impossibility of the sign to re-present something fully, in this case to bring about a recurrence of signs or, in other words, to allegorize fully the poker game, shows up as a distortion between the intertexts of the poker game and the master con. However, although the contours of the two scripts collide, apparently dissolving into one structure, they do differ in detail and outcome. Whereas the deconstruction of the master con recesses the leaking gun of the poker game into the order of simulacra, in which the real cannot be "told" from the staged, the red Cadillac cannot quite replicate this situation, instead collapsing on the weight of its own problematic as a sign, as both concealer and revealer. As in other postmodern works, where the text can only represent its semiotic functions whether as the recurrence of an embedded script or of a property, the inability to complete representation always arrives in the foreground.

Just so, the inability to complete representation in the performative sign means that the master con, the $80,000 sting that Mike has scripted, also can never be completed. As in *American Buffalo* where the burglary is always deferred both as performance and as action, the closure of the master con in which Mike should finish by escaping to Las Vegas is short-circuited. Like other Mamet characters who are involved in a teacher-student relationship, as Pascale Hubert-Leibler points out, Margaret turns out to be a model student, learning from her teacher performative abilities that turn her into a "dangerous rival" (565).

Consequently, Margaret devises a script capable of interrupting and rewriting Mike's. Now understanding the implications of his text, Margaret arrives at the airport to intercept it. As in the poker game, this new script forestalls the viewer in being able to determine just how much of the subsequent performance is already written and how much of it occurs impulsively. Up to a certain point, the viewer is placed in the position of accessory, since, as in *Glengarry Glen Ross*, we know that Margaret's initial actions are devised. Her surprise at running into Mike at the airport and her story about being followed are clearly fictions at odds with the conversation she overheard at the "House of Games." Learning from the earlier performances she had unwittingly starred in, Margaret offers Mike her confidence: "I'm so frightened. And . . . Mike: Mike: I . . . I took all my money. I took all my money out of the bank. I'm . . . and you'll help us disappear" (64). In fact, this penultimate scene attempts to allegorize the confidence games presented so far, for Margaret's text writes into Mike's in the same way the police story appeared to write into the businessman sting. And, when Margaret makes the slip of referring to the knife she took from the hotel room as "Your pocket knife" (66), the script appears to deconstruct in the manner of the poker game—Mike realizes that somehow Margaret has seen the theatricality involved in the master con and is presenting a confidence game of her own.

The collapse of Margaret's script differs, though, from the earlier breakdowns in the poker game and master con. Whereas the gun and the Cadillac revealed the functioning of the performative sign by showing themselves as stage properties, the words "your pocket knife" constitute a linguistic construct that refers back to a theatrical construct in the form of the pocket knife as stage property. In other words, "your pocket knife" refers not to the performative sign of the pocket knife as it was embodied in the *scene* in the hotel room, but to the pocket knife as signifier, as stage property that Mike had placed there. Since both the words "pocket knife" and the pocket knife come from the open range of possible signifiers for the sign, something like a chain occurs in which one signifier attempts to stand in for the other. Because there is an inevitable by-product of distortion when such a re-presentational process occurs, a certain amount of slippage occurs within the balance of meaning and intent collecting as a residue between the two signifiers. As a result, Margaret's verbal slip acts as a "tell" that tips off Mike by pointing to the opacity of the stage property rather than to its transparency. The problematics of the performative sign are once again exposed in its inability to control or absorb fully meaning and intent, especially when it has to re-present one thing as another.

Moreover, the breakdown of Margaret's script so far also suggests that the final actions between her and Mike are another attempt on the part of one text to represent others. Her linguistic error can be seen as a premeditated device much like the two earlier appearances of the gun, a device that has been written into a larger textual structure in order to usher in the denouement of a revenger's play. When Mike tries to call her bluff after she pulls out the gun, Margaret says, "It's not my pistol, I was never here" (69). A deserted baggage area makes a good setting for murder and the revving of a plane's engines conveniently covers the sound of gunshots when Margaret empties the chambers. As if making an ironic comment, these final moments in the airport again distort the poker game by almost completely reversing its ending. Mike stares into the gun in much the same way he and Margaret faced the Vegas man. The difference, of course, is that Mike has not written this script and therefore can easily misinterpret, as Margaret has previously done, the kind of theatricality involved in the performance.

For example, when the gun reappears in Margaret's hands the film returns to the question of realism in the performative sign. Realizing that Margaret is pulling some kind of confidence game of her own, Mike tries to counter the threat of the gun with the same aggressive language he used on the Vegas man in the poker game. In keeping with his sense of the gun as part of a bluff, in which realism would work to hide the harmless character of a stage property, Mike underestimates the nature of Margaret's script. He should have kept in mind the evolution of the sign to simulation begun by the gun in the poker game, in which subsequent rereadings have brought about a merging of the real with the image. In the airport, theatricality appears to blend finally with real life. The performative sign of the gun veers away from its usual relationship with the open range of possible contents, this time by allowing the signifier to dictate its contents to dangerous rather than naive effect. Instead of collapsing into a harmless stage property, the performative sign is caught in the artifice of the entire scene; it becomes a hyperreal, a loaded stage property that turns the dramatic site of a murder into the real thing.

In the final moments of his life, Mike is actually lost in the territory of simulation. Now rereading the actions that occurred before Margaret dropped her linguistic slip, Mike understands all of those signs as part of an artificial web. After the linguistic slip, though, he opts for the deconstruction of artifice into the real, failing to appreciate that the subsequent actions only situate the deconstruction of artifice within further frames of artifice. As Jean Baudrillard observes, the simulation of events turns out to have all of the features of the real: if one tries to simulate a bank robbery for instance, Baudrillard suggests that "the web of artificial signs will be inextricably mixed up with real elements" (*Selected Writings* 178). Mike makes the mistake of assuming he can "tell" the difference.

Since he is forced to act in Margaret's script, there really is no point in fighting her for control of the performance. Nevertheless, in one of the most vitriolic scenes ever staged of languages pitted against each other, Mike fires verbal salvos back at Margaret's gun: "Hey, fuck *you*. This is what you always *wanted*—you crooked bitch . . . you *thief . . .*" (69). In this case, the real is so thoroughly enmeshed with the image that neither can be isolated. The web of signs in Margaret's script, which includes the hyperrealism of the gun, cannot be separated from the web of signs in which Mike dies.

The artificiality of the penultimate scene, then, brings to a climax the artificiality that has existed throughout the film, not only in the film's focus on its own (de)construction but also as many reviewers have observed in dialogue and setting. In fact, Howie Movshovitz reads staginess right from the sign of the red dress in the opening scene. And while some reviewers critique the dialogue as "deliberately artificial" (Freedman) or as "self-consciously flat" (Rickey), most agree that *House of Games* draws on the film noir tradition with, as Anne Marie Biondo writes, its "dangerous romantic interlude, shadowy cinematography, [and] deceptive exposition" (C6).

Indeed, Mike and Margaret, who correspond to the artful characters of film noir, are played along superficial lines. As Bert Cardullo writes: "This film doesn't probe psychological depths; rather, it depicts the behavioral surfaces of characters obsessed with success, with defining themselves through achievement, be it in the world of psychoanalysis or of conning" (349). Mike and Margaret are, in fact, images of each other: the con artist demonstrates as much psychological know-how as the psychiatrist, and the psychiatrist, accused of being a con artist at the beginning of the film, learns to beat the con man at his own game. Two images lock into a revolving exchange that fosters an indeterminacy in character and identity. Who is the psychiatrist? Who is the con artist? Who is the artist?

Indeed, the scene at the airport actually shows how Margaret processes a new image out of the mirror that was Mike by playing out his role as well as her own. However, in the film's final scene appearances almost fall apart. The tension involved in the ontology of the performative sign over concealment and revelation comes back into view. Approached by a man who looks like an undercover cop (shades of the master con?), Margaret appears momentarily nonplussed as if she has somehow been found out. As it turns out, he is only asking for her autograph so that Margaret's new self, generated out of the signs of psychiatrist and con artist, remains impenetrable and intact. At this point, the performative sign has completely evolved into simulacrum, no longer in danger of collapsing into actor playing murderer: Margaret is now completely enmeshed with the real as actor *and* murderer.

The final image of Margaret that we are left with appears to present a troubling ideology about women, suggesting that feminine self-identity is achieved only as power over men, enacted through the murder of "father" and lover. Indeed, Mamet's work has been accused of anti-feminism, including plays such as *Glengarry Glen Ross* and *American Buffalo* that either have no women characters at all or recess them into fictional domains. However, I would not agree with LaPalma's claim that *House of Games* "reinscribes the woman in patriarchal ideology" (59) or Guido Almansi's that Mamet's "best plays are immune from any female contamination" (191). The depictions of women that do seem difficult (Margaret, Carol of *Oleanna*, even Karen of *Speed-the-Plow*) in terms of feminist interpretation reveal no more problematic or ambiguous characterization than what Mamet develops for the men. Ann C. Hall's Lacanian analysis of *House of Games* seems right on the mark in demonstrating that Mamet's women, including Margaret, are actually disrupting gender binaries and "creating changes concerning the representation of women" (158).

In Mamet's world, women and men are equally involved in self-serving games and in maneuvering for power. The hard shell of appearance-affects character regardless of gender. *House of Games* is about the performative sign and the processing and circulation of image in the postmodern age. The film belongs more to postfeminism than to the genre of realism, the social problem play, or what LaPalma calls the "woman's film." That we find ourselves unable to admire a female character who once had our sympathy is part of both the seductive and hard, repellant surface of signs.

House of Games is ultimately about the functioning and dysfunctioning of signs and dramatic structures and their open evolution into simulacra. While the performative sign has revealed its capacity to break down, thereby deconstructing realism and demystifying the text, the film has inevitably embedded those processes within a matrix of artificiality that progresses inexorably toward a postmodern hyperrealism. The real (and realism) finally retreats so far back into a network of signs that it effectively disappears. In fact, *House of Games* not only processes its images into the matrix of its own site but also it entraps the viewer with its manipulation of them. The scripting operations that at various times have victimized Margaret or Mike have always victimized the viewer. The film's ultimate sting lies in its identity as the postmodern "writer" itself, the (con) artist that is out to use signs *not* for communication but to wield power.

Works Cited

Almansi, Guido. "David Mamet, a Virtuoso of Invective." *Critical Angles: European Views of Contemporary American Literature.* Ed. Marc Chénetier. Carbondale: Southern Illinois UP, 1986, 191–207.

Baudrillard, Jean. *Selected Writings*. Trans. Paul Foss, Paul Patton, and Philip Beitchman. Ed. Mark Poster. Stanford: Stanford UP, 1988.

Bigsby, C.W.E. *A Critical Introduction to Twentieth Century American Drama*. Cambridge: Cambridge UP, 1985.

———. *David Mamet*. London: Methuen, 1985.

Biondo, Anne Marie. "A Whirlwind Ride in Slow Motion." Rev. of *House of Games*, by David Mamet. *Detroit News*, 18 Dec. 1987, B6.

Cardullo, Bert. "Three Ways to Play House." *The Hudson Review* 41 (1988): 348–56.

Carroll, Dennis. *David Mamet*. New York: St. Martin's Press, 1987.

Denby, David. "What's in a Game." Rev. of *House of Games*, by David Mamet. *New York* 10, 19 Oct. 1987, 101–2.

Freedman, Richard. "David Mamet Makes Superlative Debut as Director of Chilling 'House of Games.'" Rev. of *House of Games*, by David Mamet. *Star-Ledger,* 14 Oct. 1987, D4.

Hall, Ann C. "Playing to Win: Sexual Politics in David Mamet's *House of Games* and *Speed-the-Plow*." *David Mamet: A Casebook*. Ed. Leslie Kane. New York: Garland, 1992, 137–60.

Hubert-Leibler, Pascale. "Dominance and Anguish: The Teacher-Student Relationship in the Plays of David Mamet." *Modern Drama* 31 (1988): 557–70.

LaPalma, Marina deBellagente. "Driving Doctor Ford." *Literature/Film Quarterly* 24.1 (1996): 57–62.

Mamet, David. *American Buffalo*. London: Samuel French, 1975.

———. *Glengarry Glen Ross*. New York: Grove Press, 1984.

———. *House of Games*. New York: Grove Press, 1987.

———. Interview. With David Savran. *In Their Own Words: Contemporary American Playwrights*. New York: Theatre Communications Group, 1988, 132–44.

———. *Sexual Perversity in Chicago and The Duck Variations*. New York: Grove Press, 1978.

———. *Writing in Restaurants*. New York: Grove Press, 1988.

Movshovitz, Howie. "Now You Catch It, Now You Don't in Mind Game." Rev. of *House of Games*, by David Mamet. *Denver Post,* 22 Jan. 1988, C7.

Rickey, Carrie. "High Stages at the 'House of Games.'" Rev. of *House of Games*, by David Mamet. *Philadelphia Inquirer,* 18 Dec. 1987, B11.

12

More Uses of the Knife as Signifier in *The Cryptogram, The Old Religion,* and *The Edge*

THOMAS P. ADLER

Most great drama is about betrayal of one sort or another.

—DAVID MAMET

I

The title of David Mamet's 1998 book of reflections on the theater teases its readers: Why ever would three brief essay-lectures subtitled "on the nature and purpose of drama" collectively be called *Three Uses of the Knife?* What link could possibly exist between an instrument most readily associated with acts of violence and the production of art? A knife's potential, as the title passage of Mamet's modest treatise reminds us, is multifaceted and shifting, ranging from morally neutral to culpable: "Huddie Ledbetter, also known as Leadbelly, said: You take a knife, you use it to cut the bread, so you'll have strength to work; you use it to shave, so you'll look nice for your lover; on discovering her with another, you use it to cut out her lying heart" (66). Mamet, as his title may indicate, has not penned an "aspects of the drama" according to what E. M. Forster famously did for the novel; his intention here appears more sharply polemical.

Drama's "nature and purpose"—what it does and to what ends—Mamet delineates in fairly straightforward terms: by structuring events according to cause and effect, drama helps make a chaotic universe "understandable" and "comprehensible"; by moving toward an "inevitable" resolution, it helps satisfy the human desire "to order the intolerable into meaning" (27); by presenting the hero's journey to a discovery of truths earlier ignored or rejected, it (in Aristotelian fashion) "inspire[s a] cleansing awe" (69). Just *how* it accomplishes these things is where Mamet's knife comes into play.

Mamet is intent on distinguishing between two types of drama, one that he resists and another that he embraces. The first is a drama of manipulation.

Consisting of problem plays that cater to "moral superiority" and "indignation," of melodramas that "raise anxiety" only to reduce it to "safety," and
of romances that fulfill the "adolescent fantasy" of power and "triumph"
such drama "feeds the ego" and thereby "infantiliz[es]" its audience (15).
This is theater as a tool of the "entrepreneur" that provides rational solutions
for the "conscious mind" (46). If it does involve violence against an easily
identifiable villain, as is often the case, the "thrills and mutilation" can only
be compulsively repeated, which inadvertently reveals the impossibility of
ever achieving the wished for "repression" of irrational fear (52).

Against theater such as this that he regards as a commodity, Mamet proposes one that rediscovers and restores its ancient association with myth and
magic and religious ritual; one that, instead of treating its audience as "consumers," raises them to the level of "communicants" bonded together,
searching for answers. Precisely because "great art . . . stills a conflict—by
airing rather than rationalizing it" (46), such theater is troubling and disquieting. By "deal[ing] with problems of the soul, with the mysteries of human
life" (27), this variety of drama trades in recognition of "powerlessness,"
"unfairness," "quotidian calamities." Most shockingly for a post-Enlighten-
ment age, it enjoins "the worthlessness of reason" (70), which leads only to
partial truths and "wrong conclusions" and "intellectual arrogance." What it
proposes instead is "a nonrational synthesis" that permits one—in what,
from O'Neill onward in the drama, has become a peculiarly American formulation of the intersection of free will and determinism—to "perceive the
pattern wrought by our character" (80).

The answer resides, then, not in reason or the head, but in the heart. And
only the knife "comes from the heart and, so, goes to the heart" (21): "The
knife becomes, in effect, congruent to the bass line in music. For the bass
line, not the melody, gives music strength, and moves us. . . . The tragedy of
murder is affecting as the irony of the recurrent knife is affecting. The appearance of the knife is the attempt of the orderly, affronted mind to confront the awesome; to discover the hidden structure of the word. In this
endeavor, our rational mind will not be of help" (67). As Aristotle might
have put it, the chaotic violence endemic to Greek drama is somehow transcended by tragedy's cathartic power to purge emotion. If the rational mind
loses its vaunted efficacy, then what may be of help, Mamet strongly implies, is an intuition available within "the province of theater and religion"
that is attuned to and reads feelingly the suggestive nuances and gaps and
fissures within the dramatic (or literary) text, unafraid to be wounded by
what it discovers—in the same way that the text itself goes beyond the
words and rational thought processes. Mamet as a dramatist disclaims any
interest in attempting "to bring about social change" (26); he rejects the
Brechtian notion of a didactic theater committed "to teach us," creating instead a passionate drama of what might be called *felt ideas*. This disavowal

of theater as an instrument of ideology is, nevertheless, not anti-intellectual, but rather an expression of Mamet's wariness with any exclusive dependence on reason, which can so easily be misused and become distorted into an empty rationalism, devoid of affective and ethical appeal. The concern over bridging words and action, knowledge and experience, thought and feeling lies at the heart of *The Cryptogram, The Old Religion*, and *The Edge*, the dramatic, fictional, and cinematic works that immediately precede—and crystalize in—*Three Uses of the Knife*, with its antirationalist agenda and its deliberate opposition between intellection and an affective response.

These are not the first or only Mamet works in which knives figure prominently. Generalizing about the use of the knife in Mamet's plays, Linda Dorff notes that in some instances it might be "a phallus that literally and figuratively penetrates feminized Others—women, children, and gay men—in order to establish gendered difference and, thereby, power over them" (177). Yet in *Things Change*, the 1988 film written with Shel Silverstein, the knives—both Kenny's dagger and the bowie knife belonging to the retainer of the Texas Don—are purely functional, a means to enact violence like any other. In the 1979 radio play *Prairie du Chien*, however, the knife does assume phallic connotations, as the jealous husband in the Storyteller's tale uses it to castrate the hired man who has cuckolded him. In the urban inferno of *Edmond* (1983) the knife is, indeed, used in an attempt to restore phallic power and strength, exercised through both word and act. After the title character purchases the World War II survival knife (like the one in *The Cryptogram*) at a pawnshop, he—in retaliation for his own sense of having been psychologically emasculated—verbally abuses the woman in the subway station, taunts the pimp with racist and homophobic invective, and stabs Glenna to death. In prison after his violent rampage, Edmond enters into a relationship that begins in a forced homosexual act but is finally willingly embraced as he kisses his black cellmate goodnight, accepting his own Otherness that the uses of the knife initially were designed to deny and resist. As is true of *Edmond*, in *The Cryptogram, The Old Religion*, and *The Edge* the crimes of the heart are complex, the acts of violence may be as much psychological as they are physical, and the knives carry multiple significations.

II

Multiple betrayals occur in Mamet's *The Cryptogram* (1995), a play whose characters occupy points on a number of triangles: Robert/Donny/Del; Robert/Donny/the Other Woman; Robert/Del/the Other Woman; John/Donny/Robert; John/Del/Robert. Interestingly, Robert, who appears in all these triangles and who, as the audience gradually discovers, is deserting his ten-year-old son, John, and his wife, Donny, for another woman, is also the character never seen onstage, as well as the one whose knife becomes the play's central prop. The work's title raises the issue of the difficulty of decoding the meaning or significance that inheres in words and actions and objects. Most centrally, Del must decode Robert's message and motives as they are encrypted in the knife that his friend has given to him and that makes the absent father's "presence" pervade the play. Without necessarily subscribing to Martin Schaub's reading of *Cryptogram* as "a communal theatrical celebration of . . . magic meanings," it is still possible to agree that a symbol such as the knife can "give rise to thought," signify something other than itself, and communicate "truth" (334–35).

A few minutes into the play, however, Del offers the possibility that meaning does not, in fact, inhere in words but rather is a function of the speaker's intention; as if to illustrate this, several moments later Donny will use the phrase "close up" to mean "neaten up." Later still, Donny will remark on the almost universal tendency to "assume [that events] have a meaning," although "we don't know what it is" (79) and so must impose it. Her intellectually precocious son worries over the epistemological quandary of "how do we *know* the things we know?": does reality exist or does language create it? Is "nothing" (a "*book . . . buildings . . . thought*") real, or is everything true? Such Lyotardian and Derridian postmodern conundrums form but the background, however, of a homoerotically tense drama of a disintegrating nuclear family (the time is 1959) and their gay friend who positions himself as a substitute father and, albeit in a nonsexual way, surrogate husband. In what way(s) transgressive desire might be negotiated in a society that demonizes it becomes, then, a central issue in the play.

The friendship of the adults here extends back to before World War II, as evidenced in a photograph of the three of them in which Del wears Robert's shirt, perhaps as an "innocent" way of achieving physical intimacy. Del finds photography itself "seductive," quite probably because of the materiality of tangible things. Sometime after the war, when the three friends went on a trip together, Robert and Donny made love under a blanket (another object unearthed from the attic) while Del was nearby, and Donny coyly wonders now whether it "upset" Del to "hear" them. Although Robert served in the Air Force, Del confesses to not having seen combat in the war ("what would *I* know about the war? I lived in a *Hotel*" [87]), and so he was cut off from such sustaining masculine rituals and homosocial bonding. Indeed, as it finally begins to dawn on him just why Robert made him a present of the knife, Del even defines himself as Other, expressing shame over being a "geek" (unverbalized "queer") from the city whom his friend would never have imagined taking along on a camping trip, as he leads Donny to believe was the case.

Robert gives Del the knife as a gift in return for his friend's allowing him to use his bed for a week-long assignation with the other woman—during which the bookish Del, man of words rather than action, holes up in a "nook" in the library. Del romantically (mis)reads the knife as a sign of male friendship, made all the more special because Robert had supposedly been awarded it as a "Combat Trophy" for heroism in battle. Yet Donny prompts Del to consider what Robert might have been trying to tell him, what meaning accrued to the gesture of giving him an instrument that would have been used "to cut the *cords*. If his parachute snagged" (65). Employed for that purpose, the knife severs or "release[s]" its user from something he is "forced to *abandon*." Del eventually comes to realize that Robert gave him the knife as a bribe "To shut [him] up" (73). After deriding Del as a "fairy" and a "fool" and thereby, as Dorff argues, "removing him from his role as surrogate father and husband and homophobically reinscribing him as an Other on the margins of the family" (187), Donny reveals that Robert actually "bought" the knife, and so, contrary to what Del had been led to believe, it "had no meaning for him" (87) whatsoever. But whereas no special significance inhered in the object for Robert, he did nothing to discourage Del from imposing a faulty meaning upon it, as signification of homoerotic desire that it never did possess, for which Del now determines to exact vengeance.

The knife, intended to silence Del from betraying the truth about Robert and the other woman, makes its first appearance in the play innocently enough, loaned to John by Del as a means of cutting the twine around a tackle box. Later, Del uses it to open a bottle of wine for a kind of secularized communion "ceremony" to signify "interaction and togetherness" between himself and Donny; he stammers, faltering verbally yet revealingly, as he talks about their being "be-nighted" and "be-trothed" and "Close to each other" (61). As Janet Haedicke writes: "Del's trouble with the 'be's' of causality and being subverts his performance of an inscribed male epistemology; the abnegation of even illusory control reflects the position of an excluded, disempowered Other, who apparently shares Donny's desire for Robert" (10). Just as collaborating in his friend's seduction of the other woman by offering his own bed may well have been a way of experiencing some union with Robert without violating societal proscriptions, so, too, closeness to Donny may be a means of attempting to possess Robert. Finally, Del enters bearing the knife (along with a book likely inscribed to him by Donny) that he then proceeds to give to John as "a propitiation" for having been "wronged."

John has, indeed, been used badly by all three of these adults: by his father Robert who, instead of arriving to take the boy on a promised camping trip, uses the occasion to put an end to his marriage to John's mother; by

Del, who becomes an agent of Robert's adultery and desertion of his son; and, even by Donny, who turns away from and tries to thrust her emotionally fragile and quite likely psychologically disturbed son into adulthood well before his time. As John begins to hear voices and see visions and vocalize his fears about being alone and his preoccupation with death, his mother tells the boy that she is unable to "help" him and that he just needs to learn to deal with these things on his own. The offstage sound early in the play of the smashing of the teapot Donny has dropped, as well as the repeated references to the mysterious tear in the blanket that had been associated with sex between the parents and would ordinarily provide physical warmth and comfort—and even her nonfeminine name—all add to the sense of Donny as a woman who feels circumscribed by and desires to escape traditional gender roles. Not only does she look forward to having husband and son "gone" from hearth and home for awhile, but in a life she calls "trash" and a world she defines as a "shithouse" and "cesspool" she looks upon "All the men I ever met" (93) as having betrayed her. And not just, with good reason, Robert and Del, but John as well, when he backs down and fails to keep his promise about going upstairs to sleep.

If, when Del donned camping clothes only to hide out in a library, his masculinity was performative, his newly found patriarchal control turns deadly in the closing moments of the play as he dismisses John with the words, "Take the knife and go" (101). The bought object has now assumed a potent meaning for Del as an indication of Robert's final rejection and as an insult demanding retribution. And it retains an almost totemic value for the boy as the last object associated with the father in a space now totally "*denuded.*" Although John acknowledges in the play's curtain line, "They're [the voices] calling my name" (103), Mamet's text ends before he ascends to the dark at the top of the stairs. Yet the audience might certainly recall other plays—Henrik Ibsen's *Hedda Gabler*, Marsha Norman's *'night, Mother*—in which an object of destruction belonging to the father becomes an instrument of death for the child. And, what is more, Del's command to John is virtually an exact echo of Jean's to Julie in another sexually charged drama that ends in the offspring's suicide, August Strindberg's *Miss Julie*. Even if Mamet resists closure, leaving the outcome open-ended, a son here is sacrificial victim of a father, and words are shown to have the power to betray and kill as much as any knife.

In his cryptic reference earlier to a story from a children's book in which "Misfortunes come in threes" (29), John recalls that in the legend "the Lance was broken by the Lord of Night, [and] the Chalice was burnt" (30). In life, he also has seen two misfortunes so far come to pass—in the shattered teapot and the ripped blanket, for which he somehow feels guilty—and he now ominously awaits whatever the third might be. It could actually, he supposes, already have happened earlier (perhaps the play leads audiences to discover it in Robert's betrayal and insult of his friend who is sexually Other); or it might be still to come (in the fulfillment of Del's vengeance on Robert through the knife that has the potential to sever his son from life). In any event, unlike in the Old Testament story of Abraham and Isaac, no angel of the Lord seems poised and ready to save John by thwarting the knife's passage.

III

In Mamet's *The Old Religion* (1997), Leo Frank, in prison after being wrongly convicted of murdering fourteen-year-old Mary Phagan, in fact ponders the two great mythic stories from Judaism and Christianity of fathers willing to sacrifice sons. Abraham "refrained" from using the knife and "did not kill his son," whereas "*Their* [i.e., the Christians'] God did." And furthermore, whereas Jews "are told to love God," Christians conceive of god as so "lov[ing] the world . . . that he gave his only begotten son" (132). So Frank can only conclude—fully aware of its application to those who falsely condemned and will soon lynch him—"perhaps it is love of the world which leads to murder." Of course, Frank, like all Jewish males, has already been marked as Other by the use of the knife, forever defined by loss in a ritual shedding of foreskin and blood according to religious law. It is the "deformity and . . . perversion" of his circumcised penis, unseen but rumored, that the naive girls testify to at his trial. Yet like some "specimen captured by savages" (105), the text of his body also has been (mis)read as Jewish in other ways, in his physiognomy (the "hooked nose") and his gestures (the "pointing of a finger" in disputation) and his purported sexual appetites ("ravening lecher"). The society would never embrace him, even though their Saviour "was a Jew and thus the color of the wandering race" (191). Anti-Semitism is all around him. Frank becomes an avid reader while in prison, even though "In each of his books there was the Jew, the moneylender, the Shylock, the figure of fun" (118), while in the newspaper "The Kike [is called] the Nigger to the nth degree" (98). Frank, however, is a mostly nonobservant Jew: not only does he work on the Sabbath, but time spent alone in his factory office on Saturday afternoon was itself "a reward, a Sabbath" to him (75).

The Phagan murder on Confederate Memorial Day (April 26) in Marietta, Georgia, in 1913 has served as the source for several—usually critically unsuccessful—fictionalized treatments in various genres, including most recently Alfred Uhry and Jason Robert Brown's Tony Award–winning musical *Parade* (1998) and Robert Myers's drama *The Lynching of Leo*

Frank (2000). Mamet structures his narrative largely in the form of interior monologue, a dialogue with(in) the self in a gradual if necessarily foreshortened process of belated spiritual awakening, so that the crime becomes secondary. While Frank sits in the courtroom on trial in 1914, his mind wanders through a series of episodes, snapshots almost, of the way that difference from the norm results in ostracization and oppression. At times, the difference is religious, as in the case of Edgardo Mortara, recounted twice in the novel, the little Jewish boy in Italy who, in 1858, was baptized unbeknown to his parents and then abducted to be raised as a Catholic by the church, eventually becoming a priest—a story much in the news again because of the Vatican's insensitive beatification of Pius IX. Or the difference might be ethnic, as when the Klan, though bent on purifying a Southern community, still allow the businessman Weiss and his family to remain because he is "our Jew." Yet other times, it might be racial, as when the black waiter who serves drinks at the summer resort Frank's family frequents displays "the attitude of both respect and non-being in [his] demeanor. 'I am here only when and as you desire me to be,' it said" (29) or when the prosecutor can convince a jury that a black is not intelligent enough to write, let alone compose a note incriminating himself for murder. Finally, it might take the form of sexism, as in the laughter levelled at Frank's "gross" wife as if she were a "sow" rather than the vaunted ideal of Southern womanhood. Sometimes, the Jew is the victimized outcast; at other times, he is complicit in the stereotyping, as when Frank himself imposes limits upon his wife so she will keep her place, since she is "just a woman," or when he thinks derogatorily of the "fat black ass" of their household servant (34).

Frank worries repeatedly not only over whether he tries too hard to fit into the American reward system but also, and more tellingly, about whether the very idea of the American ethos is not seriously flawed, and thus he questions his own allegiance to it. As he ponders a purportedly Christian country founded on the conviction that "I Am Saved," Frank discerns an America in which a "civil religion" has been established that sanctions imperialism and discrimination and proclaims "'Go forth and kill. In the name of God'" (103)—just as "These saved folk have been convened these two thousand years to kill and hate and called it good" (155). The Puritans, themselves religious outcasts, may have identified with the biblical Hebrews and promoted religious tolerance, but somehow that tradition has been lost. When Frank studies Hebrew in prison and looks for words whose root is a source for the Latin "*amer*," he discovers a link to the word for "*ark*," suggesting the hope of a new Eden "From which they did not wish to be expelled" (151); but he also uncovers the meaning "bitter," which he sees translated into mob rule in a democracy in which law has been reduced to an "obscene travesty." In order for the Southern Christian white male ruling class to preserve, protect, and defend itself, others would need to be marginalized, if not murdered.

Frank actively resists the notion of salvation by faith alone—perpetuated in such sentimental Protestant hymns as *"He walks with me, and he talks with me/He tells me I am his own"* (154)—as a presumptuous abrogation of God's power. Instead, he attempts to reconcile the notions of fate and free will, of a higher purpose and randomness, and thereby to understand "a reason for his trial" (106). If there exists a God, then Frank should be able to find some causal connection between what he has done and what is happening to him. Failing that, if he has been accidentally "ensnared through no fault or through no error of his own" (106) by some superior "force sufficient" to "plan" what happens, then the only courageous response on his part would be "submission." Denied all resources in prison except thoughtful examination of every aspect of his existence, he seeks—in words prescient of Mamet's own in *Three Uses of the Knife*—some "clarification of apparent contradiction into simplicity" (155). The power to reason, however, has its limitations, since left unbounded, its overelaboration into a kind of rationality "must lead to evil" (169). Rather than deny the possibility of "find[ing] a hidden meaning," Frank concludes that even "If the meaning does not exist, then there is meaning in our attempts to create it" (176). As he undergoes his ritual torment, he discovers his manhood, understanding that although he will be "scorned, reviled, abandoned, humiliated, powerless, terrified, mocked," he can still "Study, live, and die" (156) as a man. When he transcends mere reason and ceases to "confront" things only "intellectually," and when he moves beyond "ratiocination regarding assimilation," then he accepts that "to them, he would always be a Jew" (148). All he can do—as did the tragic figures Mamet valorizes in his treatise on drama—is to admit to "powerlessness' and "mortality." To demand anything other is to overreach rather than participate fully in one's humanness.

In two final uses of the knife in *Old Religion*, Frank's throat is slit by a fellow inmate in the prison library, and—in an addition Mamet makes to the historical record—Frank, already metaphorically emasculated by a bigoted society, is literally unmanned by being castrated before he is lynched. The novel's final line reports that a postcard picturing him hanging from a tree "was sold for many years in stores throughout the South" (194). What began as a commodity for souvenir-seeking consumers has, however, become over time an iconic indictment of white, Christian society: the photographic image is virtually identical to similar ones of blacks who were lynched. Both, in turn, ironically may recall images of Christ (born a Jew) as sacrificial scapegoat hanging from the tree of the cross—not only condemning the mob for killing in the name of one who was himself murdered for being a criminal Other but also unveiling an anti-Semitism shamefully not excised from "the new religion." The photo of this crime, itself—or ones similar to it—familiar to most readers and the last object upon which the author fixes their gaze, becomes a kind of objective correlative for the way in which Mamet as novelist and writer for theater and film is able to convey (to use Saul Bellow's phrase) "ideas in the form of feeling."

IV

In his essay, "In the Company of Men" from *Some Freaks* (1989), Mamet alludes to Alfred Lord Douglas's coded description of homosexual love when he disparages the equation of "male bonding"—a term he does not like anyway—with "That Fun Which Dare Not Speak Its Name" (87). Dismissive of homosocial bonding as the "somewhat ludicrous reaching towards each other" of the emotionally immature or of those unready "to avow their homosexuality," Mamet valorizes instead as a necessary component of a stable and "interesting" relationship between the sexes the male prerogative of "hanging out" and "spending time with the boys": "What happened to The Lodge, Hunting, Fishing, Sports in general, Poker, Boys Night Out"— "activities" that "*are* a form of love" (88–89) and in which Mamet finds evidence of the "beautiful" and the "true." Unless one accuses Mamet of being disingenuous, it bothers him not in the least whether "men having fun . . . quite a good time with each other" is thought of as "latent homosexuality" (after all, even "overt homosexuality is No Crime"), though he would much prefer if "The Need of Men to Be Together" were simply regarded without any suspicion as being "all right" (88) and recognized for its potential for renewal: "I have felt that *beyond* the fierce competition, there was an atmosphere of *being involved* in a *communal* activity—that by *sitting there*, we, these men, were, perhaps upholding, perhaps ratifying, perhaps creating or re-creating some important aspect of our community" (89–90).

The division between the man of words and the man of action that Mamet had explored through the character of Del in *The Cryptogram* is healed in Charles Morse, the millionaire businessman in *The Edge* (1997), made from a Hemingwayesque screenplay Mamet had originally entitled "Bookworm." The film also underscores homosocial desire (to use Eve Kosofsky Sedgwick's phrase) as the play had, charting the homoerotic tension in a triangle involving the older Charles, his wife Mickey, who is a high fashion model, and Robert Green, a photographer they accompany on a shoot up into Alaska. At one point, the younger man suggests that the three of them "all get into a hot tub and bare our feelings."[1] As in the Girardian formulation of the erotic triangle, the bond between the male rivals becomes as powerful as that between either of the men and the "shared" woman; and the instances of homophobia that Bob exhibits may, in fact, be masking his own latent homosexuality—the very thing he attributes to the bookish Charles. When Bob discovers that the Native American whom he had hoped to photograph has left his cabin to pursue wild game, he remarks, "How butch, the model's gone hunting"; and in two separate scenes he camps it up by putting on effeminate speech, gestures, and gait, doing an offensive imitation belittling to gay males.

Initially, Charles's power rests in money, one of the ways, along with sexuality and hunting, that Mamet's men use to prove themselves. Money is what Charles is respected and envied and "valued for," which makes it difficult for him to know others' motives in befriending him. Two brief episodes early in the film bring this home to Charles. In one, the owner of the lodge, who up until this point has appeared admiring of and simpatico with Charles, produces a set of plans for developing the area into a vacation resort, assuming that Charles will finance the thirty or forty million dollar project. The potential encroachment of civilization upon nature finds visual expression near the beginning of the film: the great totemic eagle sculpture at the lodge, which occupies a liminal site between the two conflicting value systems, recalls the opening shots of Charles's jet. And when the smaller plane taking the men farther into the wilderness is brought down into the water by a flock of birds mangled in the engine, it is almost as if nature is taking her vengeance for being violated.

In the film's opening dialogue, an airplane mechanic says suggestively, "What I wouldn't do to get my hands on her," the "her" referring to the twenty million dollar private jet, though Charles mistakenly thinks the mechanic covets his wife. With a mixture of jealousy and taunt, Bob chides Charles, saying "You had no business with that broad," though it is he who relegates her to the status of object. Yet Mickey, as a model, participates in her own objectification: in one sequence, she costumes herself in something vaguely resembling, yet parodying through exaggeration, Native American fashion, becoming a fetish for the gaze of Bob's camera eye. Bob protests a distaste for such imitations, seeking out the "unsentimental and unselfconscious" real aborigine, though he would commodify him as well for the money and notoriety. After their ordeal in the woods, Bob wishes he could have caught it all on film, as he "would've made a fortune," no matter that such a confusion of art and commerce would have tarnished and vulgarized a near epic of survival.

En route from the city to the lodge, Charles reads a birthday present from his secretary entitled *Lost in the Wilds,* which includes much arcane information that proves unexpectedly handy, even after the book sinks to the bottom of the lake. Charles thinks that others, including Mickey, have forgotten his "special day" until they throw a surprise party, complete with Bob in a bear costume terrifying him and some additional gifts: an engraved gold pocket watch on a chain from his wife and a pocket knife, obviously phallic, from Bob. The lodgekeeper reminds him to give Bob a coin in return, lest the gift should "cut friendship"—as it had in *The Cryptogram*. Here, in fact, the knife will be used largely for sustaining or protecting life, for such things as cutting the gold chain ("the whole world longs for it") for tackle and bait; for drawing blood to lure the bear; for carving the enormous spear on which the bear, through Charles's aggressive trickery, will impale itself; for cutting the branches in order to send a smoke signal to the rescuers. That the knife need no longer be used to perpetrate violence against another human being might indicate that the arbitrary breech between words and action has been outgrown and that violence is transcended, to be replaced by forgiveness and compassion. Here the gift that galls is the one that Charles later inadvertently discovers Mickey has given to Bob, a watch engraved "For all the nights," which perhaps suggests some earlier disinterest on Charles's part and proves their joint betrayal of him.

The action begins on Charles's birthday, foregrounding that he is undergoing a rite of initiation, however belated, into full manhood, arriving at a new confidence in his ingenuity and physical prowess and endurance. Although possessor of an active and questing mind, always digesting and processing information—later, for instance, he will quickly read an old first aid manual to help the seriously injured Bob—Charles has apparently never before been expected to move from the world of books and words to function exclusively in the realm of action, supported mainly by his wits and whatever is available in the forest. He employs language, our most distinctively human social faculty, as a kind of mantra of survival to ward off passivity and despair; formerly quiet and reserved, Charles forces Bob to repeat after him, "I'm not gonna die. . . . I'm gonna kill the bear. . . . What one man can do, another can do. . . . Today. I'm gonna kill the motherfucker." Eventually, Charles and Bob will display their hard-won negotiation with nature when, after having lost many of the trappings of civilization, they don animal skins and bear-tooth talisman necklaces made by Charles. During their ordeal in the wilds, Bob observes that Charles has "never had a buddy," implying that he has never experienced the kind of homosocial dependency and community that he now does with the photographer and his dredlocked black assistant, Steve, complete with the camaraderie of mock sparring and macho vulgarity in a world of men without women. The ritual slaying of the bear ends with the dead animal falling on Charles and literally hugging him, followed by a shot of Charles and Bob in one another's arms leaning up against the carcass.

Charles admits that "all his life" he has longed to be put to the test, "to do something unequivocal." He knows the answer to the riddle, that "the prey sits unafraid because he's smarter than the panther," as well as that if people die in the wilderness they "die of shame" from "wondering what did I do wrong?" But book knowledge is useless until put into practice; knowledge untested is of no value at all. In response to Bob's query about what he will do if they survive, Charles, as much as admitting some emptiness up until now, vows to "change": "I'm gonna start my life over." Bob, on the other hand, echoing Donny from *Cryptogram* when he curses this "shithole of a world," feels that "life's a short thing, full of betrayal," and that he is "well out of it" since he "never did a goddam thing." He musters the grace, however, almost like a prodigal son returning to his father, to express remorse and to insist that Mickey "wasn't in on it, this business of doing you in."

By begging Bob, who had attempted to kill him, not to "die on me," Charles demonstrates that he now feels secure that Mickey, whom he has always loved and who is "the only woman he's ever wanted," ultimately would choose him over Bob. After he is rescued and Bob's body is brought off the plane, he surreptitiously places Bob's watch with the incriminating inscription in Mickey's hand. The gesture lets her know that he knows, but rather than being just an accusation, it more pointedly indicates his desire to go on with her despite her betrayal. He responds to the media frenzy not by casting blame but by affirming that his friends "died saving my life," offering him the opportunity to prove himself to himself, so that he can live fully and unashamed. Here maleness—a concept that has always fascinated Mamet—is not equated with simple machoism. The feeling and emotion conveyed by the film's closing scenes seems almost *Lear*-like in its intensity—a comparison made apt by the fact that Shakespeare's play, too, is about the violent severing and reestablishment of bonds. With only minimal dialogue and close-ups of Charles and Mickey, the film's ending pierces to the heart as almost nothing else in Mamet's work does.

In words that could well apply to Charles and that foretell the emphasis in *Three Uses of the Knife* on the inadequacy of the purely rational, on the need for intellectuality to give way to an affective response, Mamet asks in his essay, "In the Company of Men": "Is this male companionship about the quest for grace? Yes, it is. . . . This joy of male companionship is a quest for and can be an experience of *true* grace, and transcendent of the rational world and, so, more appropriate of the real nature of the world. . . . And the true nature of the world, as between men is, I think, community of effort directed towards the outside world, directed to subdue, to understand, or to wonder or to understand together, the truth of the world" (90–91). Might this not be seen, perhaps, as Mamet's own modern reformulation of Hamlet's remark when he affirms, "There are more things in heaven and earth, Horatio./Than are dreamt of in your philosophy" (I. v, 167–68)?

Notes

1. All dialogue from the film is based on transcription.

Works Cited

Dorff, Linda. "Reinscribing the Fairy": The Knife and the Mystification of Male Mythology in *The Cryptogram*." In *Gender and Genre: Essays on David Mamet*. Ed. Christopher C. Hudgins and Leslie Kane. New York: St. Martin's, 2000, 175–90.

Haedicke, Janet V. "Decoding Cipher Space: David Mamet's *The Cryptogram* and America's Dramatic Legacy." *American Drama* 9.1 (fall 1999): 1–20.

Mamet, David. *The Cryptogram*. New York: Vintage, 1995.

———. *The Edge*. 20th Century Fox, 1997, dir. Lee Tamahori.

———. *Edmond*. New York: Grove Press, 1983.

———. "In the Company of Men." In *Some Freaks*. New York: Viking, 1989, 85–89.

———. *The Old Religion*. New York: Free Press, 1997.

———. *Prairie du Chien*. New York: Grove Press, 1985.

——— and Shel Silverstein. *Things Change*. New York: Grove Press, 1988.

———. *Three Uses of the Knife: On the Nature and Purpose of Drama* (Columbia Lectures on American Culture). New York: Columbia UP, 1998.

Schaub, Martin. "Magic Meanings in Mamet's Cryptogram." *Modern Drama* 42.3 (fall 1999): 326–37.

13

A Theater of the Self: Mamet's *The Edge* as a *Figura* of Otherness

CLAIRE MAGAHA

David Mamet's 1997 film *The Edge* portrays a series of literal and metaphorical descents that signify its hero's achievement of self-knowledge through enlightenment. Mamet's millionaire protagonist, Charles Morse (played by Anthony Hopkins), is an allegory of self that, as the film progresses, rejects false self-reflections it had once embraced, moving from an embodiment of corporeality to spirituality, from animality to enlightenment. Showing Charles in dialectical engagement with increasingly threatening reflections of the animal-self, Mamet constructs the protagonist's experience as an allegory-in-process. The closer the hero comes to revealing his inner, animal nature the closer he comes to annihilating it, achieving the allegorical status of *being* and *doing* the self through the culminating action of auto-revelation, the slaying of the bear. Thus Mamet portrays a personal rite-of-passage that is both self-destructive and self-revelatory, putting forth the spiritual *persona* as the true one, the animal aspect as a blockage to it. While this metaphorical representation forms the film's "inner self," an outer layer of depiction illustrates Charles's experience as wilderness-survival, as a trial that places him in violent confrontation with a man-killing bear and with his wife's murderous lover, the photographer Bob (played by Alec Baldwin). Whereas the film's inner representation signifies a philosophical and creative mode of being, the outer one mirrors a postmodern yet literalist worldview. The portrayal juxtaposes the two, demonstrating and imposing the enlightenment experience. It thereby constitutes a theatrical rite that, in its attempt to incorporate the spectator in the drama of the self, forms a *figura* of primal unity, of the original love-bond between self and Other.

Constructing the spiritual self in counterpoint to capitalist and postmodern society, Mamet metaphorizes it as nature. At the same time, however, he presents the barrier to it through themes evoking nature. In this way, he shows the true persona as a function of inner animality itself, the spiritual as emanating from the material. Philosophical in his presentation of descent-as-ascent, destruction-as-rebirth, Other-as-self, he suggests that each allegorical instance of embodying a truer persona is an increasingly figurative moment, one that repeats primal unity. This theater of the self is not unlike Western culture's first imaginings of individualism, those produced by eighteenth-century French philosophers. Like Rousseau's philosophy, Mamet's cinematic work asserts the importance of a return to nature, metaphorical above all, to personal enlightenment. It implies that the individual formed by contemporary society incarnates conflict, since the values Charles adopts from postmodern society obscure and repress his inner spirituality. Specifically, his passion for the artificial is reflected in his desire for his wife, Mickey (played by Elle Macpherson), an attraction that is likewise allegorized by Bob and his relationship with her. Moreover, Charles's passion for an artificial Other and his animality converge in the symbol of the bear, the destruction of which signifies the dismantling of postmodern selfhood. Thus Mamet posits the authentic self as leaving behind the empty values espoused by materialism and artifice, as rejecting postmodern civilization.

The Edge brings to mind a story recounted by Joseph Campbell in which enlightenment is characterized as "the breakthrough of a metaphysical realization" by which "you and that other are one" (Flowers 110). Like Mamet's ideal spectator, the protagonist of Campbell's tale is one who engages in a self-sacrifice that also signals redemption. "One day," he begins,

> Two policemen were driving up the Pali Road when they saw, just beyond the railing that keeps the cars from rolling over, a young man preparing to jump [to his death]. The police car stopped, and the policeman on the right jumped out to grab the man but caught him just as he jumped, and he was himself being pulled over when the second cop arrived in time and pulled the two of them back. (Flowers 110)

Mamet and Campbell's stories are *figurae* of the unequivocal event, which is one of *being* the self through *the performance of* Otherness. They both imply that when self-sacrifice imitates salvation, the individual can transcend the limits of selfhood dictated by postmodern realities, which deform human desire. Both stories' heroes aspire to this kind of mimesis, an engagement in intersubjectivity by which they incarnate a selfhood of the Other.

As Mamet's protagonist makes the voyage by plane to a rustic lodge where his wife, a model, will participate in a photo-shoot, he feels isolated and different from the rest of the crew of the magazine. His self-contained actions both mirror theirs and contrast with them. As Bob's trivial conversation reveals his character, Charles's silent unwrapping of a birthday gift unveils his. Mamet initiates a dialectic between Charles and his alter-ego, between two competing aspects of himself that are true and false, natural and artificial. Even as this comparison between oppositional selves reflects the conflicting facets of Charles's personality, however, it supports Mamet's framing of the film, which traces a divide between the mass audience and the enlightened self-as-viewer (and as self-viewer). While Bob's conversation with the other members of the crew addresses a postmodern viewership, Charles's silent self-revelation is an introspective process that appeals to the analytical or enlightened spectator. Mamet gauges this disparity through the designation of the characters' and the spectators' objects of attention—he presents their value as signified by the things that represent them—drawing a parallel between Bob's self-worth and the watch he has recently received. Although the audience is not yet aware of it, the timepiece is a gift from Mickey on the occasion of her husband's birthday. When asked about it by one of the crew, Bob explains that it marks the time in two different zones. In response to a question about that feature's utility, he explains that if he is in LA and wants to know the time in New York, he does not have to "go through the anguish of adding three."[1] This elicits laughter from the group, and they continue with mindless talk as Charles sits alone in the front of the lodge.

Meanwhile, Charles's self-revelation occurs through his isolated unwrapping of a birthday gift from his secretary. As the others joke about trivial matters, he opens his book about wilderness-survival, *Lost in the Wilds*, leafing through it and stopping on the page introducing the topic of "traps and snares." While Bob's gift forms an artificial extension of the body, Charles's appeals to the mind and must be incorporated through attentiveness and the spending of time. Indeed, unlike the watch, Charles's book requires time and thought in order to acquire worth. Though at this point the gifts' true values remain unclear to the viewer, Charles's self-discovery progressively assigns them value based on their utility in nature. Mamet juxtaposes nature and contemporary society, then, challenging the postmodern attribution of worth even as he proposes a new scale of valuation based on a truer self.

The screenwriter poses the Alaskan wilderness as the nature-space in which Charles's authentic persona has the opportunity not only to emerge but also to suppress the influences of materialism and artifice. The lodge and the scenes in and around it signify civilization even as they introduce this transformation, which occurs through contact with nature. While the lodge welcomes Charles into the woods, a cabin by a snowy creek marks his emergence from them. These rustic interiors frame the inner experience of enlightenment, serving as the spaces of its introduction and conclusion.

Descent reverts to ascent as the group mounts the steps to the lodge after the plane's landing in the high wilderness. We view their short climb from behind the wings of a totem-angel, a figure fashioned of wood that marks their entrance into the natural order. While the airplane endures as a postmodern symbol of self-worth throughout the film, this meta-figure bears witness to Charles's arrival at the lodge and departure from it, framing his process of self-knowledge. Like the protagonist's birthday gift, the totem-angel's wood substance opposes nature to the civilized material of metal, represented both by Bob's watch and by the plane. As Charles increasingly knows himself, he places greater value on the objects that reflect this nature, dismissing the plane as the ultimate symbol of male selfhood. Like the other negative reflections of himself, that object is replaced by truer signifiers of self.

As soon as the group is inside the lodge, the innkeeper instructs them on kitchen procedures and on dealings with bears. After this instruction is complete, Charles's wife retires, pretending that she has forgotten his birthday. Upon joining her in their room, he reminds her that this is a special day for him but believes himself unsuccessful in jogging her memory. In order to make preparations for a surprise party, she asks him to go downstairs and make a sandwich for her. He dutifully agrees, descending to the kitchen. Once there, he begins sandwich-making when he spies an open door. At first he panics at the thought that a bear might have tracked the scent of the sandwich meat that sits, uncovered, on the kitchen table. He soon gathers his wits, though, closing the door and preparing the sandwich. As if to confirm his first instinct of fear, he is accosted by Bob in a bear-rug as he exits the kitchen. This act, a symbolic awakening, is accompanied by the group's shout of "Surprise!" as Charles tumbles, shocked, onto the floor.

Once Bob has helped Charles off the floor and apologized to him for the scare, the party begins. Now a second series of revelatory unwrappings occurs, providing Charles with the tools he will need to survive in the wilds. Mamet curiously presents the birthday scene as one of productive, complicit violence imposed on Charles by his wife and her lover. In offering him an old-fashioned pocket-watch and a jackknife, they make available the survival items he will need in the woods. While Bob's knife will serve to cut branches and meat, Mickey's watch must be manipulated and its function rethought in order to gain utility. Charles's enlightenment and escape from the wilderness depend on his ability to imagine it as an instrument of survival. While he avoids using one of its hands to make a compass at the outset of the journey, he eagerly employs it in that way after the bear's destruction, thereby transforming its meaning and use.

Not only do Mickey and Bob's gifts figure the unveiling of Charles's authentic, natural self, they construct its beginning and encourage its progress. The protagonist's shallow, dishonest friend and his adulterous wife shower him with gifts and praise, lauding the natural aspects of his personality. In his toast to Charles, Bob lauds his "good nature, [his] intelligence, and [his] generosity" and specifies that he is addressing "a good companion, a good friend, and a good sport." Mickey adds that Charles is a "very brave man" and presents him with a watch engraved with the message, "To my beloved husband on his birthday, from the luckiest woman in the world."

When interpreted in terms of Mickey and Bob's secret desires and criminal complicity, these compliments and gifts appear to serve as mere sham. At the same time, however, they are signifiers of Mickey and Bob's allegorical representation of Charles, simultaneous expressions of their inner voices and of his own, which push him toward self-analysis and understanding. Like the first airplane scene, the birthday-party dialogue can be read as allegory, as the encounter of various aspects of a single persona that work together to encourage the therapeutic emergence of the self-as-nature. Moreover, like the rest of the film's scenes, it not only offers a differentiation between the social self and the natural one but it is also underpinned by their potential significations and receptions—for it is written both as artifice and as nature, as an inextricable entwining of literalism and metaphor, reality and imagination, self and Other. In this way, Mamet acknowledges the idea of truth-as-construct but challenges the legitimacy of structures that form a blockage to the authentic self. In a brilliant straddling of postmodernist and Enlightenment perspectives, he resituates the dilemma of signification itself and demonstrates that philosophy can and must continue to be performed through productive self-imaginings.

While Mickey apparently functions as the mere object of Charles's physical desire, she in fact plays an instrumental role in his enlightenment. She influences his decision to join Bob and Stephen on the fateful plane ride that lands them in the high wilderness. On the first morning at the lodge, Bob discovers that the male model is ill and decides to seek out an Indian friend of the lodgekeeper for his photo layout. The search for this alternate model takes the group first to the Indian's cabin, then to his hunting-grounds, which they never reach due to the plane crash. Were it not for Mickey's words encouraging Charles to take off with Bob, he would not get any "air under [his] wings," never begin his self-discovery. Similarly, the lodgekeeper, Styles, incites Charles's desire to take the jaunt through a curious disparity between the person he seems to be and the one he truly is. While Styles's dialogue depicts him as a countrified hunter with old-fashioned values and hospitality, in reality these qualities obscure his desire for material success. On the morning after the group's arrival, Charles sits on the porch reading his book while Mickey and Bob conduct the photo-shoot. Knowing that Charles is a millionaire, Styles approaches him and begins to lament the lodge's inaccessibility to tourists. When Charles initiates a discussion having to do with wilderness survival, he diverts the conversation to the topic of his interest, noting what a shame it is that "everyone can't enjoy this [environment]." He then displays plans for the lodge's expansion, attempting to seduce Charles into investing by remarking that he can imagine the renovations "better than these folks can draw." Disgusted, the protagonist moves to the lodge's interior where Mickey and Bob are engaged in private conversation. As he prepares to leave in search of the Indian model,

Bob invites Charles to join the crew. Although the hero hesitates even when Mickey encourages him to go, upon seeing Styles reenter the lodge, he accepts the invitation.

The second descent occurs before and during the plane crash that lands Charles, Bob, and the photographer Stephen in a frigid lake of the high wilderness. On the ride preceding the crash, Charles's animalistic self-reflection begins to emerge in Bob. Their conversation forms a dialectic between conflicting selves that increasingly models oneness as they lose touch with the postmodern world. As part of that dialectic, Bob not only incarnates Charles's negative characteristic of desiring Mickey and of valuing the artificial but curiously provokes the hero's questioning of these qualities. He thereby initiates a symbolic self-analysis that operates through interior dialogue.

Bob brings into question Charles's personal worth as constructed by society, pointing out its precariousness. Referring to the previous evening's scare, he signals and promotes Charles's openness to discovering the self-as-nature by showing admiration for his reaction to that experience:

> BOB: Can I tell you something, Charles? . . . I admire the way you took that joke last night. . . . Embarrassing moment, but you handled it well.

He provokes a confrontation with the millionaire by insisting on the artificiality of his sociocultural persona. Conducting a symbolic self-attack that targets money as a personal value, he prods:

> BOB: Tough row to hoe, you think about it.
> CHARLES: What would that be?
> BOB: All that money.
> CHARLES: Ah.
> BOB: All that responsibility. Never knowing who your friends are, never knowing what people value you for.
> CHARLES: Yeah.
> BOB: Must be tough.

With his intellectual curiosity piqued and his integrity in danger, Charles makes a counterattack. He confronts Bob about his own values, implicitly accusing his companion of caring for him out of selfishness and materialism:

> CHARLES: Never feel sorry for a man who owns a plane. So, what do you value me for, Bob?

Neglecting to feign difference from what he really is, Bob replies candidly, "I tell you what, I like your style and I think your wife's pretty cute, too." This response confirms Charles's suspicion of complicity between Bob and

Mickey, and he takes it as another threat to his spiritual self, inviting the ultimate confrontation, "Yes. So how are you planning to kill me?" As the question is posed, the plane is struck by birdstrike, which causes it to go down into a lake of the high wilderness. The partial self-knowledge produced by the dialogue between Charles's integrity and his self-doubt entails a preliminary rebirth, a baptism that prepares him for the most difficult stage of his journey, in which he will lose his innocence and destroy his animality.

Escaping death and making it to the lake's shore, Charles, Bob, and Stephen make a fire with one of their signal-flares and spend their first night in the wilds. The next morning, they assess the gravity of the situation. Armed with a few matches, signal-flares, a paper clip, and their watches, they rely on Charles to make a compass out of the paper clip and a leaf to find their way out. With him as their leader, they head toward a peak that, according to the improvised compass, lies to the south.

The wilderness environment gives Charles control over Bob and Stephen, who depend on his knowledge for their survival. At the same time, the dialectic of selves formed by him and Bob shifts. While Bob is both his antagonist and his supporter in the prelude, his dependence on Charles in the woods reverses the initial configuration. Now Charles serves as his leader and protector, allegorizing the intellect's ascendancy over the physical self. This change menaces Bob's very identity, which is built on a narcissistic repression of reliance on others. The wilds place him in a state of crisis; there he cannot maintain shallow relations and he must allow his feelings and thoughts to emerge. As his true self becomes visible, it uncovers weakness and a lack of substance, which not only aids Charles's enlightenment but also partially constitutes it. While Bob attempts to embody a self based on materialism in the wilds, that environment causes the hero to invest energy in his already well-developed intellect and compassion. Thus Mamet illustrates their relationship as a paradoxically incompatible oneness of materialism and spirituality—as a persona formed by postmodern society, but unraveled by the nature-state.

As they begin a preliminary ascent up a mountainside, Charles engages in storytelling designed to focus the group on survival and to bolster spirits. Already cultivating his intellectualism as a source of energy and hope, he immediately comes into conflict with his allegorical adversary. As they reach a stopping-place at a small waterfall, Bob asserts his power over Charles through dialogue, attempting to reignite the confrontation they began in the plane. Continuing that encounter, he asks, "Is it my diseased imagination or did you say, 'How are you planning to kill me?'" He asks why he would want to murder his companion, who suggests that he would perpetrate such a crime for his wife and his money. In response, Bob cites Charles's social status and wealth as the reasons why he would never antagonize him. Feeling threatened, he reverses the initial assessment he made of Charles's personal worth; for during the recent plane ride, he indicated not that Charles's money conferred value on him, but that it undermined his integrity by falsifying his personal relationships. Now the hero's wealth is the one weapon Bob can wield against him. In its meaninglessness in the nature-state, however, the invocation of Charles's money loses its efficacy as a tactic of violence and as a defense mechanism. Initially, it nevertheless remains powerful enough to inspire Charles's self-doubt and paranoia. When Bob responds to his accusation by stating, "The rich *are* different," the millionaire buys his con, feeling regret and shame for having accused him. A few minutes later, he asks his rival, "You think I'm a fool, don't you?" Rather than making a sincere reply, Bob answers in a playful, superficial tone:

> BOB: What I think, I think that you got a whole stew of too much money, ah, latent homosexuality, lots of other good stuff, paranoia. What we'll do, we'll all get together we get back, you and me and your wife, and we'll all get into a hot tub and um, bare our feelings, and um . . . Look, even if I wanted to kill you, I need you to get home. You fuckin' idiot. Needing people, isn't it a bitch?

Now Bob's true intention emerges. Even as he attempts to express indifference to Charles, he must acknowledge his emotions—now he cares for him because his survival depends on it. While the bonds of dependence between the two appear to be a mere plot-function, they in fact figure and develop the hero's authentic selfhood.

A series of three bear attacks marks Charles's increasing contact with his animal self and his need to destroy it. The first comes as his confrontation with Bob continues, serving as a climax to their lack of communication and antagonism. As soon as the three companions sight the bear, they flee in the opposite direction. Breathless, they reach a small river flowing on a downward slope. Charles furiously improvises a bridge with their help, pushing over a tree to close the distance between the river's edges. Steve and Bob cross the log without incident, but the bear's proximity jars Charles as he attempts the crossing, causing him to fall and to catch onto the bag of signal-flares dangling from one of the log's branches. When the bag loses its hold, he plunges into the river, but he is retrieved by Bob and Stephen, who reach out to him from a nearby rock.

Charles's near-death experience shatters him and infuses him with a feeling of weakness. Compensating for his partner's shaky demeanor, Bob now retakes control and encourages him as he had before the plane crash. When Charles stalls under a tree repeating, "You saved my life," Bob teases, "Well I couldn't kill you with Stephen around. I'd have to kill him, too, and he's the only one who knows how I like my coffee." Bob's cycle of support endures until the next bear attack, which Mamet shows as depriving Charles of his innocence and as reestablishing his power.

Bob and Mickey's attentions to Charles after the mock bear attack are nurturing actions that mirror parental care. After the real attack, however, Bob and Charles take over the roles of caretaker, nurturing the innocent and naive Stephen. Many of their actions concentrate on relieving his fears and on reassuring him of their survival. They enter a cooperative relationship that replicates the one shared by Bob and Mickey in the early part of the film. When Stephen accidentally cuts himself using Charles's knife to make a spear, they nurse his wound, make him a shelter, and build a fire to keep him warm through the night. As the parental figures, they alternate between the mother and father roles, each of them occupying the male authority-position when he dominates the other's thoughts and expression. Just before Stephen's death, Bob plays the father, but Charles takes over this part once the first fatal attack occurs. From this point on, the protagonist remains in the position of authority, reassuring Bob, keeping his spirits up, and engineering their escape from the woods. While in the beginning of the wilderness-survival Stephen mirrors the childlike aspect Charles embodies in the prelude, his demise introduces the hero's maturation and his definitive rejection of the values constructed by postmodern civilization. Likewise, Stephen's death is symbolic of the repression of infantile, self-centered desires associated with postmodernity. The love of the artificial, Mamet thereby implies, parallels childlike attachment to "Mickey Morse."

Stephen's death increases Charles's power and paralyzes Bob, sapping the photographer's confidence and determination. As the two focus on catching food, the bear continues to distract them. The second blow to Bob's strength comes not from a bear attack, however, but from a sign of civilization that provides him an instant of hope that quickly shatters. Seeing a helicopter pass overhead, he and Charles run through the thick cover of trees in pursuit of it. By the time they reach a grassy clearing where the searchers might spot them, however, the helicopter is already moving into the distance. Destroyed emotionally and taxed physically, Bob falls to the ground as Charles stands over him with an expression of stoicism and compassion. Now Charles turns to his intellectualism as a means of inspiring optimism. At first Bob combats his influence by blaming his wealth. Faced with the uselessness of this defense-mechanism, however, he makes an excruciating and admirable effort to accept the hero's power over him. It is the thought that the search party will not return for them that causes him to succumb to Charles's influence:

BOB: We can't think they'd come back?
CHARLES: No. You shouldn't think they'll come back. They've scouted this area and they'll move on. (Bob cries.)
BOB: (With difficulty) All right. All right. Fire from ice. Let's have it.
CHARLES: Ice. You take it into your hands and it can be molded into a lens which will concentrate sunlight into fire, hm? (He extends his hand to

Bob, who takes it.) I doubt we'll be reduced to that because we still have
the matches and I believe that's all we'll need.

As Bob's power over Charles wanes, he fails to reflect opposition to the
spiritual self. Now the bear takes on Bob's adversarial qualities, adopting
the function that he once carried out. Accordingly, the third attack is
Charles's first lone encounter with the bear, in which he narrowly escapes
death. Afterward, his realization that it had been stalking them all along
causes him to target it as his enemy. This mental shift modifies the dialectics
of self as well. Now that he recognizes the bear as his rival, the hero places
himself squarely against the animal-self, an act of empowerment that effects
a turning point in his enlightenment. As in a dream, he can now confront the
bear and kill it without feeling like a criminal and with a sensation of finally
having attained the unequivocal.

After Charles's lone encounter with the bear, his dialogue portrays him
as completely authoritative and autonomous. Now his task is to elicit Bob's
cooperation in the bear's slaying. To gain his full support, Charles must
prime and control him. Leading his companion through a pre-hunt ritual designed to build confidence and to inspire a sense of power, he essentially
scripts his dialogue and actions. He directs Bob to repeat, "I'm gonna kill
the bear," and, "What one man can do, another can do." Telling him stories
of young native boys who confront wild beasts as a test of manhood, he prepares him for a rite-of-passage that at once signifies auto-salvation and self-
annihilation. Throughout their preparatory activities, Bob retains a certain
autonomy, but he shows little resistance to Charles's will. He works in tan-
dem with his rival, luring the bear with bloody rags and planning to injure it
with a large mace-ball made out of wood. When this strategy fails to injure
the bruin, the pair seems doomed to death and we fear the dissolution of
their teamwork. However, hope is renewed when we discover that they have
planned to retreat after the initial attack. Having pre-positioned spears at a
bend in the stream, they intend to have the bear kill itself by rearing and
landing on the weapons. Their organization proves invaluable when this tactic works. Fearlessly, Charles coaxes the bear toward him and forces it to
rear, impaling it mortally. Though the bear's fall pins him underneath it, he
survives the final attack, and the scene of his collaboration with Bob ends on
their breathless recovery while reclining against the bear cadaver.

The scene that follows the bear killing shows Bob as a participant in the
enlightenment Charles has just achieved. In effect, the hero's companion
helps him to complete the self-discovery through articulation of it. Their analytical discussion recalls the dialectical self-inquiry undertaken during the
fatal plane ride. This time, however, Bob does not provoke Charles's self-
questioning through mental assault, but he furnishes a sounding board for
his inner monologue. Their dialogue now forms an allegory of unity that allows the hero to articulate and instrumentalize his true desires:

CHARLES: So I said, I said if this is my life, then this is my life, but you can change your life.
BOB: That's what I'm telling you.
CHARLES: Yeah. Is that true?
BOB: Why wouldn't it be true?
CHARLES: Because I never knew anybody who did actually change their lives. I tell you what, I'm going to start my life over.
BOB: Yeah. You be the first.

Rather than questioning or ridiculing Charles's thoughts and emotions as he once had, Bob reinforces them. Providing an opportunity for the hero to voice his doubts and concerns, he helps Charles to gain self-knowledge and to reorganize his life in terms of that revelation. Most important, this "theater of the self," allows the protagonist to transcend the boundaries of imaginary self-conception. It signifies the performance of a transcendent authentic self that remains the same in nature and in civilization, at the interior and exterior levels.

While in this final dialogue Bob refrains from shallowness and dishonesty, as soon as they stumble upon signs of civilization, he reverts to decadence. Just as he is offering words of comfort to Charles, they reach a snowy cabin and spot a canoe stored just outside of it. This reinitiates them into civilization and triggers Bob's rejection of his new identity of Otherness. As soon as he views the cabin and intuits its contents, which includes the worldly trappings of power and utility, he makes an emotional break from Charles. He regresses to the postmodern valuation of things, reestablishing dependence on objects, which renews the conflict between him and Charles. On the other hand, Charles's dependence on intellect and sentiment has become irreversible, and it bars him from believing in the values he had once cultivated. The pair's split is represented by their parting of ways as they approach the cabin. Charles immediately notices the bear-trap, a veritable death-fall, that lies near the rustic structure and goes to examine it. Bob, however, makes for the cabin's interior in search of weapons and alcohol. By the time Charles catches up to him, Bob has already planned how to kill him. When Charles enters the cabin, Bob remarks that they must check the canoe to make sure it floats, which is a prerequisite to the murder. Knowing that Bob cannot contain his impulse either to abandon him or to kill him, Charles follows him out to the canoe. Carrying a pot along, he takes some water from the stream and offers Bob some tea. Back in the cabin, he realizes that he needs paper for a fire, so he takes out the gift-box that has remained with him throughout the wilderness trek. Inside he finds the receipt that records the engravings on his and Bob's watches, discovering that his companion's gift reads, "For all the nights." When his adversary returns, the protagonist is prepared for confrontation. Bob seems to intuit their oncoming conflict as well for he begins loading a rifle with bullets and drinking as he stares blindly out the cabin's front door. When Charles asks to see his watch, Bob's language degrades into fragments and he seems to become insensitive to Charles. He continues loading the gun and drinking as he responds, "My watch. Doesn't work. Told you. Busted." Charles insists on seeing it anyway, thereby implying his knowledge of the adulterous relationship. When Bob refuses to respond to this threat, thus acknowledging the meaning of the watch's engraving, Charles is forced to speak more plainly, demanding, "What's the matter, Bob? Can't do it sober? S'pose you don't need me any more. You can find your own way out of here without me." In response, Bob blames Charles's money for his unhappy marriage, citing it as the reason for Mickey's love. He finds justification for the murder by chiding Charles for having believed that Mickey loved him:

> BOB: Well, you had no business with that broad anyway, you know you don't. You know that you don't, Charles, I mean . . . Hey, hey, hey. Look at her, why did she go with you? Why in the hell did she go with you? Your money, for the love of God, everyone in the world knew that. Are you nuts? You went through the airport with her, everyone that saw you said, "There goes a guy with a plane. There goes a guy with a plane." So it was tough luck, Charles, that's what you drew this time.

Bob readopts the critical voice he had initially used against Charles, paradoxically aiding his companion by dismissing the marriage's validity. He suggests that Charles's desire for Mickey has not signified self-love, but an affection for the artificial. His critique symbolically threatens the love of artifice, signifying a self-annihilation that repeats his "death" of the central wilderness sequence. Indeed, this "self-destruction" echoes the bear's slaying and foreshadows the photographer's actual demise on the canoe trip out of the wilderness.

After leading Charles out of the cabin to shoot him, Bob stops and asks his companion to turn his back. When Charles refuses and continues to question him about the affair, he loses his balance and falls backward into the bear-trap located just behind him. With one of the pit's wooden spikes through his leg, Bob begs Charles to save him. The hero carefully removes the photographer from the death-trap and carries him back into the cabin, where he knocks him out to relieve the pain. He does his best to repair the wound and, the next morning, begins paddling them out of the wilds. Later that afternoon, he beaches the canoe on a rocky shore and builds a fire to keep warm.

Charles's gesture of compassion toward Bob both completes his enlightenment and redeems his friend; for the love he shows Bob rehabilitates him, causing him to repent and to wish for forgiveness. Charles's enlightened actions permit his "personal growth," eliciting his first candid and affectionate words:

BOB: Why would you want to save a piece of shit like me?
CHARLES: Well, let's say it's a challenge.
BOB: The sporting aspect of it, eh?
CHARLES: Yeah.
BOB: No. I know what it is. You never had a buddy. That's the thing, isn't it?
CHARLES: That's right.
BOB: Now I'm your pet-project. I'm your hobby-farm, eh Charles?
CHARLES: Yeah. Whatever you say, Bob.
BOB: Guy who tried to kill you, that's terrific, Charles.
CHARLES: Nah, you wouldn't have done it.
BOB: Yes I would've, you stupid son-of-a-bitch. Yes I would've.
CHARLES: Well then, you would.

Charles's interaction with Bob demonstrates total acceptance of his enemy, signaling the achievement of self-love. In displaying unconditional love, he embraces a transcendent value-system determined by sensitivity and the spirit of generosity. This second unequivocal act inspires even the depraved Bob, who makes an appeal for forgiveness that does not derive from self-pity alone:

BOB: I don't feel sorry for you, Charles. Never feel sorry for a man that owns a plane.
CHARLES: Come on. Hold on. Hold on. I'll get us out of here.
BOB: Ah, bullshit. Hey, I'm dying. I'm dying and I never did a goddam thing. But wait. Charles, I gotta tell you. Charles, I'm sorry. I'm sorry what I did. And your wife, Charles, listen to me Charles, she was never in on it, this business, doing you in. I swear it on my life, Charles. Charles.
CHARLES: Very kind of you to say so, Bob.
BOB: Never too late for a kind gesture, hey Charles?
CHARLES: Don't die on me, Bob.
BOB: Don't tell me what to do.

Just as Bob utters his last words, a helicopter is heard flying in the distance. Charles signals it by cutting fresh branches and placing them on the fire to create heavy smoke. As he furiously waves at the rescuers, Bob expires unbeknown to him. With the panoramic Alaskan wilderness in the background, Charles watches the helicopter's movement to see if it will make the turn toward him. In a moment of joyful intensity, the aircraft traces a grand curve toward him, initiating a head-on approach.

Charles's rescue by helicopter is his first authentic flight, since both literally and metaphorically, it signifies ascent. When the helicopter approaches the lodge with Charles and with Bob's corpse in tow, we view it from behind the totem-angel figure, which now holds new significance. Initially, it symbolizes an invitation on an inner, personal journey, a figure of Otherness that has yet to be internalized. Upon Charles's return, however, it denotes the Other he now incarnates; it is a sign of partnership in spirituality, of complicity in enlightenment. If the spectator recognizes the angel's new significance, it means that he or she has identified with the hero's journey at both the interior and the exterior levels, participating in the theater of self that Mamet's writing offers.

By a deliberate con game, *The Edge* affords the opportunity of a personal journey that, like the totem-angel's welcome, at first seems fearful and mysterious. For those who accept its invitation, the film functions as a *figura* of the self. For those who choose not to "get some air under their wings," it operates superficially in terms of the postmodern value-systems it otherwise clears away. Indeed, *The Edge*'s "identity" depends on the spectator's engagement in "dialogue" with it. If its façade of signification is accepted without analytical response, it serves as a postmodern self-object or a construct of narcissism. In this case, its utility resembles that of Bob's watch, which upholds passivity, the love of artifice, and the lack of intellectual curiosity. If, on the other hand, the film is analyzed and assimilated, it becomes part of the self, an instrument of personal enlightenment. Like Charles's timepiece, *The Edge* needs care and attention to acquire its true value. To those who interpret it as a failed action film unworthy of the classics of its genre, it seems to say, "The con's on you." For those who view it as an opportunity to speak and listen to themselves, however, it becomes a rehearsal in the theater of the self.

Notes

1. All dialogue from the film is based on my transcription.

Works Cited

Campbell, Joseph, and Bill Moyers. *The Power of Myth.* Ed. Betty Flowers. New York: Doubleday, 1988.

Mamet, David. *The Edge.* Dir. Lee Tamahori. Perf. Anthony Hopkins, Alec Baldwin, Elle Macpherson. 20th-Century Fox, 1997.

14
Suckered Again: The Perfect Patsy and *The Spanish Prisoner*

LESLIE KANE

Happiness . . . is the perpetual possession of being well deceived.
—JONATHAN SWIFT, *A Tale of a Tub*

Virtue never has been as respectable as money.
—MARK TWAIN, *Innocents Abroad*

A romantic, "wrong man" thriller, *The Spanish Prisoner*, his fifth film as writer/director, is the perfect vehicle for an extended examination of the gamesmanship and conartistry that characterize the best of David Mamet's work. Although Mamet has transformed a wretched childhood into deeply affecting dramas, such as *The Cryptogram and The Old Neighborhood*, he has made a name in theater and film by magically turning crime into art. In *Spanish Prisoner*, his most intricate and arguably his most arresting Hitchcockian fable, Mamet weaves a web of intrigue in which the lines between business and crime are blurred, a paradigmatic structure employed in both stage and screenplays. Mamet's original screenplay leads Everyman figure Joe Ross, a brilliant ideas man blinded by ambition and greed, into the confidences of Jimmy Dell, a process by which Ross is conned out of his lucrative business strategy and doubly gulled by those he trusts through a method that Richard Combs recognized in Mamet's *House of Games* as "complicated pieces of trickery . . . coalesce[d] into one master con" (17).

Here, the high stakes trickery played upon a credulous company man—albeit reminiscent of Mamet's earlier *Water Engine* and *Homicide*—invites assessment of the psychological process and moral ambiguities inherent in Mamet's presentation of confidence games. As the audience is led willingly down the garden path, much as the aspiring Joe Ross is duped out of his most valuable possessions—his billion dollar formula and his innocence—

Mamet plays fast and lose with the motifs of intelligence, innocence, and invention and myriad interpretations of security, including risks, safeguards, sanctuaries, and contracts (both real and fictitious). Thus, confidence tricksters trade upon Ross's trust, capitalize on his vulnerability, and make a killing on his unconscious complicity. The game as it is played by the filmmaker hooks the mark and the audience, the latter trapped by the lure of the labyrinthine plot and its own tendency to autosuggest in ways that seem logical but are inherently false. Indeed, as the filmmaker recently remarked, "We have the capacity to use our great intelligence to convince ourselves of anything in the world, true or false" (qtd. in Caro 2).

With that as a point of departure, Mamet, who has for nearly thirty years turned crime into art with a Midas touch, has struck gold in *The Spanish Prisoner*, which "takes us in as it goes along, then reveals that it's been fooling us as a way of gaining our belief" (Denby 101), the classic modus operandi of the hustler. "It's intriguing, watching films about confidence tricks," the filmmaker observes: "you see the first trick, you expect a second, but you don't see the third. The confidence trick, the magic trick, and to an extent the drama work because the audience is endeavoring to understand the play. It's that very preoccupation which enables the confidence man, the magician, the dramatist, to misdirect them" (qtd. in Gritten). And, like *The Spanish Prisoner*'s hero, a mathematician whose talent for speculation, calculation, and corroboration is inferred and whose vision is myopic, the audience proves the perfect patsy of conartistry, learning that in Mamet's world of betrayal, deceit, and shifting loyalties the acquisition of wisdom is coequal with the acquisition of skepticism.

Roland Barthes posits that, "Through the mythology of Einstein, the world blissfully regained the image of knowledge reduced to a formula. Paradoxically, the more his genius was materialized under the guise of his brain, the more the product of his inventiveness came to acquire a magical dimension" (*S/Z* 69). When viewed through the gloss of formal game theory as mathematical model, *Spanish Prisoner,* which derives its name from one of the oldest con games typically played "on . . . [the] vanity and greed" of intelligent people (90), literally turns on knowledge reduced to a formula identified merely as "the Process," a cutting edge but undefined technology with the potential to dominate "the Global Market" (*Prisoner* 6), cripple the competition, and reap billions. A Hitchcockian MacGuffin sufficiently abstract to "allow[s] audience members to project their own ideas onto an essentially featureless goal," this secret formula "has the power to excite our imagination" (*Knife* 29–30). "[A]s humans, we must dream," Jimmy Dell tells Ross. "And when we dream . . . we dream of money . . ." (*Prisoner* 17), a truism that not only informs the motivation of the film's characters but also "it connects with our larcenous side" (Carr D5).

"[S]tringing us along with ruses and red herrings" (Powers 218), *Spanish Prisoner*'s serpentine screenplay ostensibly revolves around guarded information. Yet from the first, focus is directed toward the acquisition of/or disclosure of facts on the one hand and caveats concerning security on the other. A covert conference with top executives of a major corporation in a chic Caribbean retreat establishes a paradigm for the actions of a group of corporate raiders. A case in point is the "Dog and Pony Show" (*Prisoner* 5) staged by Ross and in-house counsel George Lang for well-heeled venture capitalists to win their confidence and secure their investment in the Process developed by Ross's team. Likewise, the cabal of con artists mounts an analogous performance for Joe, albeit on a grand scale, illustrating what Mamet characterizes as "a twentieth-century version of the (Aristotelian) idea that what the hero is following and what he ends up with may be two very different things" (qtd. in Schvey 93).

Mamet describes *The Spanish Prisoner* as a "light romantic thriller," a genre we associate with Hitchcock in which an unsuspecting, intelligent man is wrongfully accused and becomes a fugitive trying to prove his innocence; he is assisted by a woman; powerful people are the villains; a denouement is set "in an extraordinarily improbable place," and a deus ex machina occurs "in the last 20 seconds" (qtd. in Denerstein 6D). In the Hitchcockian and Mametic thriller, "the hero is caught between police and criminals and not always sure which is which," portable items are emblematic, sharp or pointed, such as a knife, staircases provide transitional space and vertical perspective, and comic touches are "amusing for any audience who picks up on them but unsettling because each one arrives without warning" (Thomson 26–28; Leitch 79). Further, as Thomas M. Leitch contends in *Find the Director*, in such films "the audience's interpretation is never neutral" for it entails sympathy, apprehension, moral judgment, and the possibility of mistakes, as when audiences trust or condemn the wrong person, or when they identify closely with someone who turns out to be a victim. Hence, "every interpretation is suspect, . . . [and] interpretation itself becomes a game which pits wary audiences against the resourceful filmmaker" (Leitch 29). Armed with a bag of tricks, such as false leads, feints, plot twists, and surprises, Mamet traps us as voyeurs and virtual players into playing hide and seek, catch the con artist, and find the director. In short, his foray into Hitchcockian mystery works from familiar Mamet themes, and "ruthlessness and guile trump decency and trust in the game of life" (Matthews B11), or, as the writer has quipped, yet another opportunity to reveal that "the lumpenproletariat and the masters of industry are the same critters" (qtd. in Denerstein 6D).

The opening scene of *Spanish Prisoner* is set on a Caribbean island "so blindingly bright that we know we're being set up for dark deeds to come" (Powers 218). As Ross and Lang step off the plane for the off-premises secret meeting, Susan, a pert company secretary who has accompanied them, snaps a souvenir photograph, the first of several such photographs that induce suspicion and render evidence at odds with initial impressions and introduce a story "organized around cameras and eyes as offensive weapons"

(Leitch 53). Ross, the leader of the design team, is tense and agitated, but Lang, an attorney always ready to dispense advice, encourages him to relax. However, despite their successful presentation, Ross is rebuffed in his attempt to win specific assurances from Mr. Klein, his direct supervisor and the executive officer of the company, that his work will be both recognized and rewarded. Confirming Joe's fears, Lang admits, "Well: Alright: Nobody likes to part with money. But here's what I think" (*Prisoner* 14), a Ricky Romaesque promise of expert advice that repeatedly drives the plot.

Abruptly altering the mood, a Mysterious Stranger approaches the startled inventor who has taken his own souvenir photos of the tropical scene, proffering a thousand dollars for his camera; and Joe, surprised by the offer and opulent display of apparent wealth, makes a gift of it. "In the dark," much as the protagonist is, we are hooked by the plot and intrigued by the secrecy that cloaks the Process and the players, none more surprising than the flirtatious Susan Ricci who boasts "a Secretary Mentality" (13) but proves to be "more and less than she seems" (Matthews B11). "Shows to go you. Y'never know who anybody is . . ." (*Prisoner* 23), she warns Joe, and he doesn't know the half of it. Undercutting the initial impression that she knows little and speaks too freely, Ricci's stealth and tenacity are cloaked by affability and seductiveness, a stunning revelation that literally blindsides the audience. Although the stranger, subsequently identified as Julian Dell, and Ricci seduce Joe by diverse means, the pair of con artists share a common, hidden agenda: acquisition of the Process, a MacGuffin that Mamet writes is most captivating when least known, "Because a loose abstraction allows audience members to project their own ideas onto an essentially featureless goal" (*Three* 29).

Later that evening as Ross walks away from the bar toward the tennis courts, Dell spies him absentmindedly toying with a tennis racket. "Y'interested in Tennis . . ." (14), he asks, his seemingly aimless question revealing that "the confidence game," as Mamet suggests, "is played 'off the wall' . . . ," as it were, with "little or no props" (qtd. in Greene). Striking up a conversation that continues until dawn, Dell spins a fantastic story of a "princess," a seaplane, and his "little sister," who he claims is a champion tennis player. To solidify their budding friendship, lend veracity to the reality of his sister, and advance the con, Dell trades upon Ross's good nature, asking the latter to deliver a package to his sister, Mrs. DaSilva, who resides in New York, with the promise of a future dinner date with Dell as further inducement.

Flattered by Dell's attention and seduced by the spectacle of wealth, the conservative mathematician, who apparently succeeds in business on the strength of his precise measurements and acuity to probability and relational qualities, fails to calculate key details of Dell's story or make the requisite connections among the various players in the con game until a number of clues belatedly click into place late in the film. As Deborah R. Geis observes, "the listener is drawn in to the point where buying the story means agreeing to buy whatever the story is selling" (104), the result of which is that the listener, who in *Spanish Prisoner* is both Joe and the audience, is "gulled." In letting down his guard, a devastating error in the game of tennis and in life, this pleasure-seeker in paradise reminds us of the veracity of Teach's remark to Don in *American Buffalo*: "A guy who isn't tense, I don't want him on my side" (47).

Although this format permits little time for digression, suffice it to say that *Spanish Prisoner* shares much in common with Hitchcock's *Strangers on a Train*. In both films games "play on the audience's innate paranoia" (Leitch 105), the threat to an innocent individual comes from a villainous double or a treacherous intimate, conflict arises between the hero and the villain about who breaches rules of social conduct; a relationship between betrayer and betrayed results in an innocent individual accused of his crime; a competitive tennis game elevates the motif of games in the film, and a carousel suggests both the "childishness/naïveté of the protagonist" and "games or amusements run out of control" (Leitch 154–58). Thus, like all those purring predators in *Spanish Prisoner* Mamet plays all manner of games on the audience. This strategy not only advances the mystery and tests the viewer's skills of observation, it reinforces Christopher C. Hudgins's premise that, however elusive, "Mamet's aesthetic relies on the audience to ferret out 'conscious' structural connections and the meaning they point to" (22).

Mamet thus propels game-playing to the foreground, his choice of tennis no mere tribute to *Strangers on a Train*; neither is the mention of Don Budge, one of only two players to win the coveted grand slam within a single year. Tennis is a highly competitive game governed by rules in which the player who wins does so by overpowering his opponent with backhand, drop shot, passing shot, lobs, and aces designed to outpace his opponent, techniques that find their analogue in the trickster's bag of tricks. Played either by one player in opposition to another or by doubles, speed, strategy, and superior power dictate success while those who follow the game are forced to keep shifting their eyes back and forth to keep the ball in view. Keeping hero and viewer off-balance is exactly Mamet's intent: "I thought quite a bit about the Hitchcock formula of having danger come from a place where it can't possibly come, he told interviewers, "[a]nd of having salvation come from the place it can't possibly come" (qtd. in Clark 50). In fact, throughout *Spanish Prisoner* Mamet dazzles us with shot placement, sleight of hand, rigged performances, high jinks, and high theater (elaborate sets, villains, princesses, romance, intrigue, a femme fatale, and for good measure, a death), in a cloak-and-dagger story so clever and literal that although "You can get ahead of it once in a while," the screenplay "quickly knocks you off the track and leads you somewhere else" (Matthews B11), principally because, as Combs notes, "the slipperiness of [Mamet's] language . . . inspires a cinematic ambiguity" (17).

In fact, paralleling Mamet's work for the stage, game-playing as structure and element of plot is a controlling figure in *Spanish Prisoner*, much as it is in the playwright's critically acclaimed film noir, *House of Games*. "Games," suggests Thomas M. Leitch in his study of Hitchcock's films, "provide a frame which contains, defines or sharpens the suspense evoked by a genuinely threatening situation, or may serve as the controlling metaphor of the work relative to game-playing impulses, including the solving of a game" (8–10). In Hitchcock's and Mamet's films competitive games, games of chance, role-playing and masquerade, and games intended to disorient or induce loss of control (such as the carousel introduced late in the film) cohere in varying combinations. Thus, games such as gin rummy, poker, casino, roulette, charades, cryptograms, and tennis, which play a key role in Mamet's cons, evoke complex concordances from which the audience derives pleasure "from having to follow the director's lead" (18). Yet Mamet's films, like Hitchcock's, "beguile audiences," enticing them to follow the action as "a move in the game." These moves, as it were, surprise or disorient the audience, "encourag[ing] them to fall into misidentifications and misinterpretations which have specific moral and thematic force" (19).

Especially effective in achieving the requisite confusion in *Spanish Prisoner* are the double views the film affords of a camera bag going through airport security, a book with a red cover, Julian Dell's ersatz apartment and club, Mrs. DaSilva, a book binding store, keys to a safe, security screens and intelligence-gathering forces, and Ross's Boy Scout knife in his hand and in Lang's chest. Although Mamet has employed doubling in earlier films (i.e., *House of Games, Things Change,* and *Homicide*), here game-playing is used to particular advantage to reinforce the significance of a sign or emblem through double exposure or, alternately, to surprise an unsuspecting audience and deprive it of its expectations, thereby illustrating that for Mamet "serious play" is designed precisely as an assault on the audiences' certitudes. Employing a pattern similar to that of his screenplay for James M. Cain's *The Postman Always Rings Twice*, Mamet puts the audience in the same position as the protagonists: "led forth by events, by the inevitability of the previous actions" (qtd. in Yakir 22).

In "Playing to Win," Ann C. Hall observes: "Of course, all readers [and viewers] attempt to make meaning, to solve the puzzle, or to translate the 'tells' in the Mamet film[s] and play[s], but [Sergei] Eisenstein's method and Mamet's mimicry of that method are . . . 'readerly,'" to use Barthes's terminology (140), a premise that posits that a text "is a galaxy of signifiers, . . . we gain access to it by several entrances, none of which can be authoritatively declared to be the main one" (Barthes, *S/Z* 5). In *Spanish*

Prisoner signs and signifiers literally create confusion in the protagonist's and the audience's mind. Underscoring Ross's metaphoric journey from innocence to wisdom, signifiers (of wealth, power, knowledge, security, and passion), signs (in airports, offices, subway car, on highways, and bakery awnings), and modes of transport (airplane, seaplane, water taxi, taxi, subway train, bus, classic cars, carousel, water shuttle, paddy wagon) firmly establish a world and mind-set in transition.

Initially employed to establish place, signs foster illusion (of Dell's wealth and of Susan's status), provide directives, influence direction, or rather misdirection, and sustain credible links between an island paradise and the urban environs, Mamet's customary playground, in which fraud, theft, and felony murder occur. Implicitly underscoring the distance traveled from home and office both as a "place of shelter and an individual refuge," as well as "the stability and security of long-standing assumptions" (Leitch 25), these signifiers cumulatively bedevil the audience so that like Ross we endeavor to establish connections between the known and the unknown. In short, Mamet "lead[s] us on a Merry Chase" (Leitch 135) as Joe Ross, a kinetic company man whose given name is a common expression for "an ordinary Joe, an honest man" and an individual "easily imposed on" (Partridge 240), is seemingly in perpetual motion. While scribbling notations, running from the scene of a crime, or escaping from a trap, he is transformed before our eyes into a fugitive accused of capital crime. And just as photographs of Bobby Gold in *Homicide* provide irrefutable evidence of his criminal activity, Ross is caught red-handed. Nevertheless, suggests Steven Price, the general spreading out of suspicion onto everyone else helps to define Ross as innocent because a function of the genre is that, rather than examining clues, or even other characters, much of the pleasure derives from letting Ross/the audience be conned (15). The game as played by Mamet and Dell can thus be characterized as "*super* game control" in which Dell "maneuver[s] himself into position" of calling the shots while at the same time "creat[ing] an appearance of impartiality." He "becomes, in effect, the game's parent," assuming "decisions as to conduct-of-play" (Mamet, *Make-Believe* 16). Seen from this perspective, John Lahr correctly observes that "the con trick" has an "abiding pull on Mamet's imagination: it reverses the parental situation. In the con, the public is put in the role of the helpless child, while the con artist is the parent who knows the game and controls all the rules and the information" (79).

One of the prime ways in which the screenwriter controls information is to give the audience the impression that it possesses insider information. For example, as Ross, Lang, and Susan pass through airport security upon their return from St. Estephe to New York, Susan is instructed to place her camera on the conveyor belt for closer inspection, an act which also affords the audience a view "from the back," yielding the impression, or rather illusion, of insider information. However, this scene is a prime example of Mamet planting information before the audience has the impression that anything of what they are seeing or hearing has relevance. Likewise, as Lang sleeps on the plane, the first signs of the flu apparently incapacitate him and subsequently Dell's sister Mrs. DaSilva, keeping both out of sight later in the film, Susan animatedly engages Joe in a conversation about the mysterious stranger who in her view only appeared to get off the seaplane. Promising proof to confirm her skepticism in the form of souvenir photographs, she advances Ross's—and our—suspicions as well as the plot by keeping Dell "alive" in the conversation despite his absence. Although Susan appears full of homespun wisdom and genuine good cheer, she conceals her pivotal role in the con.

Subsequently, on the following Friday afternoon, when Susan enters Joe's office where he is in conference with Lang, she is asked to look away—much as the audience is figuratively instructed throughout the film—while Joe secures the red volume containing the Process (which we have previously spotted in his possession) in the company's safe. Subsequently when Klein leaves the office for the weekend and Joe Ross for his dinner with Dell, the former interrogates the young inventor about secrecy and security measures with respect to the formula, prompting Ross, now bolstered by Lang, to raise the issue of adequate remuneration for his valuable work product. Again, Klein's promise of compensation is characteristically cloaked in imprecision. "I'm sure we'll be rewarded, according to our Just Desserts . . ." (*Prisoner* 33), he tells the increasingly frustrated mathematician, implicitly conveying issues of merit and dueness and betrayal repeatedly raised in Mamet's works and leaving Ross and the audience convinced of the validity of his cause of action and concern. Not only is Ross rejected by Klein, he is given the cold shoulder by Dell who fails to confirm their dinner date.

Hence, when Ross goes out on an errand in his neighborhood on the following morning and spies the billionaire's bodyguard, whom we also recognize, Ross follows Dell into a garage where he is apparently engaged in the purchase of a luxury automobile. The two get into a heated argument about who showed lack of courtesy to whom and what was or was not agreed upon concerning the delivery of the book to Mrs. DaSilva. Ross uncharacteristically explodes, "And isn't it possible you misremembered . . .?" (37), he asks, prompting the audience to ask themselves, "What is it that we remember?" In fact, if it does not yet dawn on Joe that Dell could have delivered the book to his sister himself when he came to New York, the audience is also perplexed by the dinner, the sister, and the coincidence of the billionaire shopping for such automobiles in Joe's neighborhood.

We barely have an opportunity to mull over these questions when Susan, also apparently in the vicinity of Joe's apartment by chance and toting a bag of breakfast goodies, inveigles an invitation to coffee, her folksy "and aren't you courteous and all" (38) rendering ironic the heated exchange between Joe and Dell that has just transpired. Aggressively she makes a play for Joe, verbalizing that which appeals to his ego and, in the absence of resistance, to his libido, by seductively removing her sweater. Uncomfortable or indecisive at the prospect of pursuing an interoffice romance, Ross occupies himself by cutting bread, thus displaying his Boy Scout knife, whose logo "Be Prepared" speaks volumes about his lack of preparedness with Dell, Klein, and now Susan. Yet, our eye is drawn to this fetching woman whose blatant seduction ". . . Let *me* be your Good Deed Today . . ." (39) literally turns his head. However, just as it appears she might succeed in trapping him, the telephone rings, a classic Mametic trick, intruding upon the moment and their imminent coupling with Dell's apology and invitation to dinner, the lure of money obviously more enticing than sex. In parting, Susan leaves Joe with both her address and an open invitation; yet, the need for either of these Mamet leaves characteristically undisclosed. By training or disposition, rather than interest, Joe apparently commits her address and the emblem of the Sunshine Bakery to memory, a propitious act since her apartment provides the refuge that he subsequently requires after a night of terror.

Later that evening, Mamet crafts a complementary scene in which the intimacy advanced between Joe and Susan is replayed at Dell's "apartment" when the young mathematician, dressed for dinner in tie and jacket, arrives to find Dell dressed only in a robe, intended, we presume to advance the impression of intimacy and/or underscore the gulf between their mores and morality. Offering Joe a drink, Dell picks up the dropped threads of the saga of his sister and offhandedly proposes that he open a Swiss bank account for his guest, password Paddy (picked up later in the film in Susan's reference to her husband, the Mick, and the paddy wagon that carts her to jail), a grand gesture intended to impress the younger working man with his specialized knowledge. "Thus are All Men Made Equal" (42–43), he quips, a wry turn on Mamet's observation that poker is a game "played among folks made equal by their money" (*Writing* 96). Although Dell's comment, "you ever want to *impress* anybody" (42), draws attention to the action he currently undertakes with a flourish, Ross's possession of a Swiss bank account, whose principal quality is its undisclosed amount of money, will indeed impress the police that he is a man who has much to hide, as was its intent.

Meeting Dell at his tennis club on the following afternoon, where he presumes he will finally meet Dell's sister, Joe finds the former engaged in a series of telephone conversations concerning mergers and acquisitions, the charade intended to bolster the illusion of Dell's specialized knowledge in the world of high finance. Trading on his presumed business acumen, Dell moves to build up Ross's confidence by asking a series of well-placed questions about the Process while eliciting information about the extent of his legal protection. "I think you'll find, if what you have done for them is valuable," he advises, his phrases couched in the conditional as if he were ignorant of the facts, "*my* experience is that they will begin to act cruelly toward you to assuage their guilt" (*Prisoner* 49), a position that bears out the advice Lang gave him. Hence, when Joe returns to his office on Monday and is cornered by Klein and Company attorneys who want to revalidate his contract, the adversarial confrontation forewarned by Dell adds to the validity of Dell's advice, provides a credible opportunity to reflect Ross's escalating fears, and directly provokes his call to Dell formally requesting that the latter arrange a meeting with an attorney, subsequently scheduled for the following day. To repay Dell's friendship and kind offer of assistance, Ross returns to the book store to purchase a gift for Mrs. DaSilva. He had visited the store previously upon his return to New York from St. Estephe after he tore off the cover of a book on tennis by Don Budge given to him by Dell (ostensibly for Dell's "sister") in order to ascertain the contents of the package.

Arms bursting with a bouquet of flowers and a signed photograph of Don Budge, which keeps the trope of the tennis game alive in *Prisoner*, Ross goes to the San Remo where the "young" Mrs. DaSilva presumably lives to deliver his gifts. Once there he and the audience acquire a key piece of the puzzle—that Mrs. DaSilva is neither young nor a tennis player—confirming that Ross has indeed been the victim of a con. At issue for Mamet, however, is the trap that Ross has virtually built for himself, his "mixture of guilt and innocence" (Leitch 137), his confusion of illusion with reality and wealth with virtue, complicitous in the success of the conartistry. Yet, the con works in this film, as it does in many of Mamet's films and stage plays, because it plays upon trust engendered by an individual who has advised the Boy Scout Joe Ross to trust no one.

Compounding the devastating impact of his encounter at the San Remo and with his employer Mr. Klein, Ross encounters Susan upon his return to the office, the latter eager to win her bet that the "Mystery Man" was unconnected to the seaplane, as she had earlier claimed. Proffering her souvenir album from St. Estephe containing photos and icons from the trip—the FBI agent Pat McCune's card, an open ticket—Susan flips through the pages of the book revealing a photograph of a woman and Dell's launch in no proximity to the seaplane, prompting the mathematician, muttering aloud, to finally make the requisite connections among the players—or at least some of the players. But before he finishes his sentence, he is interrupted by a well-timed telephone call from Dell confirming that Dell has contacted his personal attorney on Ross's behalf and that the attorney would like Ross to bring his contract and a copy of the Process to the meeting, thus reminding us that no such copy exists. This charade, the scene staged in Dell's "apartment" and "club," and the existence of a sister, all of which are revealed later to be pure artifice, are consistent with Mamet's expressed "interest[ed] in the continuum that starts with charm and ends with psychopathology." In his view "[C]on artists deal in human nature, and what they do is all in the realm of suggestion." In fact, as the writer told *Playboy* in an interview:

> MAMET: Part of the art of the play [and film] is to introduce information in such a way, and at such a time, that people in the audience don't realize they have been given information. They accept it as a matter of course, but they aren't aware of it so that later on, the information pays off. It has been consciously planted by the author.
> PLAYBOY: And he is working a con?
> MAMET: Right. (Norman and Rezek 56)

At last, acting like the thinking man that he is, Ross seeks to outwit the con artist, who he/we presume is Dell, and thus plays right in to the cabal's hands when he turns to the FBI—McCune's card intentionally left in view to lead Joe right into the arms/trust of mock secret agents whose instructions he follows exactly, a trick employed, as well, by the hit men in *Homicide*. McCune plays fast and loose with the idiom, which lends her performance veracity, but in providing "expert" knowledge of Dell's modus operandi, alluding to others who he has swindled, and displaying a notebook containing facts and figures, she convincingly "proves" that Ross and Dell have been under surveillance. However, in contrast to Dell's increasingly overt queries about the Process, McCune plays it close to the vest, silencing Ross when trust, or nervousness, propels him to say more than he must: "Hey, don't tell *me*. 'F it's so damn secret, *I* don't wanna know. . ." (84). Insinuating that Dell has used trickery, bribes, and violence to coerce his victims, McCune elicits Ross's commitment to assist in the con man's apprehension, thereby trapping him into admitting a credible human motivation: settling the score. However, when she leaves to participate in an ersatz operation, McCune convincingly wins Joe's and the audience's trust with her parting line and sympathetic tone, "Don't worry. I'll be on top of it. Don't worry" (87).

Hence, when Dell calls to change the time and place of the meet to the carousel in New York's Central Park, just as McCune promised he would, and to instruct Ross to bring the Process, this information "confirms" her knowledge of Dell and of his operation, "proving" to the now wary mathematician that she is who she claims to be, a point credibly confirmed by her call immediately thereafter verifying the meet change and revising his instructions. One of the key elements in playing Mamet's game of "catch the director" is the dizzying series of instructions, ground rules, recommendations, directives, warnings, and guidelines that not only foil the protagonist's and audience's ability to follow the dots but also serve as figures of misdirection that abet Mamet's montage,[1] as evidenced by the success of the sting perpetrated by the FBI. On the morning of the meet with Dell, Ross is spotted approaching Bethesda Fountain, the red book that we recognize as the Process in his hand. He is guided into the men's room (implicitly a site of felonious activity and sexual assault), which has all the accoutrements of an FBI stakeout. Under the apparent guise of the press of time before the meet at the carousel, McCune's partner Kelly strips Ross of his jacket and the book and proceeds to wire him with a transmitter about which Kelly gives Ross precise directions concerning the exact wording he must elicit from Dell in order to secure a conviction and the behavior he should adopt to trap the thief and protect his life. Amid this frenetic activity, and as if in passing, Kelly acquires the single piece of information that *he* requires in the performance of his job: Ross's verification that the red volume is "the Real Thing." (66). Echoing McCune's warning, Kelly raises the ugly spectre of violence, thus riveting Ross's attention to a single instruction that the audience also digests: "if there is shooting. Stay Put. Do Not Move . . ." (66). In short, Kelly's reiterating the threat of bodily harm successfully convinces Ross and the audience of imminent danger. However, with assurances from the FBI, albeit fallacious, that agents will have Joe in sight, he is lead out of the men's toilet with repeated directions to get Dell on tape and to "*wait,* til he offers you money, *or* he threatens you . . ." (67), giving Ross the confidence that help is only a code word away. "You get in trouble," he is assured, "just say the word 'happiness'" (67). Thus McCune and Kelly commit a bloodless crime, the threat of violence a mere diversion in the con game.

Instructed to meet Dell at the appointed place and wait until he has performed the deed set before him, Ross is waved on to the carousel by bogus undercover agents, a sign confirming games out of control. As shadows lengthen, reminding us that the "FBI" transmitter's life has expired hours ago, Ross at last acknowledges that the book in his hand and the FBI agents with whom he has been dealing are fakes. Belatedly realizing with the audience that the bait and switch took place at the bathhouse hours before under cover and in front of his eyes, Ross is chastened. In giving his trust and most valued possession to the sham agents, he has advanced their plot and put his work at risk.

When two New York City police officers reveal the extent of Dell's deception, Mamet proceeds to disabuse Ross and the audience of "truths" they have held as self-evident. As the police dust Dell's stripped apartment for prints, the con man having disappeared without a trace, several probative pieces of evidence—the private club, "a coat-check room"; a membership form, an application for asylum in Venezuela; the souvenir album devoid of any evidence of Dell's existence in St. Estephe—Ross repeatedly points to his friend George Lang as the one individual who can attest to his claims and clear his name. While this longed-for release is postponed due to Lang's ill health and subsequent death, Ross's generosity, or stupidity, is revealed as human error—the ill-placed trust of a gullible man blinded by the desire for wealth and acclaim, foreshadowed when Ross squinted into the sun upon arrival in the lush Caribbean resort.

Ironically, Joe was right all along: he feared that Klein was going to rob him blind, a fact validated by in-house counsel Lang's breach of confidence. The audience, who for the most part are like Joe—undercompensated workers whose accomplishments go unrecognized—surmise that the Company (whose elusive stockholders may be seen as *Glengarry*'s mythical "bosses" Mitch and Murray, magnified exponentially) is exploitative and intends to cheat Ross, and we champion his spunk. Whether Lang was complicitous in the plan or merely an expendable witness for the defense, Mamet succeeds at film's end in leaving this point, and a myriad of questions, unresolved.

Citing a Japanese sword master in a recent interview Mamet remarked, "In combat, the trick is to see things far off as if they're very near. And to see things very near as if they're far off" (qtd. in Gritten). This is what Ross, and, for the most part, the audience fail to do, repeatedly fooled by the game of bait and switch and the trick of light that keeps us in the dark. If at film's end Mamet succeeds in leaving questions unanswered, as he does in his plays, there is no doubt, however, that Ross's first impulse was the right one. He would have done well to heed the advice of "Mr. Happiness," a talk-show host in an early Mamet one-act play of the same name: "'Follow the dictates of your heart, but Use your Head.' And keep your Two Eyes Open" (324). Or in Mamet's inimical words, "Trust everyone, but cut the cards" (*Make-Believe* 20).

Notes

1. See in particular Mamet's *On Directing Film*, in which he discusses his approach to writing for film; his writing and directing films is also the subject of myriad interviews and essays.

Works Cited

Barthes, Roland. "The Brain of Einstein." *Mythologies*. Selected and trans. from the French by Annette Lavers. New York: Noonday Press, 1991, 68–70.

———. *S/Z*. Trans. Richard Miller. New York: Hill and Wang, 1974.

Caro, Mark. "David Mamet Takes on Films, Takes No Prisoners." *South Florida Sun-Sentinel,* 4 May 1998, Arts and Leisure, D1+.

Carr, Jay. "Mamet Plays a Winning Hand in the Wily *Spanish Prisoner.*" *Boston Globe,* 10 Apr. 1998, D5.

Clark, John. "A Man of Confidence, David Mamet's *Spanish Prisoner* Extends a Favorite Theme of the Prolific Writer-Director: Con Artists and Their Games in Life." *Los Angeles Times,* 2 Apr. 1998, F50.

Combs, Richard. "Framing Mamet." *Sight and Sound* 1,7 (Nov. 1991): 16–17, 47.

Denby, David. "What's in a Game." *New York,* 19 Oct. 1987, 101.

Denerstein, Robert. "Mamet on the Games Mamet Plays." *Rocky Mountain News,* 12 Apr. 1998, 6D.

Geis, Deborah R. "The Theater as 'House of Games': David Mamet's (Con) Artistry and the Monologic Voice." *Postmodern Theatric[k]s: Monologue in Contemporary American Drama.* Ann Arbor: U of Michigan P, 1995, 89–115.

Greene, Ray. "Confidence Man: Playwright/Moviemaker David Mamet Locks Up *The Spanish Prisoner,*" 27 May 1998. http://www.boxoff.com/apr98story2.html

Gritten, David. "The Arts: Prepared for Anything as His New Film Opens, David Mamet Talks to David Gritten about Clinton, Shakespeare and Being a Boy Scout." *Daily Telegraph* [London], 7 Mar. 1998, 2 pag. Online. Westlaw. 7 May 1998.

Hall, Ann C. "Playing to Win: Sexual Politics in David Mamet's *House of Games* and *Speed-the-Plow.*" *David Mamet: A Casebook.* Ed. Leslie Kane. New York: Garland, 1992, 137–60.

Hudgins, Christopher C. "'Indirections Find Directions Out': Uninflected Cuts, Narrative Structure, and Thematic Statement in the Film Version of *Glengarry Glen Ross.*" *Glengarry Glen Ross: Text and Performance.* Ed. Leslie Kane. New York: Garland, 1996, 19–45.

Lahr, John. "Fortress Mamet." *New Yorker,* 17 November 1997, 70+

Leitch, Thomas M. *Find the Director: And Other Hitchcock Games.* Athens: U of Georgia P, 1991.

Mamet, David. *American Buffalo.* New York: Grove Press, 1977.

———. "Gems from a Gambler's Bookshelf." *Make-Believe Town: Essays and Reminiscences.* Boston: Little, Brown, 1996, 7–20.

———. *On Directing Film.* New York: Viking, 1991.

———. *The Spanish Prisoner and The Winslow Boy: Two Screenplays.* New York: Vintage, 1999.

———. *Three Uses of the Knife: On the Structure and Purpose of Drama.* New York: Columbia UP, 1988.

———. *The Water Engine and Mr. Happiness.* New York: Grove Press, 1978.

———. *Writing in Restaurants.* New York: Penguin, 1987.

Matthews, Jack. "Clean-Mouthed Mamet Does Hitchcock." *Newsday,* 3 Apr. 1998, B11.

Norman, Geoffrey, and John Rezek. "Playboy Interview with David Mamet." *Playboy,* Apr. 1995, 51+.

Partridge, Eric. *A Concise Dictionary of Slang and Unconventional English.* Ed. Paul Beale. New York: Macmillan, 1989.

Powers, John. Rev. of *Spanish Prisoner* by David Mamet. "People Are Talking About." *Vogue,* Apr 1998, 218+.

Price, Steven. "Negative Creation: The Detective Story in *Glengarry Glen Ross.*" *Glengarry Glen Ross: Text and Performance.* Ed. Leslie Kane. New York: Garland, 1996, 3–17.

Schvey, Henry. "Celebrating the Capacity for Self-Knowledge." *New Theatre Quarterly* 4, 13 (1998): 89–96.

Thomson, David. "H for Hitchcock." *Sight and Sound* 7, 1 (Jan. 1997): 26–30.

Yakir, Dan. "The Postman's Words." *Film Comment* (Mar./Apr. 1981): 21–24.

Contributors

Thomas P. Adler has been teaching since 1970 at Purdue University, where he is professor and chair of the English Department. He has published extensively on modern British and American drama, with a special emphasis on Tennessee Williams. The latest of his five books, *American Drama, 1940–60*, was reprinted in paperback in 1997. He recently contributed essays on Williams, Miller, and Hellman to three different volumes of the Cambridge Companion series, and on Mamet's children's plays to *Gender and Genre: Essays on David Mamet*.

Varun Begley holds a Ph.D. from Cornell University. At present he is an assistant professor of English at the College of William and Mary where he teaches modern drama and film. He has published on David Mamet and film and is completing a study of Pinter's work titled *The Slight Ache*.

Anne M. Dean holds an M.A. in modern English literature and a Ph.D. in theater from, respectively, Queen Mary and Royal Bedford New College, University of London. Her publications include two books on contemporary American drama, *David Mamet: Language as Dramatic Action* and *The Urban Plays of Lanford Wilson*, an essay on Mamet's *Glengarry Glen Ross*, and selected poems. Currently, she is assistant director of the Leverhulme Trust, an arts-granting organization in London.

Barry Goldensohn is professor of English at Skidmore College. A widely published poet, whose publications include *The Marrano, Dance Music*, and *East Long Pond*, Goldenson's poetry, essays, and reviews have appeared in *Salmagundi, The Iowa Review, Ploughshares*, and *The Yale Review*. He has delivered papers on the work of David Mamet, his former student at Goddard College in the mid-1960s, at the European

Association of American Studies, Warsaw, and at the Modern Language Association Convention.

Charles V. Grimes is assistant professor of English and theater at Saint Leo University. In addition to his directing seven plays by Harold Pinter, Grimes has directed work by Anton Chekhov, Tennessee Williams, and Sam Shepard. He is the author of several articles on Bernard Shaw and Harold Pinter; an article on Pinter's *The Homecoming* is forthcoming in *The Pinter Review*.

Ann C. Hall is an associate professor in the Department of English at Old Dominion College, where she is currently serving as chair. President of the Harold Pinter Society, Professor Hall has published extensively on modern drama and film. The author of *A Kind of Alaska: Women in the Plays of O'Neill, Pinter and Shepard,* she is at work on a book on *Phantom of the Opera*.

Leslie Kane, editor, is professor of English at Westfield State College. She is the author of *The Language of Silence: The Unspoken and the Unspeakable in Modern Drama* and *Weasels and Wisemen: Ethics and Ethnicity in the Work of David Mamet*. Additionally, she has edited several critical collections, including *David Mamet: A Casebook, Glengarry Glen Ross: Text and Performance, David Mamet in Conversation*, and *Gender and Genre* (with Christopher C. Hudgins). Founder and former president of the David Mamet Society, and former vice president of the Harold Pinter Society, she is the editor of *The David Mamet Review*. Her essays, reviews, and interviews on Mamet, Shepard, Pinter, and Beckett, including several in the Cambridge Companion series, have been widely published.

Kimball King is professor emeritus of English at the University of North Carolina, Chapel Hill. General editor for Garland Publishing's Casebook on Modern Dramatists and Studies in Modern Drama series for fifteen years, Professor King's publications include *Sam Shepard: A Casebook* and *Hollywood on Stage: Playwrights Evaluate the Culture Industry.* The author of numerous published essays on modern British and American dramatists, among them Shepard, Williams, Osborne, Hampton, Churchill, and Storey, Professor King serves on the editorial board of *The Pinter Review*.

Elizabeth Klaver, an associate professor of English at Southern Illinois University at Carbondale, is the author of *Performing Television: Contemporary Drama and the Media Culture* and numerous essays on modern drama and television. Her essay, "David Mamet, Jean Baudrillard and the Performance of America," appeared in *Glengarry Glen Ross:*

Text and Performance. Currently she is book review editor for *The David Mamet Review.*

Claire Magaha was a lecturer in French at the University of California, Los Angeles. The author of articles on the crisis of modern art, sexuality identity, and the discourse of utopia, she has worked as an assistant editor for the monograph series, North Carolina Studies in Romance Languages and Literature. She has also authored a CD-ROM and a revised workbook to accompany *Motifs.*

Ira B. Nadel, a professor in the Department of English at the University of British Columbia, is the author of *Biography, Fiction, Fact & Form, Joyce and the Jews* and *Various Positions: A Life of Leonard Cohen.* His biography of Tom Stoppard was recently published by Methuen. His next project is a life of David Mamet.

Penelope Prentice is an award-winning playwright and poet who has published two books on Harold Pinter, *Harold Pinter: Life, Work and Criticism* and *The Pinter Ethic: The Erotic Aesthetic.* Professor emeritus at D'Youville College, Buffalo, New York, she is the former executive director of the New York College English Association Conference. Professor Prentice's collection of poetry is titled *Capturing the Light*, and more than a dozen of her plays have been performed in New York, Washington, D.C., Australia, Alaska, and Ireland.

Steven Price, lecturer in English at the University of Wales, Bangor, has published extensively on British and American drama. He is the author of "Negative Creation: The Detective Story in *Glengarry Glen Ross*," and "Disguise in Love: Gender and Desire in *House of Games* and *Speed-the-Plow*," as well as essays on Beckett and Pinter, which appeared in *Cycnos.* A regular contributor to *The Year's Work in English Studies*, and book reviewer for *Modern Language Review*, Price serves as European editor for *The David Mamet Review.*

Marc Silverstein is Hollifield Professor of English Literature at Auburn University. A past president of the Harold Pinter Society, he is the author of *Harold Pinter and the Language of Cultural Power* (1993). His articles have appeared in *American Drama, Essays in Theatre, Journal of Dramatic Theory and Criticism, Modern Drama, The Pinter Review,* and *Theatre Journal.*

Index

Lightning Source UK Ltd.
Milton Keynes UK

175218UK00001BC/30/P

9 780415 968300